Networks Attack Detection on 5G Networks using Data Mining Techniques

Artificial intelligence (AI) and its applications have risen to prominence as one of the most active study areas in recent years. In recent years, a rising number of AI applications have been applied in a variety of areas. Agriculture, transportation, medicine, and health are all being transformed by AI technology. The Internet of Things (IoT) market is thriving, having a significant impact on a wide variety of industries and applications, including e-health care, smart cities, smart transportation, and industrial engineering. Recent breakthroughs in artificial intelligence and machine learning techniques have reshaped various aspects of artificial vision, considerably improving the state of the art for artificial vision systems across a broad range of high-level tasks. As a result, several innovations and studies are being conducted to improve the performance and productivity of IoT devices across multiple industries using machine learning and artificial intelligence. Security is a primary consideration when analyzing the next generation communication network due to the rapid advancement of technology. Additionally, data analytics, deep intelligence, deep learning, cloud computing, and intelligent solutions are being employed in medical, agricultural, industrial, and health care systems that are based on the Internet of Things. This book will look at cutting-edge Network Attacks and Security solutions that employ intelligent data processing and Machine Learning (ML) methods.

This book:

- Covers emerging technologies of network attacks and management aspects.
- Presents artificial intelligence techniques for networks and resource optimization, and toward network automation, and security.
- Showcases recent industrial and technological aspects of next-generation networks
- Illustrates artificial intelligence techniques to mitigate cyber-attacks, authentication, and authorization challenges.
- Explains smart, and real-time monitoring services, multimedia, cloud computing, and information processing methodologies in 5G networks.

It is primarily for senior undergraduates, graduate students and academic researchers in the fields of electrical engineering, electronics and communication engineering, computer engineering, and information technology.

Wireless Communications and Networking Technologies: Classifications, Advancement and Applications
Series Editor: D.K. Lobiyal, R.S. Rao and Vishal Jain

The series addresses different algorithms, architecture, standards and protocols, tools and methodologies which could be beneficial in implementing next generation mobile network for the communication. Aimed at senior undergraduate students, graduate students, academic researchers and professionals, the proposed series will focus on the fundamentals and advances of wireless communication and networking, and their such as mobile ad-hoc network (MANET), wireless sensor network (WSN), wireless mess network (WMN), vehicular ad-hoc networks (VANET), vehicular cloud network (VCN), vehicular sensor network (VSN) reliable cooperative network (RCN), mobile opportunistic network (MON), delay tolerant networks (DTN), flying ad-hoc network (FANET) and wireless body sensor network (WBSN).

Wireless Communication: Advancements and Challenges
Prashant Ranjan, Ram Shringar Rao, Krishna Kumar and Pankaj Sharma

Wireless Communication with Artificial Intelligence: Emerging Trends and Applications
Anuj Singal, Sandeep Kumar, Sajjan Singh and Ashish Kr. Luhach

Computational Intelligent Security in Wireless Communications
Suhel Ahmad Khan, Rajeev Kumar, Omprakash Kaiwartya, Raees Ahmad Khan and Mohammad Faisal

Networking Technologies in Smart Healthcare: Innovations and Analytical Approaches
Pooja Singh, Omprakash Kaiwartya, Nidhi Sindhwani, Vishal Jain and Rohit Anand

Artificial Intelligence in Cyber Physical Systems: Principles and Applications
Anil Kumar Sagar, Parma Nand, Neetesh Kumar, Sanjoy Das and Subrata Sahana

Networks Attack Detection on 5G Networks using Data Mining Techniques
Edited by Sagar Dhanraj Pande and Aditya Khamparia

For more information about this series, please visit: https://www.routledge.com/Wireless%20Communications%20and%20Networking%20Technologies/book-series/WCANT

Networks Attack Detection on 5G Networks using Data Mining Techniques

Edited by
Sagar Dhanraj Pande
Aditya Khamparia

CRC Press
Taylor & Francis Group
Boca Raton London New York

CRC Press is an imprint of the
Taylor & Francis Group, an **informa** business

Designed cover image: ZinetroN/Shutterstock

First edition published 2024
by CRC Press
2385 NW Executive Center Drive, Suite 320, Boca Raton FL 33431

and by CRC Press
4 Park Square, Milton Park, Abingdon, Oxon, OX14 4RN

CRC Press is an imprint of Taylor & Francis Group, LLC

ISBN: 978-1-032-53018-5 (hbk)
ISBN: 978-1-032-74657-9 (pbk)
ISBN: 978-1-003-47028-1 (ebk)

DOI: 10.1201/9781003470281

Typeset in Times New Roman
by SPi Technologies India Pvt Ltd (Straive)

Contents

Preface

This book begins with the basics of Network attacks and introduces the methodologies, processes, results, and challenges associated with the same. The advent of 5G technology and the exponential rise in connected devices are anticipated to make it more difficult to allocate network resources in a reliable and efficient manner. To operate on top of the same physical infrastructure, network providers are now needed to dynamically construct and deploy several services that meet different criteria in different vertical industries. It is hypothesised that current advancements in artificial intelligence and machine learning might provide a solution to the problems associated with resource allocation. Therefore, it is anticipated that the artificial intelligence components of future networks would be highly relied upon, which might make them a valuable target for assault. This book will concentrate on the application of network attacks-driven intelligent computing approaches, the state of the art, cutting-edge discoveries, and current developments in AI/ML algorithms because of new technologies and quicker user-device connection. A variety of ideas and approaches are being researched and developed in this interesting and developing multidisciplinary area of 5G networks to address difficult and complicated issues. Network analysis, machine learning, computer vision, and deep learning-enabled assessment of the suggested solutions are likely to be included in applications-oriented development. More instances of possible use issues are provided throughout the book, along with probable solutions. It is difficult to thoroughly examine every technique and/or solution due to the topic's depth.

OBJECTIVE OF THE BOOK

The main aim of this book is to provide a detailed understanding of Network Attacks Detection on 5G Networks assisted applications with involvement of distinct intelligent computing methods and optimized algorithms in the field of computer science. This book will also concentrate on applications utilizing Network Attacks and AI/ML in various domains/perspectives.

ORGANIZATION OF THE BOOK

The book is organized in 10 chapters with the following brief description:

1. Enhancing 5G and IoT Network Security: A Multi-Model Deep Learning Approach for Attack Classification

   The Internet of Things (IoT) is expanding quickly and their incorporation into daily life have made it possible for unprecedented connectedness and creativity. The Chapter emphasizes the effectiveness of deep learning in safeguarding IoT networks and extending this protection to 5G networks. This could help researchers consider previous applications, problems, challenges, and threats in the healthcare field. The presented work also includes an overview of the CICIoT2023 dataset to provide a robust security framework.

2. Networks Attack Detection on 5G Networks using Data Mining Techniques

   This chapter introduces approach for achieving dynamic deployment of the user plane in the 5G core network, a multi-stage planning technique based on Bender's decomposition is provided for the deployment and traffic scheduling of the User Plane Function (UPF) in an edge network context.

3. Spatial Federated Learning and Blockchain based 5G Communication Model for Hiding Confidential Information

   This chapter suggests a covert blockchain communication methodology that incorporates spatial federated learning and spatial blockchain as a means of fixing these issues. By utilizing Cipher-text-Policy Attribute-Based Encryption (CP-ABE) to encrypt the sensitive document and uploading it to the Inter Planetary File System (IPFS), the technique conceals sensitive files and the sender's identity.

4. Mining Intelligence Hierarchical Feature for Malware Detection over 5G Network

   This chapter trains mining malware classifiers using byte feature layers, PE (Portable Executable) structure feature layers, and mining operation execution feature layers, respectively, from the perspective of mining malware threat intelligence.

5. Enhancing Reliability and Security of Power Monitoring Systems in the Era of 5G Networks

   This chapter suggested method entails using network security classification standards and an industrial system vulnerability database to create a set of evaluation indicators that include network communication reliability, operational reliability, and overall system dependability.

6. Passive Voice in 5G Mobile Edge Computing: Optimizing Energy Efficiency and Resource Utilization

   This chapter proposed a hybrid integer nonlinear stochastic optimization model that minimizes the long-term average energy consumption while ensuring task buffer queue stability. The optimization problem is decomposed into two stages: relay node selection and relay offloading decision.

7. Exchange Matching Algorithm for Low-Complexity Traffic Scheduling for 5G Fronthaul Networks

    This chapter presents a low-complexity traffic scheduling algorithm based on exchange matching for a power + 5G fronthaul network, focusing on ensuring deterministic latency and differentiated quality of service for power communication services.

8. Attack Path Discovery in Dynamic Network Environments for Automated Penetration Testing Over 5G Networks

    This Chapter describes The Attack Path Discovery using Bidirectional Ant Colony Algorithm (APD-BACO) network attack path discovery method to resolve this problem and increase the efficiency of path discovery.

9. Enhancing Electric Vehicle Charging Efficiency in Urban Areas with 5G Network Integration and Network Attack Mitigation

    This Chapter introduces the Charging Priority (CP) preemptive charging scheduling strategy. This approach, founded on queuing theory, prioritizes the charging of electric vehicles with the highest charging priority, determined by factors such as charging demand and remaining parking time, to maximize overall charging efficiency.

10. Next-Generation Intrusion Detection System for 5G Networks with Enhanced Security Using Updated Datasets

    This Chapter presents an indetailed analysis of the CIC-IOT 2023 dataset. A comprehensive collection of network traffic data specifically designed for evaluating IoT device behaviors and their interactions within a 5G network environment. The primary objective of this analysis is to uncover potential vulnerabilities and security challenges that may arise in 5G-connected IoT ecosystems.

Contributors

Haewon Byeon
Department of Digital Anti-Aging Healthcare
Inje University
Gimhae, Republic of Korea

Jitendra Kumar Chaudhary
School of Computing, Graphic Era Hill University
Bhimtal Campus
Dehradun, India

Sandeep Kumar Davuluri
Department of Information Technology
University of the Cumberlands
Williamsburg, Kentucky

Sheshang Degadwala
Department of Computer Engineering
Sigma University
Vadodara, India

Krishan Dutt
School of computer application
Lovely professional university
Phagwara, India

Nishanth Gadey
School of Computer Science & Engineering (SCOPE)

VIT-AP University
Amaravati, India

Manvitha Gali
Doctor of Information Technology
University of the Cumberlands
Williamsburg, Kentucky

Komal Shyamsundar Jakotiya
School of Engineering
ADYPU
Pune, India

Amit Jain
Computer science and engineering department
O P Jindal University
Raigarh, India

Rajan John
Department of Computer Science
College of Computer Science and Information Technology
Jazan University
Jazan, Kingdom of Saudi Arabia

Ismail Keshta
Computer Science and Information Systems Department
College of Applied Sciences,
AlMaarefa University
Riyadh, Saudi Arabia

Aditya Khamparia
Department of Computer Science
Babasaheb Bhimrao Ambedkar
   University (A Central
   University)
Lucknow, India

Ihtiram Raza Khan
Computer Science Department
Jamia Hamdard
Delhi, India

Chaitanya Kulkarni
VPKBIET
Baramati, India

Pramod Kumar
Computer science and Technology
Ganga Institute of Technology and
   Management
Jhajjar, India

Ravi Kumar
Department of Electronics and
   Communication Engineering
Jaypee University of Engineering
   and Technology
Guna, India

Saurabh Kumar
College of computing science and
   information technology
Teerthankar Mahaveer University
Moradabad, India

M. Ramkumar Raja
Department of Electrical
   Engineering
College of Engineering,
   King Khalid University
Abha, Saudi Arabia

Raj Gaurav Mishra
School of Engineering, ADYPU
Pune, India

Renato R. Maaliw III
College of Engineering
Southern Luzon State University
Lucban, Quezon, Philippines

Sujeet More
Department of Computer
   Engineering
Trinity College of Engineering and
   Research
Pune, India

Sagar Dhanraj Pande
Department of Computer Science
   and Engineering
School of Engineering and
   Technology, Pimpri Chinchwad
   University (PCU)
Pune, Maharashtra, India

Mukesh Soni
Dr. D. Y. Patil Vidyapeeth, Pune
Dr. D. Y. Patil School of Science &
   Technology
Tathawade, Pune

Betty Elezebeth Samuel
Department of Computer Science
College of Computer Science and
   Information Technology
Jazan University, Jazan, Kingdom of
   Saudi Arabia

Arijeet Chandra Sen
Joint Director, Government of
   India, Mtech
MSc (Independent Researcher),
   BITS Pilani
Pilani, India

**Zekrifa Djabeur Mohamed
   Seifeddine**
Centre of Excellence for
   Quantum Computation and
   Communication Technology
Sydney, Australia

Rajiv Sharma
Department of Computer Science &
   Engineering
Faculty of Engineering,
   Baba Mastnath University
Asthal Bohar
Rohtak, India

Vishal Shirsath
School of Engineering
ADYPU
Pune, India

S. A. Sivasankari
Department of ECE
Vignan's Foundation for Science,
   Technology & Research (Deemed
   to be University)
Guntur, India

Ajeet Kumar Srivastava
Department of Electronics and
   comm. Engg.
C S J M University
Kanpur, India

Herison Surbakti
Information and Communication
   Technology
Rangsit University International College
Lak Hok, Thailand

Chintureena Thingom
Department of CSE
Alliance College of Engineering &
   Design, Alliance University
Anekal, India

V. Mahalakshmi
Department of Computer Science
College of Computer Science &
   Information Technology
Jazan University
Jazan, Saudi Arabia

Vibhor Kumar Vishnoi
College of Computing Sciences and
   Information Technology
Teerthanker Mahaveer University
VIBHU, Moradabad, India

About the editors

Dr. Sagar Dhanraj Pande

Assistant Professor, Department of Computer Science and Engineering, School of Engineering and Technology, Pimpri Chinchwad University (PCU), Pune, Maharashtra, India.

Dr. Sagar Dhanraj Pande has expertise in Teaching, Innovation, Research & Development of more than 8 years. He has received his **Ph.D.** in Computer Science and Engineering from Lovely Professional University, Phagwara, Punjab, India in 2021. He was **2nd University Topper** during his Master of Engineering in 2016 at Sant Gadge Baba Amravati University, Amravati, Maharashtra, India. He has been awarded with "**BEST PAPER AWARD**" in 2023 from International Knowledge Research Foundation in collaboration with Eminent College of Management and Technology (ECMT), West Bengal, India. He has received the "**Young Researcher Award**" and "**Best Ph.D. Thesis Award**" in 2022 from Universal Innovators, New Delhi, India. Also, he has received the "**Emerging Scientist Award**" in 2021 from VDGOOD Professional Association, Pondicherry, India. He has been **Session Chair** of Multiple International Conferences. His research interest is Deep Learning, Machine Learning, Network Attacks, Cyber Security, and the Internet of Medical Things (IoMT). He has published and presented more than **85 papers** in IEEE, Springer, Elsevier, Taylor & Francis, and other reputable journals which are SCI, SCIE, Scopus indexed & peer-review journals. Also, he has published more than **48 Patents** on the topics of Computer Vision, Natural Language Processing, Generative AI, IoT, and its applications. He is currently supervising 4 Ph. D Scholar in the domain of AIML. He has also supervised several postgraduate students in cybersecurity, computer networks, and AI. He is responsible for teaching Artificial Intelligence, Deep Learning, Machine Learning, Cyber Crime and Security, and Python Programming courses to undergraduate and post-graduate students. He is also sharing his knowledge through his YouTube channel named **sdpguruj** https://www.youtube.com/c/SDPGuruji/playlists.

Dr. Aditya Khamparia

Assistant Professor

Coordinator of Department of Computer Science, Babasaheb Bhimrao Ambedkar University, Satellite Centre, Amethi, India.

Dr. Aditya Khamparia has expertise in Teaching, Entrepreneurship, and Research & Development of 8 years. He is currently working as Assistant Professor and Coordinator of Department of Computer Science, Babasaheb Bhimrao Ambedkar University, Satellite Centre, Amethi, India. He received his Ph.D. degree from Lovely Professional University, Punjab in May 2018. He has completed his M. Tech. from VIT University and B. Tech. from RGPV, Bhopal. He has completed his PDF from UNIFOR, Brazil. He has around 95 research papers along with book chapters including more than 15 papers in SCI indexed Journals with cumulative impact factor of above 50 to his credit. Additionally, He has authored, edited and editing 5 books. Furthermore, he has served the research field as a Keynote Speaker/Session Chair/Reviewer/TPC member/ Guest Editor and many more positions in various conferences and journals. His research interest includes machine learning, deep learning, educational technologies, computer vision.

Chapter 1

Enhancing 5G and IoT network security

A multi-model deep learning approach for attack classification

Nishanth Gadey
VIT-AP University, Amaravati, India

Sagar Dhanraj Pande
School of Engineering and Technology, Pimpri Chinchwad
University (PCU), Pune, Maharashtra, India

Aditya Khamparia
Babasaheb Bhimrao Ambedkar University (A Central University),
Lucknow, India

1.1 INTRODUCTION

The Internet of Things (IoT) encompasses a diverse array of interconnected objects with limited resources, such as wireless sensor networks (WSNs). To fulfill shared objectives and applications, these devices, which frequently include actuators, sensors, and processors, interact with one another using unique identification numbers that correspond to the Internet protocol (IP). Intelligent buildings, telecommunications, healthcare and medicine, aeronautical and aviation, monitoring the environment, related to agriculture, and manufacturing operations are just a few of the many industries that might benefit from IoT applications. Three layers make up the basic IoT architecture: the perception layer, which is where devices at the edge communicate with the surroundings in order to identify physical elements and intelligent objects; the network layer, which consists of network equipment connecting devices to one another for data the transmission of information; and the application layer, which oversees various IoT services and applications, as well as managing data storage and processing [1].

The successor to 4G, 5G is the next generation of mobile network technology. It offers diverse applications, including product development and high-speed data transfer. It aims to solve issues from 4G's widespread adoption by providing wide coverage and high throughput using millimeter waves. Advanced antennas and modulation methods enable high-bandwidth bidirectional communication. 5G enables downloading full movies, potentially rendering technologies like Bluetooth obsolete. 5G smartphones are expected to resemble tablets in size and features, and security is a significant concern [2].

DOI: 10.1201/9781003470281-1

The successor to 4G, 5G is the next generation of mobile network technology. These technologies enable network operators to shift toward service-focused management, improve customer service, and aid in network optimization. ML, a subset of AI, facilitates predictions based on historical data, while AI helps recover costs for network upgrades. Despite its advantages, AI introduces data challenges. Incorporating ML enhances traffic forecasting, analytics, network visibility, and security against intrusions, making AI a powerful ally in the evolving 5G landscape [2].

A network monitoring technology called an IDS, or intrusion detection system, can identify potentially dangerous traffic. It can be put into practice using both anomaly-based detection and signature-based identification. A signature-based IDS relies on a database of known attack signatures to detect attacks, whereas an IDS based on anomalies checks network traffic for abnormal patterns compared to typical traffic. Signature-based detection is a significant drawback since it is vulnerable to zero-day breaches or changed assaults that do not exist in the signature database. However, anomaly-based IDS is better at separating legitimate traffic from attack traffic, especially when it uses Machine Learning (ML). Integration of ML with IDS, however, is difficult. Issues were identified by Sommer and Paxson's research, with false positives becoming a particular worry. False positives occur when normal data triggers the IDS to raise alerts, reducing its reliability. Identifying models with the least number of false positives is crucial for successful ML-based IDS implementations [3].

The IoT envisions a society in which connected entity with sensors may talk to one another. They handle activities like item tracking, remote patient monitoring, and autonomous warehousing for a variety of businesses, including retail, healthcare, and manufacturing. IoT devices are multiplying quickly and are anticipated to reach 75.44 billion by 2025. This growth attracts attackers who employ automated methods like scripts and malware to exploit IoT networks. The autonomous nature of attacks and the limited processing power and bandwidth of IoT devices create challenges in ensuring adequate security, potentially leading to network layer attacks like denial of service (DoS). To address these concerns, it is necessary to research and develop effective prevention systems capable of identifying and countering such malicious traffic on IoT networks. Achieving a balance between detection precision and false alarm reduction remains a major priority in IoT security [4].

Due to the fast increase of wireless network traffic and the emergence of 5G technology, this research chapter focuses on enhancing 5G network security. It presents a novel cybersecurity model, incorporating machine learning algorithms like firewalls and IDS/IPS, integrated into the existing 5G architecture. Rigorous testing in a controlled laboratory environment demonstrates its superior performance recognizing and reducing DDoS and DoS attacks. The study not only addresses current security concerns but also outlines future enhancements for ongoing security evolution. In the context of 5G networks, a critical concern arises during both design and deployment phases. Every network component requires authentication before initiating any operation. Moreover, trustworthiness is essential for physical layer network components. DoS assaults DDoS, which affect both the application and network layers of the OSI model, are a specific danger posed by intrusion-based assaults [5].

The IoT anticipates a society in which connected objects with sensors may talk to one another. They handle activities like item monitoring, monitoring patients remotely, and autonomous warehousing for a variety of businesses including retail, healthcare, and manufacturing. IoT devices are projected to number 75.44 billion by 2025, which is a significant rise. Attackers who use automated techniques like scripts along with malware to hack IoT networks are drawn to this increase. It is difficult to provide effective security due to the autonomous nature of assaults and the constrained computing power and bandwidth of IoT devices, which could lead to network layer assaults like DoS attacks. To ease these concerns, it is crucial to do research and create systems for intrusion detection and prevention that can identify and stop such harmful activities on IoT networks [3].

Meeting the rising demand for IT services raises a critical concern: internet security. DDoS assaults, a potent technique that disrupts web-based services, thereby prohibiting genuine users from accessing resources, are one of the most significant dangers encountered. These attacks can be executed utilizing protocols like TCP, UDP, ICMP, and HTTP across multiple network layers. Researchers are actively examining a range of strategies to solve this issue, including AL and DL knowledge-based, and statistical methods, with the goal of developing robust detection and defense mechanisms. Nonetheless, each approach has drawbacks; statistical methods fail to reliably determine normal packet distribution, while ML techniques struggle to define the best appropriate feature-set [6].

By suggesting a DL-based IDS for IoT and 5G attack classification using CICIoT2023 dataset, this research study significantly advances the field of IoT and 5G network security. There are two key goals for this study. First, using the CICIoT2023 dataset, create and deploy an IDS for efficient IoT and 5G attack classification. Second, to assess how well the cutting-edge deep learning algorithms, such as ANN, DNN, RNN, Random Forest based feature selection and applying the same models and finally other proposed model for attack classification, to identify the most fitted model for IoT and 5G attack classification. The research methodology involves extensive exper- imentation and evaluation of deep learning algorithms on the CICIoT2023 dataset, which comprises comprehensive IoT and 5G traffic, both benign and malicious. The training process includes an in-depth hyperparameter search to optimize the performance of each deep learning model. The exper- imental setup employs various algorithms to classify different types of IoT and 5G attacks, and their accuracy and performance are rigorously assessed.

This study is unique in that it proposes an approach based on deep learn- ing for IoT and 5G attack classification that is specifically built to handle dynamic and developing IoT and 5G attack scenarios. Our research presents unique insights into the usefulness of cutting-edge deep learning algorithms for IoT and 5G security by investigating a wide range of cutting-edge deep learning methods. Furthermore, by defining the most precise and effective model for IoT and 5G attack classification, our research contributes to the progress of intrusion detection technologies. Using our proposed methods, we expect to attain best accuracy in categorizing diverse IoT and 5G attacks. The expected results will demonstrate the effectiveness of the proposed IDS technology and the ability of DL to handle diverse and complex IoT and 5G attacks.

This study's findings have important implications for increasing IoT and 5G security by offering a strong and reliable intrusion detection system. As the count of IoT devices and 5G networks grows, contributions of our study can improve the resilience of IoT and 5G networks to evolving cyber threats. Furthermore, determining the best deep learning algorithm for IoT and 5G attack classification might spur innovations in intrusion detection approaches, hence improving the overall cybersecurity of IoT and 5G networks.

The remaining section of the chapter is structured as follows: The related works are shown in Section 1.2, and Section 1.3 demonstrates the methodologies and working on the dataset for the attack classifications via enriching IoT datasets. In Section 1.4, we provide our experimental findings, including how well our machine learning algorithms performed. In Section 1.5, we wrap up the chapter and discuss our future goals.

1.2 LITERATURE SURVEY

Due to the complexity and breadth of the growing cyber threats, intrusion detection systems (IDS) are crucial protections for many industries, including IoT networks, software-defined networks (SDNs), web services, and industrial environments. Techniques like ML and DL in Table 1.1 have shown promise for creating intrusion detection and classification systems. In this literature review, we provide a comprehensive assessment of recent research publications that compare and analyze several techniques for anomaly-based intrusion detection in various datasets.

1.2.1 Summary of Table 1.1

Recent studies on anomaly-based intrusion detection utilizing ML and DL approaches are compiled in Table 1.1. Studies focus on diverse datasets and domains, including IoT, SDN, web, and industrial environments. Impressive performance metrics, such as high accuracy (up to 99.99%), precision (up to 99.6%), and R-Score (up to 99.87%), underscore the effectiveness of the proposed approaches. These findings highlight the potential of ML and DL methods in enhancing intrusion detection systems and bolstering cybersecurity in various contexts.

Table 1.1 ML and DL techniques for intrusion detection in IoT, SDN, web, and industrial environments: Comparative analysis

Reference paper	Year	Dataset	Techniques	Performance (Best)	Domain
[7]	2021	CICIDS2017	KNN, NB, RF, SVM	99.54 (Accuracy)	IDS
[8]	2022	CICDDOS2019	DT, RF and XGBoost, MOCA	96.67 (Accuracy)	IOT
[9]	2022	CICDDoS2019	CNN-LSTM	99.02 (Accuracy)	SDN
[10]	2022	CICDDoS2019, DDOS attack SDN Dataset	DNN (Hyper Parameter tuning)	99.53 (Accuracy) 99.96 (Accuracy)	SDN
[11]	2020	CICDDoS2019	Proposed EDSA with two hidden layers and fine tuning	98 (Accuracy)	IDS
[12]	2020	CICDDoS2019	DDoSNet	99 (Accuracy)	SDN
[13]	2021	CICDDoS2019	EFC	97.5 (F1-Score)	IDS
[14]	2021	NSL-KDD	Spectral clustering algorithm based on NJW algorithm.	98.01 (Accuracy)	WEB
[15]	2020	State-of-the-art dataset	Novel deep neural network	98 (Accuracy)	IOT
[16]	2021	Novel SDN Intrusion	hybrid CNN LSTM IDS mode	96.23 (Accuracy)	SDN
[17]	2019	CICIDS2017	Shallow NN, DNN, AE	98.45 (Accuracy)	IDS
[18]	2022	CICDDoS2019	(FwBw) with (RF)	99.99 (Accuracy)	SDN
[19]	2021	ISCXIDS2012, KDDCUP99, CICIDS2017, CICDDOS2019	Proposed, SVM, NB, RF	99.6 (Precision)	IDS
[20]	2020	CICDDoS 2019	LSTM-FUZZY	99.87 (R-Score)	SDN
[21]	2021	CICDDos 2019	Bagging, Boosting, and Stacking-based	97.3 (Accuracy)	IDS

1.3 METHODOLOGY

a) Dataset description

A significant contribution to the field of IoT security, the CIC IoT Dataset 2023 aims to facilitate the creation of reliable security analytics. This unique and sizable dataset includes real-time attacks made against a network of 105 linked IoT devices. The dataset, which includes 33 different attacks, offers a wide range of attack scenarios that have been painstakingly arranged into seven areas, including DDoS, DoS, Recon, Web-based, Brute Force, Spoofing, and Mirai attacks. Notably, every attack targets other IoT devices individually and is carried out by rogue IoT devices.

In the directory of multiple csv files of the CICIOT2023 dataset, the first csv file is considered for the project implementation which comprises 238,687 instances and 47 features; the dataset offers a substantial volume of data, presenting ample opportunities for in-depth analysis and testing of security analytics models. The target column boasts 34 unique values, reflecting the multitude of attack types covered in the dataset. This extensive dataset can be used by researchers and professionals to create and assess creative intrusion detection, classification, and mitigation techniques, fostering the advancement of IoT security solutions. As a result, the CIC IoT Dataset 2023 serves as a valuable resource, facilitating advancements in safeguarding IoT ecosystems against a wide array of potential cyber threats.

b) Pre-processing

Prior to model training, a series of pre-processing steps were meticulously executed to ensure data quality and prepare the dataset for analysis. The dataset, denoted as "df," contains both feature attributes and target labels.

1. **Random Forest feature selection**: To determine the factors that have the greatest impact on attack classification, a Random Forest Classifier was employed. The model was fitted to the dataset, and feature importance was computed.

2. **Feature importance ranking**: Based on the relevance scores that were obtained from the Random Forest model, where the features were arranged in descending order. This ranking allowed for the selection of the top 40 features, a number adaptable to specific research requirements.

3. **Feature selection**: The features with the highest importance scores were chosen, resulting in a new DataFrame, "X_new," that exclusively included the selected features. This strategic feature selection process aimed to enhance model efficiency and reduce dimensionality.

4. **Label encoding**: To facilitate multi-class classification, the target column "label" was converted into numerical values using LabelEncoder. This transformation ensured compatibility with machine learning algorithms.

5. **Data splitting**: Using an 80–20 split ratio, the dataset was divided. This partitioning allowed for model training on one subset and evaluation on another to assess generalization performance.

6. **Feature scaling**: To ensure consistent scaling across features, StandardScaler was applied to normalize the feature values in both the training and testing datasets. This step is crucial for models that are sensitive to feature scale variations.

7. **Target label encoding**: The target labels were encoded into numerical format using LabelEncoder to prepare them for multi-class classification.

8. **One-hot encoding**: For multi-class classification, the target labels were further transformed into categorical format using one-hot encoding. This transformation transformed the target labels into a binary matrix, facilitating model training and evaluation.

9. These pre-processing steps collectively ensured that the dataset was appropriately prepared for model training and evaluation, enhancing the robustness and accuracy.

c) **Analysis of dataset**

Unveiling Crucial Insights from Figures 1.1 and 1.2, Delving into Target Class Distribution and Correlation Patterns

d) **Deep learning algorithms used**

1) **Artificial Neural Network (ANN):**

These are a type of DL algorithms that take their cue from the neural architecture of human brain. Every neuron process input data using weighted connections and an activation function. The network learns to adjust these weights through backpropagation, minimizing the error between predicted and original outputs during training. The output of a neuron is computed as follows:

$$z = \sigma\left(\sum_{j=1}^{m} a_j b_j + C\right) \tag{1.1}$$

where z is the neuron's output, σ is the activation function, a_j are input features, b_j are corresponding weights, and C is the bias term.

2) **Deep Neural Network (DNN):**

Having a multitude of concealed layers, DNNs are an extension of ANNs that can learn intricate representations from data. Every hidden layer record higher-level pattern and feature, contributing to the network's ability to model intricate relationships. DNNs excel at tasks like image and speech recognition. The output of a DNN with L layers can be represented as:

$$y = f_L\left(f_{L-1}\left(\cdots f_2\left(f_1\left(\sum_{i=1}^{m} a_j b_j + C_1\right)\cdots + C_L - 1\right)\cdots + C_L\right)\right) \tag{1.2}$$

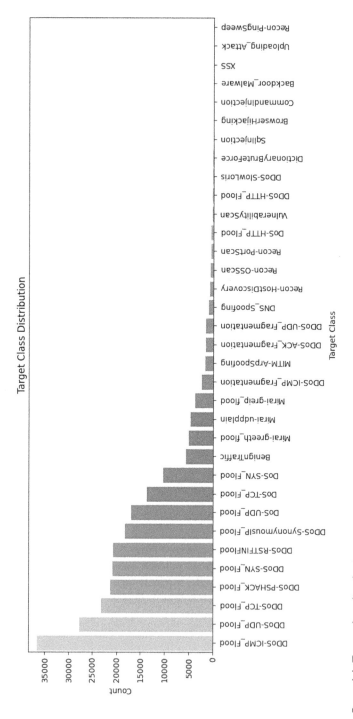

Figure 1.1 Target class distribution.

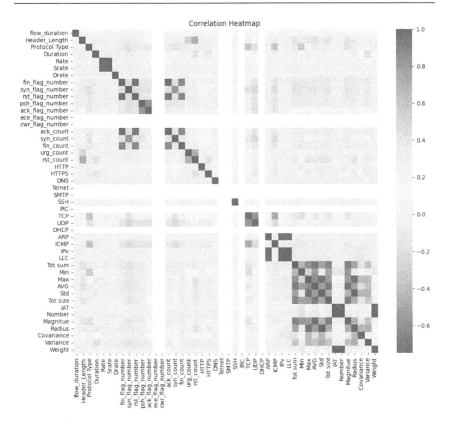

Figure 1.2 Correlation heatmap.

where f_i denotes the activation function at layer i, a_i are the layer-specific weights, and C_i are the bias terms

3) **Recurrent Neural Network (RNN):**

The purpose of RNNs is to process sequential data with time-dependent patterns. They feature feedback connections that allow them to preserve hidden states throughout different time steps. This property makes RNNs suitable for sequential tasks like NLP and time series analysis. The computation denoted is as follows:

$$ht = \sigma\left(W_h{\cdot}k_{t-1} + W_x{\cdot}T_t + C\right) \tag{1.3}$$

where T_t is input time, W_h and W_x are recurrent and input weight matrices, respectively, and C is the bias term.

e) **Proposed model**

In this section, we introduce three novel intrusion detection models along with the proposed model that leverage Random Forest (RF) as a feature selection mechanism, followed by deep learning techniques, namely, ANN, DNN, and RNN. The main objective of these models is to improvise accuracy along with robustness.

1.3.1 Feature selection by Random Forests

To choose the dataset's most pertinent features, Random Forest is used. This step of feature selection enhances the efficiency of the model and reduces the input's dimensionality.

1. **RF + ANN model**:
   The RF + ANN model synergizes the strength of Random Forest feature selection with its inherent power of ANN for ID in IoT and 5G networks.
   Model architecture:
   - The RF + ANN (Random Forest + Artificial Neural Network) aims to combine the strength of both approaches combining the Random Forest feature selection method with an ANN's deep learning capabilities.
   - The model initiates with an input layer, which takes as input the features selected by the Random Forest feature selection step.
   - A hidden layer with 64 units and ReLU (Rectified Linear Unit) is placed after the input layer. The activation function used to add nonlinearity to the model is ReLU.
   - Subsequently, there is another hidden layer with 32 units and ReLU.
   - The output layer utilizes the Softmax. It is employed for jobs involving multi-class classification. Each class is assigned a probability, and the one with the highest probability is chosen as the final classification.

2. **RF + DNN model**:
   The RF + DNN model synergizes the strength of Random Forest feature selection with the adaptability of DNN for ID in IoT and 5G networks.
   Model architecture:
   - The RF + DNN (Random Forest + Deep Neural Network) model incorporates Random Forest for feature selection and a DNN for intrusion detection.
   - It starts with an input layer that receives the features selected by Random Forest.
   - The DNN architecture comprises multiple layers – input, two hidden, output layers.
   - The input layer consists of 128 units and utilizes the ReLU activation function.
   - The first hidden layer consists of 64 units with ReLU activation, followed by the next hidden layer with 32 units, collectively enhancing the model's capability to learn intricate patterns.

- The output layer employs Softmax for multi-class classification, like RF + ANN model.

3. **RF + RNN model**:

The RF + RNN model synergizes the strength of Random Forest feature selection with the adaptability of RNN for ID in IoT and 5G networks.

Model architecture:

- The RF + RNN (Random Forest + Recurrent Neural Network) model combines the feature selection capabilities of Random Forest with the sequential data processing power of a RNN.
- Before feeding the data into the RNN, the input data is reshaped to align with the RNN's input shape.
- The RNN architecture consists of an LSTM layer with 64 units and ReLU. LSTMs are particularly well suited for managing sequential data.
- The output layer's final step uses Softmax activation, accommodating multi-class classification tasks.

Training and optimization:

The model is constructed using the "adam" optimizer, a popular choice for gradient-based optimization techniques. For multi-class classification tasks, the appropriate loss function to use is categorical cross-entropy. It is trained with a batch size of 64 over 30 epochs to develop the capability to make precise predictions for all the above three models.

4. **Proposed model**

Model architecture:

The architecture of the proposed model is specifically created to effectively classify IoT attacks. It consists of several layers, each serving a specific purpose:

Input Layer:
- Units: 128
- Activation Function: ReLU
- Input Shape: Determined by the input features in the training data

Hidden Layer 1:
- Units: 64
- Activation Function: ReLU
- Regularization: L2 Regularization (0.00001) to prevent overfitting

Hidden Layer 2:
- Units: 32
- Activation Function: ReLU
- Regularization: L2 Regularization (0.00001) to enhance model robustness

Output Layer:
- Activation Function: Softmax
- Units: Match the number of classes in the dataset

Model configuration

The configuration of the proposed model involves the use of the Adam optimizer and the employment of the Categorical Cross-Entropy loss function and evaluating performance based on the accuracy metric. These choices in model configuration lay the foundation for its effectiveness in training and prediction.

Model training

In the training phase, the model undergoes 40 epochs, where each epoch involves processing a batch size of 64 data points. Additionally, a crucial aspect of model development is the inclusion of a validation split. In this setup, 10% of the training data is set aside for validation, enabling continuous evaluation of the model's performance and aiding in the prevention of overfitting during the training process.

Simplified pseudo code

Here is a simplified pseudo code representation of the proposed model for reference:

Create a deep neural network model (new_model)
Add input layer with 128 units and ReLU activation
Add hidden layer 1 with 64 units, ReLU activation, and L2 regularization (0.00001)
Add hidden layer 2 with 32 units, ReLU activation, and L2 regularization (0.00001)
Add output layer with Softmax activation

Compile the model
Use Adam optimizer for efficient optimization
Employ categorical cross-entropy as the loss function
Track accuracy as a metric during training

Train the model
Input training features (X_train_scaled) and one-hot encoded labels (y_train_categorical)
Perform 40 training epochs with a batch size of 64
Allocate 10% of the training data for validation

Common evaluation metrics:
- For all proposed models, common evaluation is computed.
- Confusion matrices and classification reports provide a comprehensive view of model performance.

These proposed models harness the strengths of both Random Forest and utilizing DL for the improvement of precision and optimization of computational efficiency of intrusion detection for IoT and 5G networks. The subsequent sections provide detailed insights into the experimental results, demonstrating the effectiveness of each model in classifying diverse intrusion patterns.

1.4 RESULT ANALYSIS

In this section, a detailed examination is conducted on the performance metrics and training outcomes for each of the seven models utilized in this study. The models have been evaluated rigorously to assess their effectiveness.

Performance metrics comparison:
Table 1.2 provides a comprehensive comparison of the key performance metrics across all models:
Model comparison and observations
In this section, we delve into a detailed comparison of the seven models based on the performance metrics:

1. **Proposed model**: The RF + Proposed model emerges as the top-performing model across all metrics. It achieves an impressive test accuracy of 98.45%, highlighting its capacity for precise classification IoT and 5G network intrusions. This model exhibits excellent precision, recall, and F1 Score, emphasizing its overall effectiveness.
2. **RF + DNN**: The RF + DNN model also performs exceptionally well, with a high test accuracy of 98.28%. It demonstrates excellent precision, recall, and F1 Score, making it a good contender for intrusion detection.
3. **RF + ANN**: The RF + ANN model showcases a commendable performance with a test accuracy of 98.16%. It demonstrates a well-balanced trade-off between precision, recall, and F1 Score, making it a reliable choice for intrusion detection.
4. **RF + RNN**: The RF + RNN model delivers competitive results with a test accuracy of 98.23%. While it excels in accuracy and recall, its precision and F1 Score are slightly lower compared to the top-performing models.

Table 1.2 Performance metrics comparison for seven models

Metric	ANN score	DNN score	RNN score	RF + ANN score	RF + DNN score	RF + RFF score	Proposed model score
Test Accuracy	0.9812	0.9821	0.9801	0.9816	0.9828	0.9823	0.9845
Precision	0.9802	0.9808	0.9790	0.9804	0.9810	0.9810	0.9829
Recall	0.9812	0.9821	0.9801	0.9816	0.9828	0.9823	0.9845
F1 Score	0.9802	0.9806	0.9790	0.9802	0.9810	0.9810	0.9831

5. **DNN**: The stand-alone DNN model performs impressively, achieving a test accuracy of 98.21%. It demonstrates excellent precision, recall, and F1 Score, highlighting its effectiveness in intrusion detection.
6. **ANN**: The stand-alone ANN model delivers strong results, with a test accuracy of 98.12%. It exhibits excellent precision, recall, and F1 Score, making it a valuable component in the model ensemble.
7. **RNN**: The stand-alone RNN model showcases robust performance, with a test accuracy of 98.01%. It excels in accuracy and recall, though its precision and F1 Score are slightly lower compared to the top models.

Overall observations

- All models achieve exceptionally high test accuracies, highlighting their effectiveness in intrusion detection for both IoT and 5G networks.
- The RF + Proposed model stands out as the top-performing model, with the highest evaluation metrics. It offers a comprehensive solution for intrusion detection in evolving attack scenarios.
- The ensemble models (RF + ANN, RF + DNN, RF + RNN) demonstrate consistent performance, indicating the strength of combining random forests with neural network architectures.
- Stand-alone ANN, DNN, and RNN also exhibit strong intrusion detection capabilities, making them valuable alternatives for specific use cases.
- The results emphasize the potential of ensemble models when dealing with intricate security challenges.

Training outcome visualizations

To gain deeper insights into the training process of each model, we present visualizations depicting the training and validation trends over multiple epochs. These visualizations provide a dynamic view of the model's learning process (Figure 1.3).

Discussion and Implications:

The findings from this extensive evaluation have several implications:

- The RF + Proposed model showcases the potential for achieving superior intrusion detection in IoT and 5G networks through a well-crafted combination of Random Forests and Deep Neural Networks.
- The observed patterns in training outcomes emphasize the importance of selecting the appropriate model architecture, as well as monitoring metrics like accuracy, loss, and validation performance.
- The variations in model performance across metrics highlight the trade-offs involved in intrusion detection, where different models excel in different aspects.

In conclusion, this comprehensive analysis underscores the efficiency of the suggested models in addressing the complex challenges of ID in the ever-evolving landscape of IoT and 5G networks. The results provide valuable insights seeking to fortify the security of these critical domains.

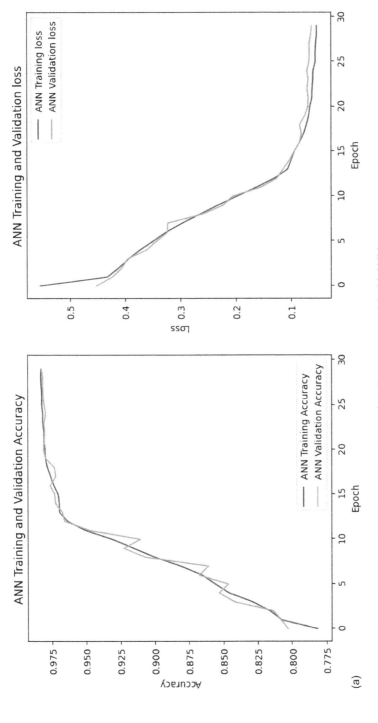

Figure 1.3 Training vs validation graphs for accuracy and loss for all the seven models. (a) ANN.

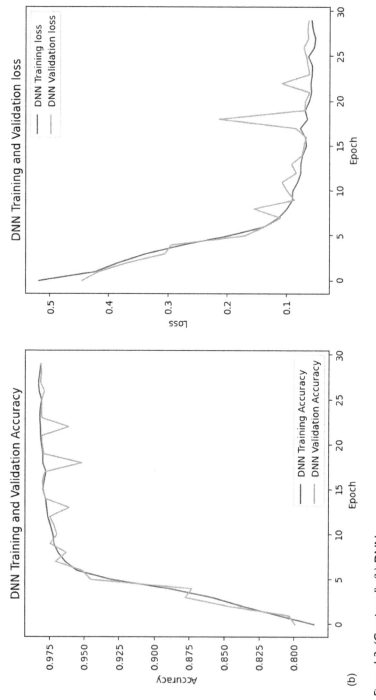

Figure 1.3 (Continued) (b) DNN.

(b)

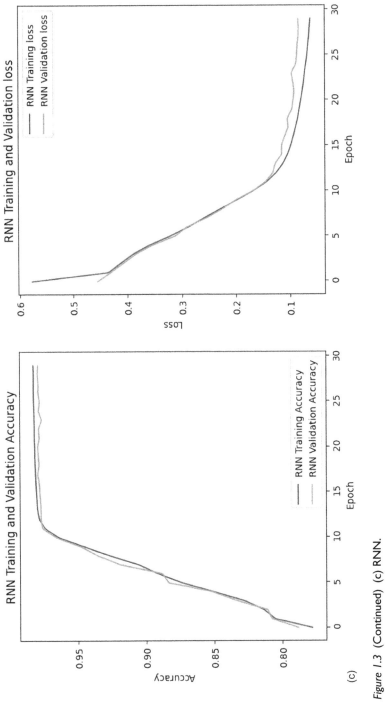

Figure 1.3 (Continued) (c) RNN.

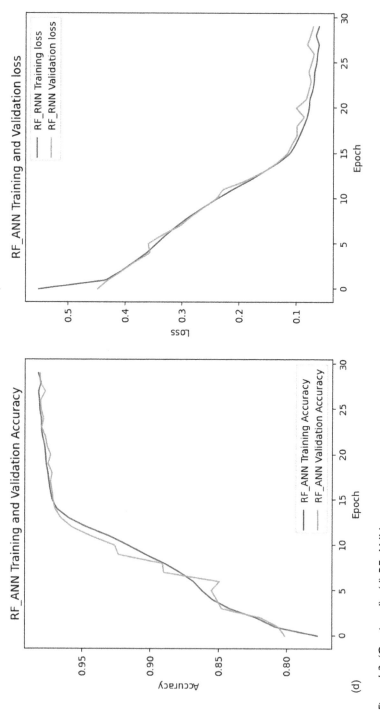

Figure 1.3 (Continued) (d) RF_ANN.

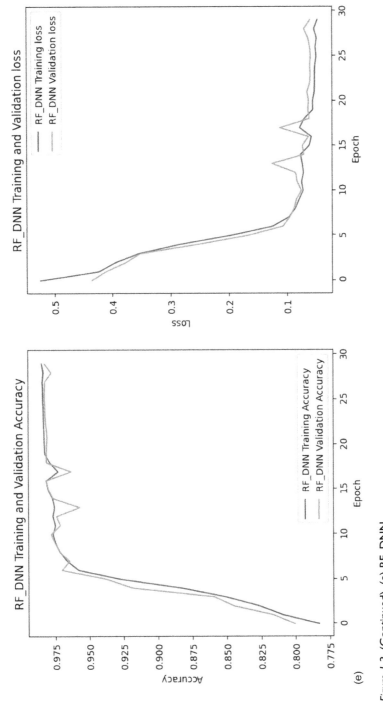

Figure 1.3 (Continued) (e) RF_DNN.

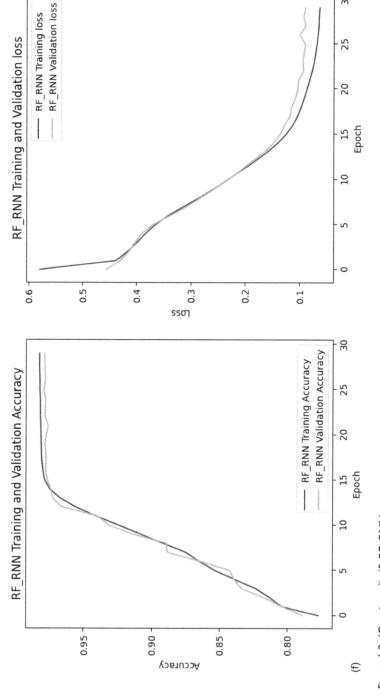

Figure 1.3 (Continued) (f) RF_RNN.

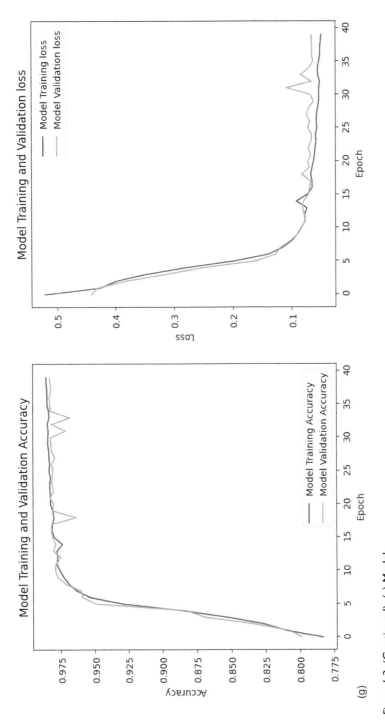

(g)

Figure 1.3 (Continued) (g) Model.

1.5 CONCLUSION AND FUTURE SCOPE

This study advances the realm of Intrusion Detection Systems (IDS) by focusing on classifying both IoT and 5G network attacks using the expansive CICIOT2023 dataset – first csv file. Seven distinct models, including ensemble techniques and deep learning algorithms, were rigorously evaluated. Among them, the RF + Proposed model exhibited remarkable performance, achieving an impressive 98.45% test accuracy, firmly establishing its position as the most effective IDS in this context. This study highlights the potential of combining traditional machine learning with cutting-edge neural networks.

Future endeavors can explore ensemble methods, transfer learning, hyperparameter fine-tuning, and real-time deployment, enhancing IDS robustness. Continuous monitoring is pivotal for proactively safeguarding IoT and 5G networks against emerging cyber threats. This study demonstrates that leveraging various models and algorithms significantly enhances network security, fortifying the resilience of IoT and 5G networks against potential intrusion attempts and ensuring a secure digital future.

REFERENCES

[1] Abu Al-Haija, Qasem, and Saleh Zein-Sabatto. "An efficient deep-learning-based detection and classification system for cyber-attacks in IoT communication networks." *Electronics* 9.12 (2020): 2152.

[2] Keserwani, Hitesh, et al. "Security enhancement by identifying attacks using machine learning for 5G network." *International Journal of Communication Networks and Information Security* 14.2 (2022): 124–141.

[3] Churcher, A., R. Ullah, J. Ahmad, S. Ur Rehman, F. Masood, M. Gogate, … and W. J. Buchanan. An experimental analysis of attack classification using machine learning in IoT networks. *Sensors* 21.2 (2021): 446.

[4] Tama, Bayu Adhi, and Kyung-Hyune Rhee. "Attack classification analysis of IoT network via deep learning approach." *Research Briefs on Information and Communication Technology Evolution* 3 (2017): 150–158.

[5] Yadav, Neha, et al. "Intrusion detection system on IoT with 5G network using deep learning." *Wireless Communications and Mobile Computing* 2022 (2022): 1–13.

[6] S. Jin, and D. S. Yeung. "A covariance analysis model for DDOS attack detection." *2004 IEEE International Conference on Communications* 4 1882–1886, 2004.

[7] Z. K. Maseer, R. Yusof, N. Bahaman, S. A. Mostafa, and C. F. M. Foozy. "Benchmarking of machine learning for anomaly based intrusion detection systems in the CICIDS2017 dataset." *IEEE Access* 9 (2021): 22351–22370.

[8] Fuhr, J., F. Wang, and Y. Tang MOCA: A network intrusion monitoring and classification system. *Journal of Cybersecurity and Privacy* 2 (2022): 629–639. https://doi.org/10.3390/jcp2030032

[9] Zainudin, Ahmad, Dong-Seong Kim, and Jae-Min Lee. "A lightweight deep learning-based anomaly detection and classification in software-defined industrial network." 한국통신학회 학술대회논문집 (2022): 1116–1117.

[10] Bennet, Deepthi, Preethi Tabitha, Samantha Bennet, and D. Anitha. "Securing smart city networks-intelligent detection of DDoS cyber attacks." *2022 5th International Conference on Contemporary Computing and Informatics (IC3I)*. IEEE, 2022.

[11] Sindian, Samar, and S. Samer. "An enhanced deep autoencoder-based approach for DDoS attack detection." *WSEAS Transactions on Systems and Control* 15 (2020): 716–725.

[12] Elsayed, Mahmoud Said, et al. "Ddosnet: A deep-learning model for detecting network attacks." *2020 IEEE 21st International Symposium on" A World of Wireless, Mobile and Multimedia Networks" (WoWMoM)*. IEEE, 2020.

[13] C. F. T. Pontes, M. M. C. de Souza, J. J. C. Gondim, M. Bishop, and M. A. Marotta. "A new method for flow-based network intrusion detection using the inverse Potts model." *IEEE Transactions on Network and Service Management* 18.2 (Jun. 2021): 1125–1136.

[14] Yu, X., W. Yu, S. Li, X. Yang, Y. Chen, and H. Lu. WEB DDoS attack detection method based on semisupervised learning. *Security and Communication Networks* 2021 (2021): 1–10.

[15] M. Asad, M. Asim, T. Javed, M. O. Beg, H. Mujtaba, and S. Abbas. "Deepdetect: Detection of distributed denial of service attacks using deep learning." *The Computer Journal* 63.7 (2020): 983–994.

[16] M. Abdallah, N. An Le Khac, H. Jahromi, and A. Delia Jurcut. "A hybrid CNN-LSTM based approach for anomaly detection systems in SDNs." *The 16th International Conference on Availability, Reliability and Security*, pp. 1–7, Vienna, Austria, August 2021.

[17] Ustebay, Serpil, Zeynep Turgut, and M. Ali Aydin. "Cyber attack detection by using neural network approaches: Shallow neural network, deep neural network and autoencoder." *Computer Networks: 26th International Conference, CN 2019, Kamień Śląski, Poland, June 25–27, 2019, Proceedings 26*. Springer International Publishing, 2019.

[18] Ibrahim, Zainab A., and Imad J. Mohammed. "Analysis of features selection effects on different classification algorithms with performance metrics improvement based on PortScan-attack of CICDDoS2019 dataset." *Journal of Algebraic Statistics* 13.3 (2022): 1712–1723.

[19] Adhao, Rahul B., and Vinod K. Pachghare. "Support based graph framework for effective intrusion detection and classification." 01 November 2021, PREPRINT (Version 1) available at Research Square https://doi.org/10.21203/rs.3.rs-1035364/v1

[20] Novaes, Matheus P., et al. "Long short-term memory and fuzzy logic for anomaly detection and mitigation in software-defined network environment." *IEEE Access* 8 (2020): 83765–83781.

[21] Khoei, Tala Talaei, et al. "Ensemble learning methods for anomaly intrusion detection system in smart grid." *2021 IEEE international conference on electro information technology (EIT)*. IEEE, 2021.

Chapter 2

Dynamic deployment and traffic scheduling of UPF in 5G networks

Renato R. Maaliw III
Southern Luzon State University, Lucban, Quezon, Philippines

Haewon Byeon
Inje University, Gimhae, Republic of Korea

Ravi Kumar
Jaypee University of Engineering and Technology, Guna, India

Mukesh Soni
Dr. D.Y. Patil Vidyapeeth, Pune, Dr. D.Y. Patil School of Science & Technology, Tathawade, Pune

2.1 INTRODUCTION

The proliferation of mobile data traffic and Internet-connected gadgets in the 5G era has forced a revision of the tried-and-true design of the backbone of wireless networks [1]. The control plane and user plane, as well as the software and hardware, are connected in this design [2]. To overcome these restrictions, new core network architecture has been introduced as part of the 3GPP's 5G technology specifications. By isolating the control plane from the user plane and introducing network function virtualisation and software-defined networking technologies into core network deployment, this design increases network flexibility and scalability [3, 4]. Traditional centralised core network user plane deployment, on the other hand, results in high round-trip latency since it cannot meet the low-latency requirements of 5G services.

Leveraging upcoming technologies like mobile edge computing and fog computing gives a possible answer to these problems. UPF deployment on edge servers nearer users allows for much lower end-to-end latency [5]. Putting in place UPF is a standard example of a challenge while deploying a VNF. Dynamic VNF deployment needs have been largely ignored, while the static deployment of VNFs has received a lot of attention in recent years [6–9]. Joint optimisation techniques for VNF migration costs and network energy usage [10] have been proposed in certain research. These methods, however, ignore the effect that deployment choices have on delay. While other studies have attempted to solve the dynamic VNF deployment problem under

DOI: 10.1201/9781003470281-2

time-varying traffic conditions by breaking it down into smaller problems [11], the solution accuracy of these approaches is subpar. To deal with fluctuating needs for service function chain resources, deep deterministic policy gradient-based VNF migration algorithms have been developed [12], although training on these algorithms is time-consuming. Additionally, some research has focused on the monetary losses associated with moving VNF instances, and optimisation models for moving VNF instances have been developed, taking energy consumption and reconfiguration costs into account using heuristic algorithms based on the MDP [13].

Energy economy and latency must be considered when deploying UPF because they are two of the most crucial KPIs for 5G networks [14]. UPF network components should be installed as close to the user equipment (UE) as possible to reduce user plane data latency, and UPF network parts should be integrated into as few edge servers as possible to minimise energy usage. The cost of UPF deployment must also be taken into account. Costs related to decisions on deployment made during one time slot may have an impact on those made during the next, and vice versa. The current approaches to time slot optimisation ignore the influence of deployment decisions on delays, which increases the cost of UPF installation.

The overarching goals of this research are to minimise the total energy consumption of edge servers, lessen the expense of UPF deployment, and lessen the impact of operational latency on user plane data. We do this by developing a staged approach for rolling out the user plane UPF and traffic scheduling in the network's core. The model is broken down into its component parts using the Benders decomposition algorithm, with the UPF deployment challenge serving as the major focus. We find the best strategies for UPF deployment and traffic scheduling by iterative, alternating solution of the main problem and subproblems.

Due to the exponential development of mobile data traffic and the rising number of Internet-connected devices, the traditional architecture of wireless network infrastructure must be re-evaluated in the 5G era. The coupling of the control plane and user plane, as well as the software and hardware, limits both flexibility and scalability. As part of the 5G technology specifications, the 3GPP has designed a new central network architecture that incorporates software-defined networking and network function virtualisation. Traditional, centralised deployment of the user plane of the core network results in significant round-trip latency and falls short of the low-latency requirements of 5G services.

This study aids in the design of effective UPF deployment techniques that boost the functionality of 5G networks by taking into account energy usage, latency, and deployment costs. To overcome the difficulties of real-time UPF deployment, a new multi-stage planning model is proposed, which employs the Benders decomposition technique. The results of this research give important information for network operators and researchers working to improve 5G networks through optimised UPF deployment and traffic scheduling.

This research focuses on utilising cutting-edge technology to improve the deployment of the user plane function (UPF) in 5G networks in order to address the aforementioned difficulties. The criteria for dynamic VNF deployment have largely been ignored, despite the fact that static VNF deployment has received a lot of attention. Decomposition-based methods for dynamic VNF deployment in time-varying traffic conditions do not provide appropriate solution accuracy, and existing optimisation approaches do not take the impact of deployment choices on latency into account. Deep deterministic policy gradient-based VNF migration algorithms nevertheless require time-consuming training procedures despite being effective.

Given these limitations, the goal of this study is to lower the amount of energy that edge servers use, the cost of deploying UPF, and the effects of operational latency on user plane data over the whole network operational cycle. In order to do this, a new multi-stage planning method is made for UPF implementation and traffic scheduling in the core network. The Benders decomposition algorithm is used to break the model into a major UPF deployment problem and a number of traffic scheduling subproblems. By solving the main problem and its subproblems one at a time, you can get to the best UPF deployment and traffic scheduling methods.

The findings of this study aid in the development of efficient UPF deployment methods that improve the performance of 5G networks while taking energy efficiency, latency, and deployment costs into account. The problems with real-time UPF deployment are addressed by the multi-stage planning approach that is being suggested, which makes use of the Benders decomposition method. For network operators and researchers trying to optimise UPF deployment and traffic scheduling to boost the performance of 5G networks, the study's conclusions are extremely insightful.

2.2 UPF DEPLOYMENT AND TRAFFIC SCHEDULING MULTI-STAGE PLANNING MODEL

Figure 2.1 depicts the edge network's deployment of the 5G core network's user plane. To drastically cut down on user plane latency, the UPF is deployed on edge servers, one of which is placed at each base station (assuming the base station distribution is a Poisson point process). The graphic depicts how the energy optimisation technique consolidates traffic onto a small number of edge servers. By routing connections to closer-by edge servers, latency for the user plane is minimised. This research builds a multi-stage planning model for UPF deployment and traffic scheduling, taking into account the energy consumption and user plane delay of edge servers as well as the cost of redeployment and rescheduling under time-varying load conditions.

2.2.1 Edge network environment

Let I be the set of edge servers, J be the set of edge server resource types, R_{ij} represents the capacity of type j resources on edge server i (where $i \in I$ and

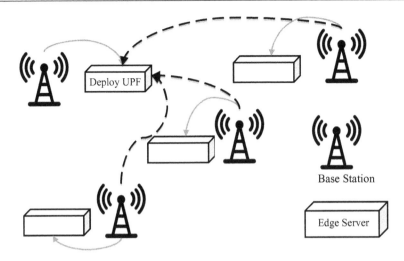

Figure 2.1 Deployment of 5G network.

$j \in J$). Let K be the set of UPF virtual network function types, r_{kj} represents the demand for type j resources of UPF instances of type k (where $k \in K$), and u_K^{UPF} represents the processing capacity of UPF instances of type k. Let M be the set of base stations. The data traffic of base stations exhibits a clear day-night pattern and is usually periodic [15]. Let T be the set of time slots for a single period, and Δt be the duration of each time slot. Let u_{mt}^{gNB} represent the data traffic of base station m (where $m \in M$) in time slot t (where $t \in T$).

2.2.2 UPF deployment and traffic scheduling problem

Let $y_{it} \in \{0, 1\}$ determine whether edge server i is enabled in time slot $t \in T$: $y_{it} = 1$ indicates it is enabled, $y_{it} = 0$ indicates it is not enabled. n_{ikt} (where ($n_{ikt} \in N$)) represents the number of UPF instances of type k deployed on edge server i in time slot t. $u_{mit} \geq 0$ denotes the data traffic between base station m and edge server i in time slot t. Consider the following three optimisation objectives: edge server energy consumption, UPF deployment cost, and user plane data latency.

2.2.2.1 The edge server energy

The edge server energy consumption adopts a linear power consumption model based on CPU utilisation [16]. The power consumption of edge server i is represented as:

$$P_i = P_i^{idle} + \left(P_i^{peak} - P_i^{idle} \right) u_i^{CPU} \tag{2.1}$$

In the equation: P_i^{idle} and P_i^{peak} represent the idle power consumption and peak power consumption of edge server i, respectively. u_i^{CPU} denotes the CPU utilisation of edge server i. The energy consumption of edge server i in time slot t is represented as:

$$E_t = \sum_{i \in I} y_{it} \left(P_i^{\text{idle}} + \left(P_i^{\text{peak}} - P_i^{\text{idle}} \right) \sum_{k \in K} n_{ikt} r_k^{\text{CPU}} / R_i^{\text{CPU}} \right) \Delta t \qquad (2.2)$$

In the equation: R_i^{CPU} represent the CPU capacity of edge server i, and r_k^{CPU} represents the demand of UPF virtual network function of type k for CPU resources.

2.2.2.2 UPF deployment cost

UPF deployment cost includes the energy cost of deploying new UPF instances and the revenue loss caused by deployment delay. Let C_k^{UPF} be the deployment unit cost of UPF instances of type k. Let Δn_{ikt} be the number of newly deployed UPF instances of type k on edge server i in time slot t, represented as:

$$\Delta n_{ikt} = \max \left\{ n_{ikt} - n_{ik(t-1)}, 0 \right\} \qquad (2.3)$$

Therefore, the UPF deployment cost in time slot t is represented as:

$$C_t^{\text{dep}} = \sum_{i \in I} \sum_{k \in K} \Delta n_{ikt} C_k^{\text{UPF}} \qquad (2.4)$$

2.2.2.3 User plane data latency

User plane latency is mainly composed of four components: processing latency, queuing latency, transmission latency, and propagation latency. Among these, only propagation latency is affected by the geographical location of UPF deployment. Therefore, this study considers only the propagation latency of the user plane. Let δ_{mit} represent the propagation latency between base station m and edge server i. The propagation latency between a base station and an edge server is proportional to the geographical distance between them. The user plane data latency in time slot t is represented as:

$$D_t = \sum_{m \in M} \sum_{i \in I} u_{\text{mit}} \cdot \Delta t \cdot d_{\text{mi}} \qquad (2.5)$$

With the objective of minimising the total edge server energy consumption, UPF deployment cost, and user plane data latency over the operating cycle, the UPF deployment and traffic scheduling problem can be formulated as follows:

$$\min \sum_{t \in T} \left(\beta_e \cdot E_t + C_t^{\text{dep}} + \beta_d \cdot D_t \right) \tag{2.6a}$$

$$\&\text{s.t} \sum_{k \in K} n_{ikt} \cdot r_{kj} \leq y_{it} \cdot R_{ij}; \ t \in T, \ i \in I, \ j \in J \tag{2.6b}$$

$$\& \sum_{m \in M} u_{mit} \leq \sum_{k \in K} n_{ikt} \cdot u_k^{\text{UPF}}; \ t \in T, \ i \in I \tag{2.6c}$$

$$\& u_{mt}^{\text{gNB}} = \sum_{i \in I} u_{mit}; \ t \in T, \ m \in M \tag{2.6d}$$

$$\Delta n_{ikt} \geq n_{ikt} - n_{ik(t-1)}; \ t \in T, \ i \in I, \ k \in K \tag{2.6e}$$

$$\& y_{it} \in \{0,1\}; \ t \in T, \ i \in I \tag{2.6f}$$

$$\& n_{ikt} \in N; \ t \in T, \ i \in I, \ k \in K \tag{2.6g}$$

$$\& u_{mit} \geq 0; \ t \in T, \ m \in M, \ i \in I \tag{2.6h}$$

$$\& \Delta n_{ikt} \geq 0; \ t \in T; \ i \in I; \ k \in K \tag{2.6i}$$

Equation (2.6b) represents the resource capacity constraint of the edge servers, ensuring that the resource allocation for each edge server does not exceed its resource capacity. Equation (2.6c) represents the processing capacity constraint of the edge servers, ensuring that the data traffic scheduled to each edge server does not exceed its processing capacity. Equation (2.6d) represents the flow conservation constraint, indicating that the data traffic from base station m is equal to the sum of the data traffic scheduled to all edge servers. Equations (2.6e) and (2.6i) are derived from the definition of auxiliary variables, where λ and φ are the cost factors for energy consumption and unit data latency, respectively, used to convert energy consumption and data latency into monetary costs. It can be observed that Equation (2.6) represents a mixed-integer linear programming problem.

Theorem 1

The UPF deployment and traffic scheduling problem described in Equation (2.6) is an NP-hard problem.

Proof: We will prove this by constructing a special case of the problem using a reduction method [17] and showing that this special case is a known NP-hard problem.

Let $C_k^{\text{UPF}} = 0$ and $\delta = 0$, which allows us to decompose the problem into time slots.

Let $\beta_d - 0$ be set to such values that the traffic scheduling becomes irrelevant.

Consider a restriction where only a single edge server and a single resource type are considered. Thus, Equation (2.6a–2.6h) transforms into an integer minimum knapsack problem.

Since the integer minimum knapsack problem is known to be NP-hard [18], it follows that Equation (2.6) is also NP-hard.

2.3 TRAFFIC SCHEDULING ALGORITHM BASED ON BENDERS DECOMPOSITION

The Benders decomposition approach is used to resolve the UPF deployment and traffic scheduling problems. Equation (2.6) is divided into several smaller problems for traffic scheduling and one primary problem for UPF deployment in order to effectively reduce the computational complexity of the issue.

Theorem 2

The deployment and scheduling of traffic in the user plane of the 5G core network is a mixed-integer linear programming problem with complicated variables [19].

Proof: From Equation (2.6e), it can be observed that the deployment cost for each time slot depends not only on the deployment decisions for the current time slot but also on the deployment decisions for the previous time slot. The decision variable δ hinders the decomposition of Equation (2.6) into time slots. If the variable δ is fixed to a given value, Equation (2.6) can be decomposed into a series of subproblems for traffic scheduling. Therefore, the variable δ is a complex variable in Equation (2.6).

Equation (2.6) is resolved using the Benders decomposition procedure in accordance with Theorem 2. Iterative algorithms include the Benders decomposition algorithm. To determine the lower and upper bounds of Equation (2.6), the main problem and the subproblem are each solved independently in each iteration. When the lower and higher boundaries are sufficiently near, the process stops.

2.3.1 Traffic scheduling subproblem

By fixing the complex variable δ to a given value, Equation (2.6) can be decomposed into a series of traffic scheduling subproblems based on time slots. In the iteration, the traffic scheduling subproblem for time slot is given by:

$$\min D_t \tag{2.7a}$$

$$\text{s.t.} (6c).(6d).(6h) \tag{2.7b}$$

$$\& n_{ikt} = n^*_{iktv}; i \in I, k \in K \tag{2.7c}$$

The optimisation objective is to minimise the user plane data latency for time slot. Equation (2.7b) represents the constraints related to traffic scheduling and it is fixed for the given value which is obtained from solving the main problem in the current iteration. In Equation (2.7), the variable is treated as a continuous variable. It can be observed that the traffic scheduling subproblem is a continuous linear programming problem.

Consider the user plane data latency for time slot obtained from solving the subproblem in Equation (2.7). The total operational cost for the user plane in the core network over the running period is represented as:

$$z_v^{ub} = \sum_{t \in T} \left(\beta_e \cdot E_{tv}^* + C_{tv}^{dep*} + \beta_d \cdot D_{tv}^* \right)$$

The energy use of the edge servers during the time slot determined from solving the primary issue in the current iteration is represented in the equation E_{tv}^*. After resolving the key issue in the current iteration, C_{tv}^{dep*} is the deployment cost of UPF for time slot. An upper limit on Equation (2.6)'s ideal value is given by z_v^{ub}. The Benders optimal cut in the main problem is produced using λ_{iktv}^*, the best value of the dual variable connected to Equation (2.7c).

2.3.2 The problem of UPF deployment

In iteration v, the UPF deployment master problem is

$$\min \sum_{t \in T} \left(\beta_e \cdot E_t + C_t^{dep} + \beta_d \cdot \alpha_t \right) \tag{2.8a}$$

$$\& \text{s.t.Mode}(6b).(6e) \sim (6g).(6i), t \in T \tag{2.8b}$$

$$\alpha_t \geq D_{tj}^* + \sum_{i \in I} \sum_{k \in K} \lambda_{iktj}^* \left(n_{ikt} - n_{iktj}^* \right) t \in T, j = 1, \cdots, v - 1 \tag{2.8c}$$

$$\alpha_t \geq \alpha_t^{\text{down}}; t \in T \tag{2.8d}$$

The objective function in Equation (2.8a) corresponds to Equation (2.6a), which represents the estimated value of the user plane data latency in time slot. Equation (2.8b) represents the constraints related to UPF deployment. Equation (2.8c) represents the Benders optimal cut set generated in previous iterations. Equation (2.8d) sets the lower bound, which accelerates the convergence of the Benders decomposition algorithm. It can be observed that the main problem is an integer linear programming problem.

From Equations (2.6c) and (2.6d), it is known that the variable must satisfy the constraints:

$$\sum_{i \in I} \sum_{k \in K} n_{ikt} u_k^{\text{UPF}} \geq \sum_{m \in M} u_{mt}^{\text{gNB}}, t \in T \tag{2.9}$$

Because Equation (2.9) is not a component of the main issue, obtaining the values of the complex variables generated from the main problem solution may make the subproblem infeasible. In such cases, a feasibility cut is applied to the fundamental issue, increasing the computing cost of the Benders decomposition technique significantly. Equation (2.9) is attached to the core issue to guarantee that the subproblem is always doable. When a feasibility cut is removed from the fundamental issue, the computing cost of the Benders decomposition procedure is greatly decreased.

Let z_v^{lb} be the optimal solution to the main problem at the vth iteration, which functions as a lower bound for the optimal solution of Equation (2.6). Let θ represent the optimal solution to the main problem in the vth iteration, which will serve as the fixed value for the complex variables in the current iteration of the subproblem.

2.3.3 Benders decomposition algorithm

As shown in Figure 2.2, the specific steps to solve the UPF deployment and traffic scheduling problem using the Benders decomposition algorithm are as follows:

(1) Initialise parameters: Set the upper bound of the objective function of the UPF deployment and traffic scheduling problem, $z^{\text{ub}} = \infty$, and set the lower bound, $z^{\text{lb}} = -\infty$. Set the Benders optimal cut set in the UPF deployment master problem to empty.

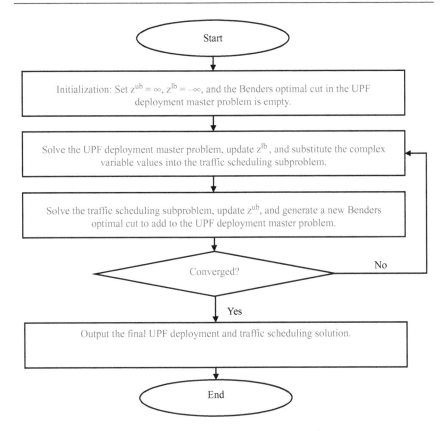

Figure 2.2 Flow chart based on Benders decomposition approach.

(2) Solve the UPF deployment master problem: Obtain z_v^{lb} and n_{iktv}^* as the optimal solution. Update the lower bound of the objective function of the UPF deployment and traffic scheduling problem to $z^{lb} = z_v^{lb}$ and replace n_{iktv}^* in the traffic scheduling subproblem.

(3) Solve the traffic scheduling subproblem: Obtain D_{tv}^* and λ_{iktv}^* as the optimal solution. Update the upper bound of the objective function of the UPF deployment and traffic scheduling problem.

$$z^{ub} = \min\left\{ z^{ub}, z_v^{ub} = \sum_{t \in T} \left(\beta_e \cdot E_{tv}^* + C_{tv}^{dep*} + \beta_d \cdot D_{tv}^* \right) \right\} \qquad (2.10)$$

(4) Check if the convergence condition is satisfied. Let ε be the predetermined error tolerance. If $(z^{ub} - z^{lb})/z^{lb} \leq \varepsilon$, then terminate the iteration. Otherwise, generate the Benders optimal cut.

$$\alpha_t \geq D_{tv}^* + \sum_{i \in I}\sum_{k \in K} \lambda_{iktv}^* \left(n_{ikt} - n_{iktv}^*\right), t \in T \tag{2.11}$$

And add Formula (2.11) to the main problem of UPF deployment, return to step 2).

2.3.4 Complexity analysis

The proposed algorithm in this research separates the traffic scheduling problem into $|T|$ subproblems, one of which is the UPF deployment master problem. Assuming that each edge server can host a maximum of n_{max} UPF instances, the UPF deployment master problem is an integer programming problem in which just a single UPF type is taken into account. The UPF deployment master problem has a complexity of $O(2^{|I||T|}(n_{max} + 1)^{2|I||T|})$. Linear programming problem of complexity $O((|M||I|)^3)$ describes the traffic scheduling subproblem. Each iteration has a complexity of $O(2^{|I||T|}(n_{max} + 1)^{2|I||T|} + |T|(|M||I|)^3)$ in terms of computation. Where L is the number of iterations needed for the algorithm to converge, the overall computational complexity is written as $O(L(2^{|I||T|}(n_{max} + 1)^{2|I||T|} + |T|(|M||I|)^3))$. Our experiments show that only a few iterations are needed to reach convergence. $O(|T|2^{|I|}(n_{max} + 1)^{2|I|}(|M||I|)^3)$ is the computational complexity of the direct solution of Equation (2.6). Therefore, the computing complexity of Equation (2.6) is much reduced by the proposed technique. The suggested algorithm is evaluated in a simulation experiment alongside a staged solution approach and an MDP-based heuristic algorithm. The staged solution approach has an $O(|T|2^{|I|}(n_{max} + 1)^{2|I|}(|M||I|)^3)$ computational complexity. The computational complexity of the MDP-based heuristic algorithm is $O(|T|2^{|I|}(n_{max} + 1)^{2|I|}(|M||I|)^3)$ for determining the action set via the staged solution method, and $O(L'|T|^3(|M||I|)^3)$, for determining the optimal policy via policy iteration, where L' is the number of iterations required for algorithm convergence. $O(|T|2^{|I|}(n_{max} + 1)^{2|I|}(|M||I|)^3 + L'|T|^3(|M||I|)^3)$.

2.4 SIMULATION EXPERIMENT

The effectiveness of the UPF deployment and traffic scheduling algorithm in the user plane of 5G core network based on Benders decomposition is verified by simulation experiments.

2.4.1 Experimental setup

In a 4.0 km × 4.0 km area, the positions of base stations are assumed to follow a Poisson point process [20] with a density of 1 station/km². Each base station is equipped with one edge server for deploying 5G core network user-plane UPF elements. Each edge server has 48 CPU cores (considering only CPU as the bottleneck resource) with a peak power consumption of 1,000 W. The idle power ratio (the ratio of idle power consumption to peak power consumption) is set to 0.4. Only one type of UPF is considered, which requires 1 CPU core and has a throughput of 0.1 Gb/s. The backhaul link between the base station and the edge server is established using millimetre-wave communication, and the propagation delay is proportional to the geographical distance [21]. The traffic of the base stations exhibits periodic variations with a cycle of 1 day. Therefore, we set $\Delta t = 24$ hours, and we take $\Delta = 1$ hour. The traffic of the base stations is randomly selected from the set {0.5, 1.0, 1.5, 2.0, 2.5} Gb/s with a uniform distribution.

2.4.2 Experimental results

We examine the convergence of the proposed algorithm. Figures 2.3 and 2.4 illustrate the variations of the upper and lower bounds of the UPF deployment and traffic scheduling problem with the number of iterations. In the figure, C represents the total cost, and η denotes the iteration number. The energy price is set to 1 yuan/(kW·h), the cost of unit data latency is 5 Unit/(Gb·ms), the unit price for UPF instance deployment is 0.02 Unit, and the error tolerance is set to 0.01. It can be observed that as the number of iterations increases, the upper and lower bounds gradually converge. The relative error between the upper and lower bounds approaches 0. After 29 iterations, the relative error drops below the error tolerance.

The proposed algorithm was compared to the sequential solution method and the MDP (MDP) heuristic algorithm [13]. The stepwise optimisation approach optimises each time period in sequence without considering the delayed effect of deployment choices. The MDP-based heuristic approach represents the original issue as a MDP and solves it using the policy iteration process, although its accuracy is restricted by the action sets used. The total cost of the three techniques for varied UPF instance deployment costs (cUPF) is shown in Figure 2.4. The suggested method has the lowest overall cost, and its advantage rises as the cUPF becomes larger. as cUPF = 0.06

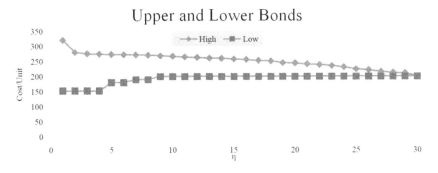

Figure 2.3 Cost estimation using iterations.

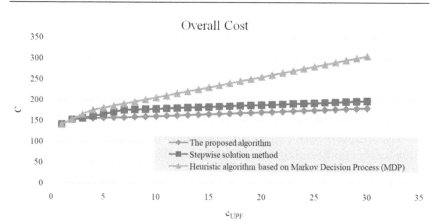

Figure 2.4 Comparative cost analysis (a) average number of servers used, (b) average user plane delay, (c) average number of servers used, (d) average user plane delay.

yuan, the suggested approach cuts overall operating expenses by 10.4% and 5.1%, respectively, as compared to the sequential solution technique and the MDP-based heuristic algorithm.

The effects of the inactive power coefficient and the latency cost on the algorithm's performance were analysed. Figure 2.5(a–d) depicts the average number of edge servers utilised per time interval and the average user-facing latency for various parameter values. Us represents the average number of server requests, while Du represents the average user-facing latency. As the idle power coefficient () increases or decreases, it is observed that the UPF instances are consolidated onto fewer edge servers, resulting in a smaller average number of edge servers used per time slot but a higher average user-facing latency. Inversely, eitherdecreasingor increasing, the UPF instances are deployed to a larger average number of edge servers per time interval, resulting in a smaller average user-facing latency.

2.5 CONCLUSION

This study examined the issue of dynamic UPF (UPF) implementation in peripheral networks for 5G core networks. A multi-stage planning algorithm for UPF deployment and traffic scheduling using Benders decomposition was developed. We were able to achieve the optimal UPF deployment and traffic scheduling by considering how much energy edge servers consume, how much UPF deployment costs, how long user plane data takes to arrive, and the delayed effects of deployment choices. The Benders decomposition method was used to determine how to solve the UPF deployment and traffic scheduling multi-stage planning model. Simulations demonstrated that the proposed algorithm decreased the amount of energy used by peripheral servers, the cost of deploying UPF, and the time required for user plane

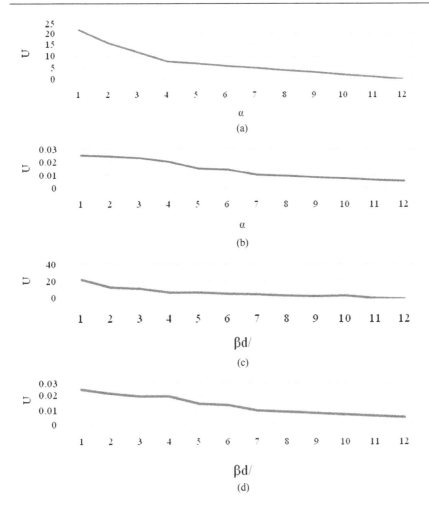

Figure 2.5 Analysis of latency cost. (a) Average number of servers used. (b) Average user plan delay. (c) Average number of servers used. (d) Average user plan delay.

data to arrive. However, it should be noted that the suggested algorithm is still difficult to implement for large problems. Future research will concentrate on determining how to implement user plane functions in large-scale core networks.

REFERENCES

[1] J. Kang, O. Simeone and J. Kang, "On the Trade-Off between Computational Load and Reliability for Network Function Virtualization," in *IEEE Communications Letters*, vol. 21, no. 8, pp. 1767–1770, Aug. 2017, doi: 10.1109/ LCOMM.2017.2698040

[2] J. Gil Herrera and J. F. Botero, "Tabu Search for Service Function Chain Composition in NFV," in *IEEE Latin America Transactions*, vol. 19, no. 01, pp. 17–25, January2021, doi: 10.1109/TLA.2021.9423822

[3] Q. Chen, X. Xu and H. Jiang, "Online Green Communication Scheduling for Sliced Unlicensed Heterogeneous Networks," in *IEEE Transactions on Vehicular Technology*, vol. 70, no. 10, pp. 10657–10670, Oct. 2021, doi: 10.1109/TVT.2021.3110823

[4] S. Agarwal, F. Malandrino, C. F. Chiasserini and S. De, "VNF Placement and Resource Allocation for the Support of Vertical Services in 5G Networks," in *IEEE/ACM Transactions on Networking*, vol. 27, no. 1, pp. 433–446, Feb. 2019, doi: 10.1109/TNET.2018.2890631

[5] X. Wang, G. B. Giannakis and A. G. Marques, "A Unified Approach to QoS-Guaranteed Scheduling for Channel-Adaptive Wireless Networks," in *Proceedings of the IEEE*, vol. 95, no. 12, pp. 2410–2431, Dec. 2007, doi: 10.1109/JPROC.2007.907120

[6] K. M. Zuberi and K. G. Shin, "Design and Implementation of Efficient Message Scheduling for Controller Area Network," in *IEEE Transactions on Computers*, vol. 49, no. 2, pp. 182–188, Feb. 2000, doi: 10.1109/12.833115

[7] R. Casellas, R. Vilalta, R. Martínez and R. Muñoz, "Highly Available SDN Control of Flexi-Grid Networks with Network Function Virtualization-Enabled Replication," in *Journal of Optical Communications and Networking*, vol. 9, no. 2, pp. A207–A215, Feb. 2017, doi: 10.1364/JOCN.9.00A207

[8] J. Zhanget al., "Aeronautical $Ad~Hoc$ Networking for the Internet-Above-the-Clouds," in *Proceedings of the IEEE*, vol. 107, no. 5, pp. 868–911, May2019, doi: 10.1109/JPROC.2019.2909694

[9] Z. Wang, J. Zhang and T. Huang, "Determining Delay Bounds for a Chain of Virtual Network Functions Using Network Calculus," in *IEEE Communications Letters*, vol. 25, no. 8, pp. 2550–2553, Aug. 2021, doi: 10.1109/LCOMM.2021.3065147

[10] C. Bu, X. Wang, M. Huang and K. Li, "SDNFV-Based Dynamic Network Function Deployment: Model and Mechanism," in *IEEE Communications Letters*, vol. 22, no. 1, pp. 93–96, Jan. 2018, doi: 10.1109/LCOMM.2017.2654443

[11] K. Mebarkia and Z. Zsóka, "Service Traffic Engineering: Avoiding Link Overloads in Service Chains," in *Journal of Communications and Networks*, vol. 21, no. 1, pp. 69–80, Feb. 2019, doi: 10.1109/JCN.2019.000007

[12] L. Linguaglossaet al., "Survey of Performance Acceleration Techniques for Network Function Virtualization," in *Proceedings of the IEEE*, vol. 107, no. 4, pp. 746–764, April2019, doi: 10.1109/JPROC.2019.2896848

[13] G. M. Saridiset al., "Lightness: A Function-Virtualizable Software Defined Data Center Network With All-Optical Circuit/Packet Switching," in *Journal of Lightwave Technology*, vol. 34, no. 7, pp. 1618–1627, 1April1, 2016, doi: 10.1109/JLT.2015.2509476

[14] Al-Shuwaili, O. Simeone, J. Kliewer and P. Popovski, "Coded Network Function Virtualization: Fault Tolerance via In-Network Coding," in *IEEE Wireless Communications Letters*, vol. 5, no. 6, pp. 644–647, Dec. 2016, doi: 10.1109/LWC.2016.2611510

[15] S. Cherrared, S. Imadali, E. Fabre, G. Gössler and I. G. B. Yahia, "A Survey of Fault Management in Network Virtualization Environments: Challenges and Solutions," in *IEEE Transactions on Network and Service Management*, vol. 16, no. 4, pp. 1537–1551, Dec. 2019, doi: 10.1109/TNSM.2019.2948420

[16] S. Yang, F. Li, S. Trajanovski, R. Yahyapour and X. Fu, "Recent Advances of Resource Allocation in Network Function Virtualization," in *IEEE Transactions on Parallel and Distributed Systems*, vol. 32, no. 2, pp. 295–314, 1Feb. 2021, doi: 10.1109/TPDS.2020.3017001

[17] Y. Tao, J. Wu, X. Lin and W. Yang, "DRL-Driven Digital Twin Function Virtualization for Adaptive Service Response in 6G Networks," in *IEEE Networking Letters*, vol. 5, no. 2, pp. 125–129, June2023, doi: 10.1109/LNET. 2023.3269766

[18] R. Mijumbi, J. Serrat, J.-L. Gorricho, N. Bouten, F. De Turck and R. Boutaba, "Network Function Virtualization: State-of-the-Art and Research Challenges," in *IEEE Communications Surveys & Tutorials*, vol. 18, no. 1, pp. 236–262, First-quarter 2016, doi: 10.1109/COMST.2015.2477041

[19] T. Lin, Z. Zhou, M. Tornatore and B. Mukherjee, "Demand-Aware Network Function Placement," in *Journal of Lightwave Technology*, vol. 34, no. 11, pp. 2590–2600, 1June1, 2016, doi: 10.1109/JLT.2016.2535401

[20] Y. Liu, H. Lu, X. Li and D. Zhao, "An Approach for Service Function Chain Reconfiguration in Network Function Virtualization Architectures," in *IEEE Access*, vol. 7, pp. 147224–147237, 2019, doi: 10.1109/ACCESS.2019.2946648

[21] L. Ge, J. Zhou and Z. Zheng, "Dynamic Hierarchical Caching Resource Allocation for 5G-ICN Slice," in *IEEE Access*, vol. 9, pp. 134972–134983, 2021, doi: 10.1109/ACCESS.2021.3116602

[22] V. Petrov et al., "Dynamic Multi-Connectivity Performance in Ultra-Dense Urban mmWave Deployments," in *IEEE Journal on Selected Areas in Communications*, vol. 35, no. 9, pp. 2038–2055, Sept. 2017, doi: 10.1109/JSAC.2017.2720482

Chapter 3

Spatial federated learning and blockchain-based 5G communication model for hiding confidential information

Sandeep Kumar Davuluri

University of the Cumberlands, Williamsburg, Kentucky

Haewon Byeon

Inje University, Gimhae, Republic of Korea

Ismail Keshta

AlMaarefa University, Riyadh, Saudi Arabia

Herison Surbakti

Rangsit University International College, Lak Hok, Thailand

3.1 INTRODUCTION

Traditional covert communication is a technology that hides secret information in commonly used carriers for confidential transmission [1] and plays a vital role in information security, data communication, etc. Widely used pages include images, text, audio, and video, among which Image is a widely used carrier format because of its high payload capacity [2]. However, in the traditional covert communication process, the carrier information may risk being deleted or tampered with, destroying embedded secret information. In addition, during this process, the identities of both parties to the communication are exposed on the network, and attackers can carry out targeted interference and blocking of communication.

Compared with other communication media, blockchain has the features of anti-forgery, anti-tampering, and anonymity [3–5]. Anti-tampering makes it invalid for attackers in covert communication to delete and tamper with secret information; because of anti-forgery the attackers of the covert communication cannot forge the content of the personal data; anonymity enables the two parties of the covert communication to communicate anonymously without revealing their real identities. Therefore, some studies use blockchain as a communication medium to solve the problems traditional clandestine communication faces. Literature [6] first suggested and demonstrated the secure

DOI: 10.1201/9781003470281-3

encoding of confidential data into the most innocuous part of a blockchain transaction address, allowing for its covert transfer. In Gao et al. [7], authors hid transactions using blockchain technology. In Gao et al. [7], authors hide the transactions using blockchain technology and combining cypher text with steganographic images to provide a secret means of transmission. To ensure the confidentiality of blockchain transaction data, literature [8] encrypts and conceals the private information in HEVC video. In order to implement double steganography, authors [9] in the literature integrated blockchain technology with IPFS (Interplanetary File System).

Technology solves the storage problem of private carriers of large files in the blockchain. These studies are all about the covert transmission of a short message. With the quickgrowth of applications and applications, the amount of data required for confidential communication is increasing. The underground information of short messages is unsuitable for large amounts of sensitive data.

To circumvent these issues, this study presents a blockchain-based covert communication paradigm for concealing both the sender's and the recipient's identities and sensitive data. Store the encrypted document in IPFS using picture steganography based on Generative Adversarial Networks (GAN) [10–15] after acquiring the encrypted document using H-SD&SI.-Based Encryption, CP-ABE). To acquire the encrypted Image, the value is hidden inside the carrier image produced by the GAN. After obtaining a ring signature [16], the sender will launch a transaction that will include the hash value of the encrypted Image. Node synchronization has been achieved [7]. The receiver extracts the hash value of the encoded Image carried in the local transaction and searches. Finally, it downloads the encoded document from IPFS through the reverse process of the above method. Since the access control strategy of CP-ABE is used, only specific recipients can decrypt encrypted documents and obtain sensitive documents.

This study aims to suggest a blockchain-based covert communication paradigm that overcomes the drawbacks of existing covert communication techniques. Sensitive data is protected during transmission while the sender and recipient's identities are kept secret. The project employs picture steganography based on Generative Adversarial Networks (GAN) and Ciphertext-Policy Attribute-Based Encryption (CP-ABE) to securely store encrypted documents in IPFS. The objectives include large-scale sensitive data transmission while maintaining privacy and access control. The main contribution of the work is as follows:

1. Blockchain integration: The study investigates the usage of blockchain as a communication medium to offer anti-tampering, anti-forgery, and anonymity capabilities. By utilizing the benefits of blockchain, it is possible to protect the integrity of confidential information, stop content forgery, and keep the names of the communication parties a secret.

2. The suggested covert communication paradigm combines photo steganography and CP-ABE to hide sensitive information and sender identities. The secret information is safely concealed and transferred covertly by employing GAN-based steganography to insert the encrypted document in a carrier image.

3. IPFS is used in the study to store and retrieve documents that have been encrypted. Sensitive data can be accessed securely and quickly thanks to the recipient's ability to retrieve the encrypted document from IPFS and extract the hash value of the encoded image from the local transaction.

4. Access Control and Confidentiality: The deployment of access control measures is made possible by adopting CP-ABE, ensuring that only particular recipients with the required qualifications can decrypt the encrypted documents and gain access to sensitive data. This strategy improves privacy and prevents unauthorized access.

5. Scalability and Application: This work addresses the issue of safely communicating vast volumes of sensitive data, in contrast to earlier studies on short message covert transmission. The suggested approach is scalable and adaptable to numerous circumstances that call for the covert transmission of substantial amounts of sensitive data.

3.2 RELEVANT KNOWLEDGE

This section mainly introduces the knowledge of covert communication based on blockchain and IPFS, steganography based on GAN, CP-ABE, and ring signature.

3.2.1 Covert communication and IPFS based on blockchain

A distributed ledger having a chain topology, in which the data on the chain cannot be altered in any way [17, 18], is known as blockchain. Once data in a block has been recorded, it cannot be changed without impacting subsequent blocks as well. This prevents any node from being able to modify its own data. Instead, then relying on individuals' identities, nodes generate transactions using just their addresses. Transactions are first confirmed by unsuspended Transaction Outputs, also known as UTXOs, after being broadcast to each and every node in the network. Later when these transactions have been validated, they will then be bundled together into blocks. When other nodes in the league confirm that all of the league's transactions are legitimate, the block will be eligible for addition to the blockchain. In the end, all of the nodes are responsible for recording the transactions and achieving information synchronization.

Figure 3.1 presents the covert communication concept that may be used inside the blockchain. The sender, Alice, uses a specialized embedding method

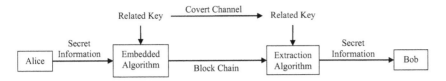

Figure 3.1 Blockchain covert communication model.

in order to insinuate the secret information into the public carrier. This results in the development of a page that contains the secret, and this page will be delivered through the covert channel. Following the procedure of embedding the confidential information, Alice encrypts the private message by using the key K. To get his personal statement, Bob is the only one who can use K or a key that is connected to it. Through the process of sending a transaction, the sender does not interact directly with the recipient. Instead, the sender uses a random selection method to determine the receiving address, which it then uses to communicate with additional regular nodes in the blockchain system. Because of the broadcast nature of the transaction, the information of hidden significance may also be received by the end receiver. This will not only guarantee that the communication process remains hidden, but it will also prevent the identity of the receiver from being exposed.

IPFS is a decentralized storage system that assigns a random hash to each file using content addressing. Merkle DAG (Directed Acyclic Graph) and Distributed Hash Table (DHT) are two of the index structures that IPFS uses. Data structure (graph, Merkle DAG) [19]. If the size of an IPFS object's data exceeds 256 KB, that data will be divided into several chunks of 256 KB. Each block's hash value serves as a unique identifier (Content-ID, CID) for the league and may be used to check for tampering in the data. In a Merkle DAG, the root hash value is equivalent to the whole file. IPFS will provide a file to the sender with the file's calculated hash value when the sender transfers the file to IPFS. A file's hash value is all that's needed to be entered into IPFS when the receiver wants to download it, and the system will return the actual file. The recipient may use the hash value to download IPFS files after the sender and receiver have established an IPFS cluster. There are two types of IPFS collections: those that are open to the public, and those that are not. Any IPFS node in the globe may join a general IPFS cluster since they are decentralized networks. Nodes in IPFS small groups only react to requests from other peers and are only linked through shared key. If a node fails in an IPFS network, other nodes may still provide access to the necessary data. Data saved on IPFS is protected in this manner, essentially.

3.2.2 GAN-based image steganography

GAN is a generative model proposed by Literature [20], widely used in image generation. The model includes a generator (Generator) and a discriminator

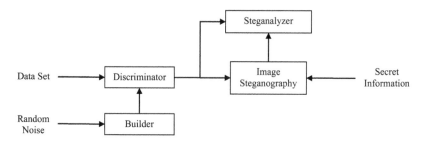

Figure 3.2 GAN-based image steganography.

(Discriminator) [21]. The generator's task is to sample noise from a random distribution and then output a synthetic image. The discriminator takes an actual or artificial image as input and outputs the result of the judgment. The generator and the discriminator continue to play an adversarial game until the discriminator synthesizes. Then, the image is judged to be an actual image, and the final output is to generate a fake image.

GAN-based image steganography draws on confrontation and introduces information-hiding technology. Literature [22] combined GAN and information steganography for the first time, adding an image and steganalysis module based on GAN, as shown in Figure 3.2. The generator generates a synthetic image that conforms to the statistical characteristics of natural images. Then, the discriminator judges the authenticity of the picture. If the synthetic image is considered an actual image, the synthetic image is input to the image steganography module. They are used as a cover images. The image steganography module implantstop-secret information into the cover image. The steganalysis module distinguishes the protection image from the concealed image. If it cannot be determined, the personal image is output; if it is distinguished, continue training.

To guarantee that hidden data can be recovered, the actual steganography process employs a tried-and-true steganographic technique known as the Least Significant Bits (LSB) method. LSB is a popular steganographic method for concealing picture data. Each pixel's least significant bit is swapped out for identifying data. The RGB (red-green-blue) color model is represented by 8 bits per pixel. When the secret information is to be embedded, the method requires changing the bottommost bit of the pixel from "1" to "0" or from "1" to "0" when the bit is dissimilar from the bottommost bit of the pixel. The altered pixel value has no noticeable impact on the final product. In addition to being simple to construct, the method is capable of concealing a great deal of sensitive data.

3.2.3 CP-ABE and ring signature

To protect sensitive documents, it is necessary to encrypt the sensitive documents before the covert transmission of the secret documents, ensuring concealment and improving security.

The first CP-ABE approach, as suggested in the literature [23], enables data owners to impose granular control over who may access their data via the definition of access rules. The key stands in for characteristics, whereas the ciphertext represents an authorization scheme. The attribute set may be decrypted if and only if its details conform to the access structure [24]. The steps involved in CP-ABE are as follows.

(1) Initialization: Input security parameters, public output parameters PK and a master key MK.
(2) Encryption: Ciphertext E is generated given a message m, an access structure A, and public parameters PK.
(3) Key generation: The proper decryption key SK is created after the master key MK, public parameters PK, and attribute Y are all given.
(4) Decryption algorithm input: By giving the algorithm the public parameters PK, ciphertext E, and user decryption key SK, the algorithm will convert ciphertext E to plaintext M if the user decryption key SK has the same traits as the access structure A in ciphertext E.

Ring signature is a completely anonymous and unforgeable anonymous method that was initially put forth by literature [25]. The signer signs using both his private key and the public keys of the other ring signature participants. Even if the attacker gets hold of the ring signature's private key, he will be unable to identify which ring member created the signature. In this study, the sender creates a blockchain transaction using the ring signature in order to conceal their identity during covert communication. In addition, this article introduces the concept of ring signature and the sender in order to prohibit all ring signature members other than the communication parties from authenticating the trade. Alice creates many accounts as ring signature members on the blockchain network, but only uses one of the accounts. Create a transaction with Bob as the recipient and the final ring member. If Bob is able to successfully validate the transaction, it will be transmitted to Bob.

3.3 H-SD&SI FRAMEWORK

This section introduces CP-ABE, GAN-based image steganography and ring signature in the blockchain network and proposes a blockchain covert communication model that can hide sensitive documents and sender identities: H-SD&SI. The framework of H-SD&SI is exposed in Figure 3.3, which comprises three parts: embedding, transmission, and extraction.

3.3.1 Embedding process

Technologies that hide information are distinct from those that encrypt it. Technologies like information concealing keep secrets from prying eyes, while

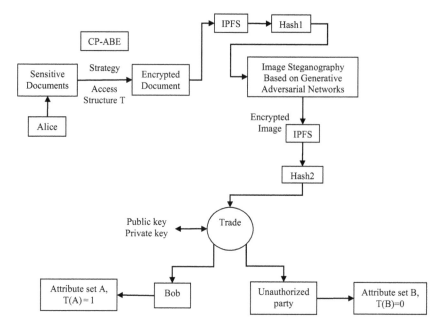

Figure 3.3 Framework of H-SD&SI.

technologies like information encryption transform data into meaningless. When information concealing and information encryption are used together, not only is the model's security enhanced but the concealment is also assured. Therefore, in this paper, sensitive documents are first processed into encrypted documents through information encryption technology. Then the encrypted documents are hidden in a specific carrier through information-hiding technology and entered into the next. The one-stage page conceals the transmission process in the blockchain.

At this stage, the sender, Alice, must first perform CP-ABE encryption on the sensitive document secret.pdf to obtain the encrypted document secret. pdf.cpabe. Then Alice uploads the encrypted document to IPFS. After that, Alice and the receiver, Bob, only need to establish an IPFS cluster; Bob can download files from IPFS according to the hash value, so this article shows a private IPFS cluster to store files. Then, Alice establishes a collaborative critical swarm. Bob receives the shared key and transmits it to the other nodes. In the event that Alice and Bob have already agreed upon the following: When Bob gets the hive, he expects Alice to provide a secret file since he has the key to unlock it. In this study, we provide a timing technique to signal to Bob when it is safe to read the secret file.

In order to obtain encrypted documents, CP-ABE encrypts them; nevertheless, it is inconvenient to utilize information-hiding technology to embed encrypted documents in a particular carrier. For the purpose of this paper, IPFS is introduced as a repository for encrypted documents, and the mess

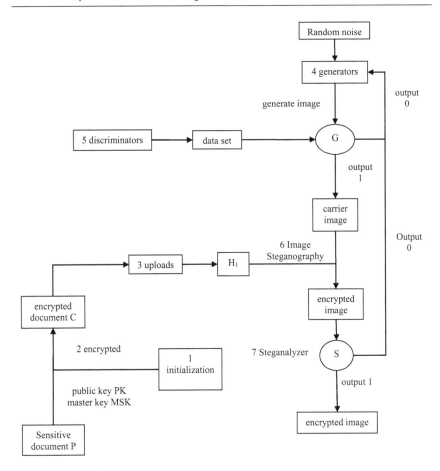

Figure 3.4 Embedding process.

value of the encrypted document is implanted into the steganographic page as the only piece of information to be hidden. This prevents sensitive private data from being uploaded to the chain in plain text and guarantees anonymity.

After Alice sends the encrypted copy of the document to IPFS, IPFS sends back the encrypted copy's hash value. Next, Alice uses GAN to make a carrier image that looks like a natural picture. She then uses the LSB algorithm to hide the document's hash value in the carrier image to get a secret image. Figure 3.4 shows the embedding method, and the following are the steps of embedding.

(1) Initialization. Setup(λ)$\rightarrow$PK, MSK: This method takes a security parameter as input and makes a set of keys: a public key (PK) and a master secret key (MSK).

(2) Encryption. Encrypt(PK, M, P)$\rightarrow$C: This encryption method takes the public key PK, the sensitive document M, and the access policy P

as inputs and outputs the encrypted document C. It encrypts the sensitive document M based on the access policy P.

(3) Upload. Upload(C)→H₁: Sends the encrypted document C to IPFS and returns the document's hash value H1.

(4) Generator. Gen(noise)→cover - image: This algorithm is a neural network called Generator, which receives a random noise and tries to generate an image close to the real one for subsequent steganographic operations.

(5) Discriminator. Dis(actual - image, cover - image)→0/1: This algorithm is a discriminator neural network. Its task is to distinguish authentic images, and the generated carrier image cover - image returns the judgment result. When the return result is "0", it means that the discriminator can discriminate between the actual - image and the cover - image; when the return result is "1", it means that the discriminator cannot determine between the actual - image and the body – image; the generated image at this time can be used as a carrier image for subsequent steganographic operations.

(6) Image steganography. Embed(H₁, cover - image)→stego -image: This step mainly uses the LSB algorithm to implant the hash value H₁ of the encrypted document C into the cover image cover - image to obtain the secret image stego - image.

(7) Steganalysis (cover-image, stego-image)→0/1: The task of this algorithm is to distinguish the generated cover image cover-image from the top-secret image stego-image and return the judgment result. When the return result is "0", the discriminator can discriminate between protection-image and stego-image; when the return result is "1", the discriminator cannot distinguish between stego-imageand cover-image.

3.3.2 Transmission process

If the encrypted image is directly stored on the blockchain, the overhead is too high; if the image is compressed and stored on the blockchain, the embedded secret information may be lost due to image distortion, Consequently, this piece integrates IPFS and the blockchain to provide off-chain, collaborative storage. The blockchain keeps track of the mess value of the file supplied by IPFS, which allows for off-chain loading of encrypted photos. The blockchain's capacity issue is efficiently addressed by this cooperative paradigm. And you may rest assured knowing that the encrypted photographs are secure and genuine.

In this procedure, Alice extracts the mess value of the encrypted image and uploads it to IPFS. Then Alice creates a transaction, sends the encrypted image to a random receiving address rather than directly to Bob's address. The data field of the trade contains the exact value of the transaction. The transaction is published to the blockchain system after the transaction ring has been signed. Bob might also get the marketing after verification and

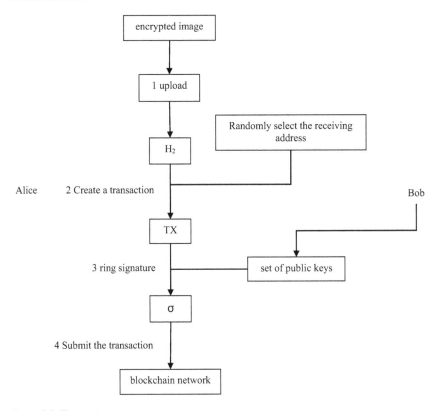

Figure 3.5 Transmission process.

packing. Figure 3.5 illustrates the transmission in use. Here are the specific steps that made up the exchange.

(1) Upload. Upload(stego - image)→H_2: Upload the stego - image to IPFS, and return the hash value H_2 of the stego - image.

(2) Create a transaction. Transaction(H_2)→TX: In this stage, Alice creates a transaction TX, and the transaction data field carries the value H_2 of the stego-image.

(3) Ring signature. Sign(TX, P_1, P_2, ..., P_n)→σ: The signature algorithm includes six steps. P_1, P_2, ..., P_n represent the public keys of all ring signature members, including Alice's public key P_s and Bob's public key P_b. In the first step, k = Hash(H) is calculated using a cryptographic hash function, with k as the symmetric encryption key. In the next step, a random value, v, is chosen. In the third step, a random value x_i is selected for n − 1 ring signature members except for the sender, and the corresponding y_i is calculated according to $y_i = g_i(x_i)$. In the fourth step, the ring equation $C_{k,v}(y_1, y_2, ..., y_n) = v$ is solved to get y_s. In the fifth step, according to $x_s = g_s^{-1}(y_s)$, use the sender's private key

to calculate x_s. Finally, in the sixth step, the ring signature σ is a $(2n + 1)$ tuple $\{P_1, P_2,..., P_n; v; x_1, x_2,..., x_n\}$.

(4) Submit the transaction. Submit(TX, σ): Alice publishes the ring-signed transaction to the blockchain system, the transaction is broadcast in the blockchain, and then UTXO verifies whether the transaction is valid. When the transaction is confirmed as accurate, It will be packaged into a block through mining. Once the legitimacy of all league transactions has been confirmed, the newly created block will be updated throughout the blockchain network. Last but not least, the recipient might receive financial transactions that the sender has filed.

3.3.3 Extraction process

Ten minutes after, Bob accepts the swarm. The Key, he traverses the transactions in the newly generated block and tries to verify the ring signature. If the verification is successful, the transaction is sent to Bob. The extraction process is represented in Figure 3.6; the specific extraction steps are as follows.

(1) Verify the signature. For example, verify $(\sigma, P1, P2, ..., P_n) \to 0/1$: The signature verification algorithm includes three steps. In the first step, calculate $y_i = g_i (x_i)$ for each x_i to get the corresponding y_i. The second step estimates the symmetric key k = Hash(H). The third step is to verify whether the loop equation $C_{k,v} (y_1, y_2, ..., y_n) = v$ is valid. If the loop equation is correct, consider the signature is correct. Otherwise, the signature is considered wrong.

(2) Read. Read(payload) $\to H_2$: Read the hash value H_2 of the stego-image stego-image from the transaction data field.

(3) Download. Download(H_2) $\to$ stego-image: Bob feeds H2 into IPFS, which then utilizes it to locate the DHT index structure pertinent to the stego-image and, finally, the node that stores the data block. IPFS will get the encrypted image data block from the node, reassemble it in the direction of the DHT hash array, and then send the whole encrypted image stego - picture back to Bob.

(4) Extract. Extract(stego - image) $\to H_1$: The stego - print may be used to get the encrypted document's hash value H1 using an approach that is the inverse of the LSB embedding procedure.

(5) Download. Download(H_1) $\to$ C: When Bob enters H1 into IPFS, IPFS first examines the node's location that stores the data block through DHT before determining the file structure of DHT related to the encrypted document C through H1. Download the node's encryption. Following the complete data blocks of document C, Bob, IPFS will compile the data blocks according to the DHT hash array's order.

(6) Key production. KeyGen(PK, MSK, A) $\to$ SKA: This algorithm is a key generation algorithm that requires a public Key PK, a master key

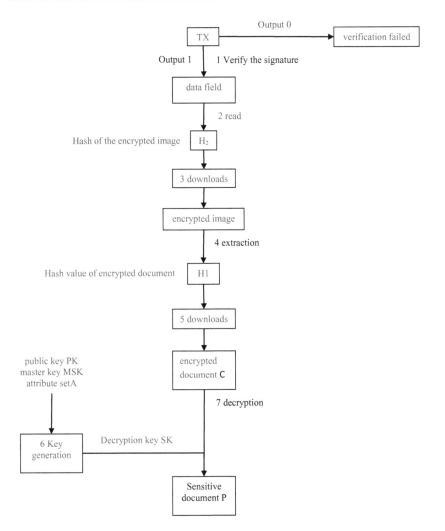

Figure 3.6 Extraction process.

MSK, and an attribute set A of the requester, output, and request as inputs. The SKA decryption key is associated with the attribute set of the proprietor.

(7) Decryption. Decrypt(PK, C, SKA)→M: This algorithm is used to break encryption. The inputs consist of a public key PK, an encrypted document C, and a decryption key SKA. Let's say that when the admissions policy P is included in the encrypted document C, the attribute in the user's decryption key SKA is happy. The

technique then transforms the plaintext-sensitive document M from the encrypted document C.

3.4 SIMULATION EXPERIMENT AND EXPERIMENT ANALYSIS

3.4.1 Simulation experiment

This experiment uses FISCO BCOS to simulate the blockchain and creates 20 accounts in the Ubuntu system.

Alice configures a local IPFS node and utilizes JS-IPFS API to use IPFS services, assuming account 1 is Alice's account for making transactions and account 2 is Bob's account. A collective vital swarm is produced by Alice and passes it to the secure channel with the key. The following is the precise content of the hive.key that was delivered to other nodes, including Bob. swarm.key.

(1) /key/swarm/psk/1.1.0/
(2) /base32/
(3) 8c45603441c4e23f70714a492f011fa1056e82124f73643 7f28481155ce46ef

As shown in Table 3.2, Alice uses the public key pub_key to encrypt 100 sensitive documents of different sizes, including secret1.pdf, secret2.pdf, secret3.pdf,…, and secret100.pdf. The encrypted document [secret1.pdf.cpabe, secret2.pdf.cpabe, secret3.pdf.cpabe,…, secret100.pdf.cpabe] is obtained, and the encrypted copy denotes the access control policy. To create Bob's decryption key, bob_priv_key, use his characteristics, public key pub_key, and master crucial master_key.

The blockchain network includes numerous users (User1, User2, and User3, etc.), and each user can have various account addresses (Address1, Address2, Address3, etc.). In addition, multiple accounts can be built in the blockchain network – a private IPFS cluster (IPFS1, IPFS2, and IPFS3, etc.). Therefore, the optional scope of attribute definition in data access control in this paper is represented in Table 3.1.

Table 3.1 Definition of user attributes and attributes values

Attributes	attribute value
User ID	User1, User2,…
Account Address ID	Address1, Address2,…
IPFS cluster ID	IPFS1, IPFS2,…

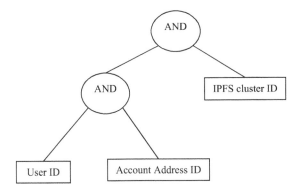

Figure 3.7 Access control policy.

A policy is an access structure composed of attributes. For example, this article customies an exclusive access policy for Bob only to allow the authorized party Bob to decrypt encrypted documents. The policy is defined as: (user ID=Bob) and (address ID=0x91CB0D322ba3817CAE7b00f42C004f 9C1aFd8bCc) and (IPFS cluster ID=IPFS*), as shown in Figure 3.7.

Alice uses the add(·) method to upload the encrypted documents [secret1. pdf.cpabe, secret2.pdf.cpabe, secret3.pdf.cpabe, …, se-cret100.pdf.cpabe] to IPFS, and IPFS returns their Hash value, as shown in column 4 of Table 3.2. Then Alice converts the returned hash value into a binary sequence, which is convenient for subsequent embedding into the generated carrier image. For example, the following operations take the hash value H_1 of secret1.pdf.cpabe and convert H_1 into a second sequence BS; the specific content of H_1 and BS is shown in Table 3.1. To let the receiver know when the embedding ends, the two parties agree to add a separator d after the hash value H1, where the specific content is "/n#", d and the binary sequence BS_d of d.

To create cover-image 1 and cover-image 2, Alice employs GAN-based picture steganography, training on the MNIST dataset, and the CelebA face dataset, respectively (Figures 3.8(a) and 3.8(c)). After generating cover

Table 3.2 100 sensitive documents of different sizes

sensitive documents	encrypted document	Hash value of encrypted document
secret1.pdf	secret1.pdf.cpabe	QmQpvkABZ6hDg5UxcWK-NUqS9Nwjoc9YYztLpb62wcsboWY
secret2.pdf	secret2.pdf.cpabe	QmaehxqkiH7Ez2nuXVH8JKqZUCVN-sdC4LVmTk3B2GUBqaZ
secret3.pdf	secret3.pdf.cpabe	QmdVy6SBejwp57uiBbrSnbvDapQFsx-SqjuUWn3ZYjrRTyU
…	…	…
Secret100.pdf	secret100.pdf.cpabe	QmRpXkRacz3NfdwsoWAeDyyLGBQ-spNHqpsoknGVY4HN2vF

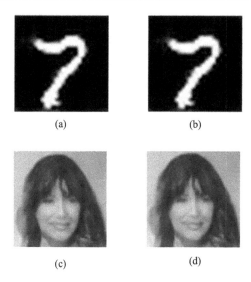

(a)   (b)

(c)   (d)

Figure 3.8 Comparison before and after embedding (a) cover-image I, (b) stego-image I, (c) cover-image 2, (d) stego-image 2.

pictures 1 and 2, Alice embeds BS and BSd into them to create stego-images 1 and 2, as shown in Figures 3.8(b) and 3.8(d), respectively, before and after embedding. Figure 3.8 depicts the contrast. Finally, Alice uses IPFS to store the secret images (stego-image 1 and stego-image 2), and IPFS responds with stego-image 1's hash value (H12). Table 3.1 displays the individual contents of the hash values H22, H12, and H22.

Alice does not directly select Bob's account but randomly selects a receiving address to create a transaction. The data field in the transaction carries the hash value H_2 of the stego-image. Alice performs a ring signature on the transaction, and the ring signature result is written into the transaction's extraData field and published the transaction to the blockchain system. Afterward the transaction is confirmed, it is packaged into a block. The freshly created block is sent to all blockchain nodes for updating. At long last, Bob may participate in Alice's transaction. Transaction See the diagram of the building as follows:

① signedTransaction ={
② nonce=1,
③ gasPrice=300000000,
④ gas=300000000,
⑤ blockLimit=502,
⑥ receiveAddress=accounts[random.randint (1,20)].address,
⑦ value=0,
⑧ data='QmVUPp1SWGA9nsBwvjdrb6oFNyhe28hu hpw4W4B9CHUAJQ',

⑨ extraData= '{"message":"QmVUPp1SWGA9ns-Bwvjdrb6oFNy he28huhpw4W4B9CHUAJQ"\, "param_info": "{\"g\":\"2. \"\,\"p\" :"116629146130897…085687.\" \,\"q\":"58314573065448517876…542843 .\"}"\, "ret_code": 0\, "sig":"{\"C\":\"596934492704…849502.\"\, \"Y\":\" 631573589796…098535.\"\,\"num\":\"3\"\,\"pk0\":\"114228877694…654739.\ "\,\"pk1 \":\"4751250745535584…301670. \"\,\"pk2\":\"7401228587…502970. \"\,\"s0\":\"53226645683501…384828.\"\,\" s1\":\"2403484418121…539097.\"\ ,\"s2\":\"1610471047…137130.\"}"}'}

For Bob to find out the transaction submitted by Alice, the two parties agreed in advance that the transaction starting with "Qm" in the data field was the transaction proposed by Alice after 10 minutes of receiving the shared vital swarm. The key, which Bob starts to traverse in the channel, is produced again and looking for commerce, beginning with "Qm" in the data field. After finding the transaction, Bob first verifies the ring signature. After the verification is passed, he reads the data field of the trade and enters the content of the data field into IPFS to obtain the complete encrypted image. According to the LSB algorithm's extraction algorithm, the encrypted document's hash value is extracted from the encrypted image. Then the hash value of the encrypted copy is input into IPFS, and IPFS returns the complete encrypted document, IPFS*) to obtain the decryption key and decrypt the encrypted document to get the sensitive paper.

3.4.2 Experimental analysis

This section mainly analyzes the investigational results from the three aspects of hiding capacity, concealment, and security.

(1) Transmission of secret information capacity
    This paper conducts simulation experiments on 100 sensitive documents of different sizes, encrypts these sensitive documents, and uploads them to IPFS, and successfully embeds the hash value returned by IPFS into the carrier image for covert transmission. In the study of transmitting a message, the method proposed in the text has dramatically improved the transmission order of magnitude, and the amount of secret information transmitted can reach MB. The comparison of the amount of personal information shared by each method in the blockchain covert communication model is shown in Table 3.3.

(2) Concealment
    Comparing the carrier and hidden images on a number of statistical metrics, such as Peak Signal-to-Noise Ratio (PSNR) and Structural Similarity Index (SSIM), allows for the measurement of concealmentas well as mean square error (MSE).

Table 3.3 Comparison of the amount of secret information transmitted

method	capacity
Literature [6]	bit
Document [7]	KB
Literature [8]	bit
Literature [9]	bit
This article	MB

The degree of discrepancy between the cover image and the secret image is mostly reflected by the mean square error. This indicator evaluates the level of the personal image that was created once secret information was embedded. The sum of squared deviations between the cover image and the hidden image is divided by the total number of pixels in order to calculate the mean square error. The steganography technique performs better, the lower the MSE value. The MSE formula is written as follows:

$$\text{MSE} = \sum_{l=1}^{M} \sum_{m=1}^{N} \frac{\left(I(l,m) - I'(l,m)\right)^2}{M^*N} \tag{3.1}$$

Literature [26] uses the traditional image steganography LSB, and this paper uses GAN-based image steganography. The MNIST dataset generates the carrier and the 100 carrier images and calculates the MSE between the carrier image and the secret image, as shown in Figure 3.9(a). The MSE of the method in this paper is about 0.2, much lower than the traditional steganography MSE of the technique. Similarly, the secret information is embedded in the common carrier, the CelebA face dataset generates 100 carrier images, and the MSE between the carrier image and the personal image is calculated, as shown in Figure 3.9(b). The MSE of the method in this paper is much lower than the MSE of the literature [27]; that is, the concealment of the steganographic process in this paper is better than that of the literature [28].

After the secret information has been implanted in an image, the quality of the image may be evaluated using a metric called the peak signal-to-noise ratio (PSNR). Contrary to MSE, the larger the PSNR value, the better the image quality. Its unit is dB when the value of PSNR is high. At 40 dB, the picture quality is excellent, very close to the novel image; when the PSNR value is between 30 dB and 40 dB, the image superiority is respectable, and the image distortion is perceptible but satisfactory; when the PSNR value is between 20 dB and

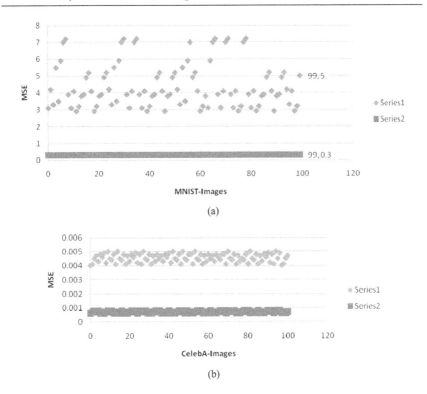

Figure 3.9 Comparison of mean square error (a) MNIST dataset and (b) CelebA face dataset.

30 dB, the image is Poor good quality; when the PSNR value is lower than 20 dB, the idea is unacceptable.

The formula for PSNR is expressed as follows:

$$PSNR = 10 \lg \frac{255^2}{MSE} \tag{3.2}$$

This paper compares the steganography method in literature [29] with the way this paper embeds the secret information into the common carrier and 100 carrier images generated by the MNIST dataset, respectively, and calculates the PSNR between the carrier image and the personal image, As shown in Figure 3.10(a). Similarly, the personal information is embedded in the common carrier, and the CelebA face dataset generates 100 carrier images. Finally, the MSE between the airline and intimate images is calculated, as shown in Figure 3.10(b). As a result, the PSNR of the method in this paper is much higher than that of the steganographic method used in the literature [30]; that is, the concealment of the steganographic process in this paper is better than that of the steganographic form in the literature [31–37].

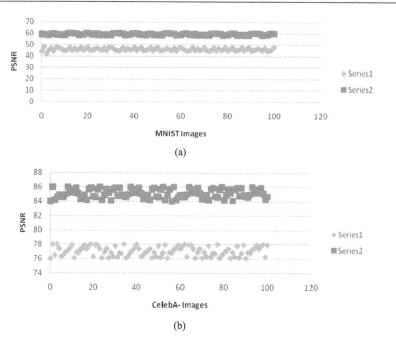

Figure 3.10 Comparison of peak signal-to-noise ratio (a) MNIST dataset and (b) CelebA face dataset.

Structural similarity (SSIM) is an index to measure the similarity between two images [38]. The maximum value of SSIM is 1. The more significant the SSIM value, the higher the carrier's and secret ideas' similarity. The formula of SSIM is expressed as follows:

$$\text{SSIM}(x, y) = \frac{\left(2\mu_x\mu_y + C_1\right)\left(\sigma_{xy} + C_2\right)}{\left(\mu_x^2 \cdot \mu_y^2 + C_1\right)\left(\sigma_x^2 + \sigma_y^2 + C_2\right)}a \tag{3.3}$$

This paper compares the steganography method in literature [9] with the way this paper embeds the secret information into the common carrier and 100 carrier images generated by the MNIST dataset, respectively, and calculates the SSIM between the carrier image and the personal image, as shown in Figure 3.11(a). The SSIM of the method in this paper is close to 1 and higher than the SSIM of the steganographic method used in ref. [39]. Therefore, the performance is better than the steganographic method in the literature [37]. Similarly, the secret information is embedded in the common carrier, the CelebA face dataset generates 100 carrier images, and the SSIM between the airline and personal photos is calculated. As shown in Figure 3.11(b). The SSIM of the method in this paper is higher than the SSIM of the

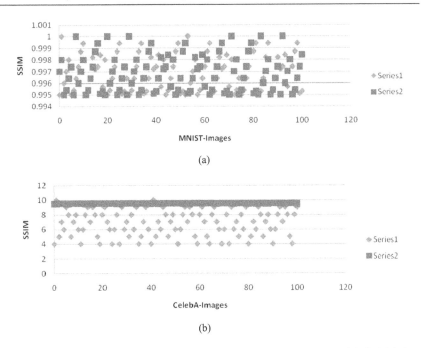

Figure 3.11 Comparison of structural similarities (a) MNIST dataset and (b) CelebA face dataset.

steganographic method used in the literature [37]. Therefore, it can also be concluded that the concealment of the technique in this paper is better than that of the steganographic method in the literature [35].

(3) Security

Definition 1: (S1 security) means that the attacker does not have enough information to prove that secret information is hidden in the carrier information passing through the transmission channel.

This type of security requires covert communication to be indistinguishable. The cover image used for steganography in this paper is generated by GAN-based image steganography. The statistical characteristics of the cover and private photos are very similar. During transmission, it is not easy for attackers to find information. The carrier of confidential information ensures security.

Definition 2: (S2 security) means that the secret information can still be received correctly even when the communication information is actively attacked.

This type of security means that the attacker cannot damage the secret information hidden in the communication information passing through the transmission channel; the personal data can still be recovered from the communication information under the attacker's attack. First, the non-tamperable modification of the blockchain makes the deletion and tampering of secret information invalid for the attacker of covert communication. Second, this paper uses CP-ABE to encrypt sensitive documents before steganography. When the user's attributes pass the verification of the access control policy, then the user is able to decrypt the encrypted document. Moreover, the security of the model depends to a certain extent on the confidentiality of the key used. CP-ABE generates the decryption key according to the user attribute, which avoids the leakage of the private key. Finally, in the blockchain covert communication in this paper, the identities of both the sender and the receiver are hidden, and it is difficult for the attacker to discover the transaction containing the secret information. Therefore, even if the attacker suspects the personal data in the image, he cannot. Consequently, it is challenging to extract confidential information, and sensitive documents cannot be obtained without knowing the decryption key. Thus, the security of covert communication is guaranteed.

3.5 CONCLUSIONS

This paper proposes a blockchain covert communication model H-SD&SI that can conceal sensitive documents and the identity of the submitter to enable the secure transmission of sensitive documents in the blockchain. This model employs CP-ABE technology to improve the security of sensitive documents and ring signature technology to sign the transaction in order to conceal the identity of the originator, thereby enhancing the secrecy of transmission. Furthermore, during embedding, the model utilizes GAN-based picture steganography to transform the encrypted document's embed hash value into the resulting cover image, so improving its concealment. This paper evaluates the efficacy of the model by comparing the MSE, PSNR, and SSIM of cover and intimate photographs. The investigational findings indicate that the model has significantly increased the quantity of transmitted personal information. And its concealment and security are exceptional.

REFERENCES

[1] Rasha Al-Huthaifi, Tianrui Li, Wei Huang, Jin Gu, Chongshou Li, Federated learning in smart cities: Privacy and security survey. *Information Sciences*, Vol. 632, pp. 833–857, 2023, https://doi.org/10.1016/j.ins.2023.03.033
[2] X. You, C. X. Wang, J. Huang et al., Towards 6G wireless communication networks: Vision, enabling technologies, and new paradigm shifts. *Science China Information Sciences*, Vol. 64, 110301, 2021, https://doi.org/10.1007/s11432-020-2955-6

[3] H. Sheng et al., Near-online tracking with co-occurrence constraints in blockchain-based edge computing. *IEEE Internet of Things Journal*, Vol. 8, no. 4, pp. 2193–2207, 15 Feb., 2021, https://doi.org/10.1109/JIOT.2020.3035415

[4] D. De, Fed lens: Federated learning-based privacy-preserving mobile crowdsensing for virtual tourism. *Innovations in Systems and Software Engineering*, 2022, https://doi.org/10.1007/s11334-021-00430-6

[5] Rishu Chhabra, Saravjeet Singh, Vikas Khullar, Privacy enabled driver behavior analysis in heterogeneous IoV using federated learning, *Engineering Applications of Artificial Intelligence*, Vol. 120, 105881, 2023, https://doi.org/10.1016/j.engappai.2023.105881

[6] Aimin Yang, Zezhong Ma, Chunying Zhang, Yang Han, Zhibin Hu, Wei Zhang, Xiangdong Huang, Yafeng Wu, Review on application progress of federated learning model and security hazard protection, *Digital Communications and Networks*, Vol. 9, no. 1, pp. 146–158, 2023, https://doi.org/10.1016/j.dcan.2022.11.006

[7] L. Gao, T. Cheng, L. Gao, TSWCrowd: A decentralized task-select-worker framework on blockchain for spatial crowdsourcing. *IEEE Access*, Vol. 8, pp. 220682–220691, 2020, https://doi.org/10.1109/ACCESS.2020.3043040

[8] M. Abdel-Basset, N. Moustafa, H. Hawash, I. Razzak, K. M. Sallam, O. M. Elkomy, Federated intrusion detection in blockchain-based smart transportation systems. *IEEE Transactions on Intelligent Transportation Systems*, Vol. 23, no. 3, pp. 2523–2537, March 2022, https://doi.org/10.1109/TITS.2021.3119968

[9] Y. P. Tsang, C. H. Wu, W. H. Ip et al., Federated-learning-based decision support for industrial Internet of Things (IIoT)-based printed circuit board assembly process. *Journal of Grid Computing*, Vol. 20, p. 43, 2022, https://doi.org/10.1007/s10723-022-09637-8

[10] J. An, S. Wu, X. Gui et al., A blockchain-based framework for data quality in edge-computing-enabled crowdsensing. *Frontiers in Computer Science*, Vol. 17, p. 174503, 2023, https://doi.org/10.1007/s11704-022-2083-8

[11] X. Chen, D. Zou, G. Cheng et al., Blockchain in smart education: Contributors, collaborations, applications and research topics. *Education and Information Technologies*, Vol. 28, pp. 4597–4627, 2023, https://doi.org/10.1007/s10639-022-11399-5

[12] Chenxi Huang, Gengchen Xu, Sirui Chen, Wen Zhou, Eddie Y. K. Ng, Victor Hugo C. de Albuquerque, An improved federated learning approach enhanced internet of health things framework for private decentralized distributed data. *Information Sciences*, Vol. 614, pp. 138–152, 2022, https://doi.org/10.1016/j.ins.2022.10.011

[13] Yuan-Cheng Lai, Jheng-Yan Lin, Ying-Dar Lin, Ren-Hung Hwang, Po-Chin Lin, Hsiao-Kuang Wu, Chung-Kuan Chen, Two-phase defense against poisoning attacks on federated learning-based intrusion detection, *Computers & Security*, Vol. 129, p. 103205, 2023, https://doi.org/10.1016/j.cose.2023.103205

[14] A. Giuseppi, S. Manfredi, A. Pietrabissa, A weighted average consensus approach for decentralized federated learning. *Machine Intelligence Research*, Vol. 19, pp. 319–330, 2022, https://doi.org/10.1007/s11633-022-1338-z

[15] L. Foschini, G. Martuscelli, R. Montanari, et al., Edge-enabled mobile crowdsensing to support effective rewarding for data collection in pandemic events.

Journal of Grid Computing, Vol. 19, p. 28, 2021, https://doi.org/10.1007/s10723-021-09569-9

[16] D. Liu, J. Ni, X. Lin, X. Shen, Transparent and accountable vehicular local advertising with practical blockchain designs. *IEEE Transactions on Vehicular Technology*, Vol. 69, no. 12, pp. 15694–15705, Dec. 2020, https://doi.org/10.1109/TVT.2020.3032375

[17] L. Soltanisehat, R. Alizadeh, H. Hao, K.-K. R. Choo, Technical, temporal, and spatial research challenges and opportunities in blockchain-based healthcare: A systematic literature review. *IEEE Transactions on Engineering Management*, Vol. 70, no. 1, pp. 353–368, Jan. 2023, https://doi.org/10.1109/TEM.2020.3013507

[18] H. Cheng, Q. Hu, X. Zhang, Z. Yu, Y. Yang, N. Xiong, Trusted resource allocation based on smart contracts for blockchain-enabled Internet of Things. *IEEE Internet of Things Journal*, Vol. 9, no. 11, pp. 7904–7915, 1 June, 2022, https://doi.org/10.1109/JIOT.2021.3114438

[19] Rajesh Kumar, Jay Kumar, Abdullah Aman Khan, Hub Ali Zakria, Cobbinah M. Bernard, Riaz Ullah Khan, Shaoning Zeng, Blockchain and homomorphic encryption based privacy-preserving model aggregation for medical images. *Computerized Medical Imaging and Graphics*, Vol. 102, p. 102139, 2022, https://doi.org/10.1016/j.compmedimag.2022.102139

[20] A. Velez-Estevez, P. Ducange, I. J. Perez, M. J. Cobo, Conceptual structure of federated learning research field. *Procedia Computer Science*, Vol. 214, pp. 1374–1381, 2022, https://doi.org/10.1016/j.procs.2022.11.319

[21] Subir Halder, Thomas Newe, Radio fingerprinting for anomaly detection using federated learning in LoRa-enabled industrial Internet of Things. *Future Generation Computer Systems*, Vol. 143, pp. 322–336, 2023, https://doi.org/10.1016/j.future.2023.01.021

[22] H. Lin, S. Garg, J. Hu, G. Kaddoum, M. Peng, M. S. Hossain, Blockchain and deep reinforcement learning empowered spatial crowdsourcing in software-defined internet of vehicles. *IEEE Transactions on Intelligent Transportation Systems*, Vol. 22, no. 6, pp. 3755–3764, June 2021, https://doi.org/10.1109/TITS.2020.3025247

[23] P. Weerapanpisit, S. Trilles, J. Huerta, M. Painho, A decentralized location-based reputation management system in the IoT using blockchain. *IEEE Internet of Things Journal*, Vol. 9, no. 16, pp. 15100–15115, 15 Aug., 2022, https://doi.org/10.1109/JIOT.2022.3147478

[24] M. Kadadha, R. Mizouni, S. Singh, H. Otrok, A. Ouali, ABCrowd an auction mechanism on blockchain for spatial crowdsourcing. *IEEE Access*, Vol. 8, pp. 12745–12757, 2020, https://doi.org/10.1109/ACCESS.2020.2965897

[25] K. N. Mishra, V. Bhattacharjee, S. Saket et al., Security provisions in smart edge computing devices using blockchain and machine learning algorithms: A novel approach. *Cluster Computing*, 2022, https://doi.org/10.1007/s10586-022-03813-x

[26] A. Kareem, H. Liu, P. Sant, Review on pneumonia image detection: A machine learning approach. *Human-Centric Intelligent Systems*, Vol. 2, pp. 31–43, 2022, https://doi.org/10.1007/s44230-022-00002-2

[27] A. Belhadi, Y. Djenouri, G. Srivastava et al., SS-ITS: Secure scalable intelligent transportation systems. *The Journal of Supercomputing*, Vol. 77, pp. 7253–7269, 2021, https://doi.org/10.1007/s11227-020-03582-7

[28] Saurabh Singh, Shailendra Rathore, Osama Alfarraj, Amr Tolba, Byungun Yoon, A framework for privacy-preservation of IoT healthcare data using federated

learning and blockchain technology. *Future Generation Computer Systems*, Vol. 129, pp. 380–388, 2022, https://doi.org/10.1016/j.future.2021.11.028

[29] Xi Zhu, Junbo Wang, Wuhui Chen, Kento Sato, Model compression and privacy preserving framework for federated learning. *Future Generation Computer Systems*, Vol. 140, pp. 376–389, 2023, https://doi.org/10.1016/j.future.2022.10.026

[30] W. Li, S. Wang, Federated meta-learning for spatial-temporal prediction. *Neural Computing and Applications*, Vol. 34, pp. 10355–10374, 2022, https://doi.org/10.1007/s00521-021-06861-3

[31] Y. Ren, F. Zhu, J. Wang, P. K. Sharma, U. Ghosh, Novel vote scheme for decision-making feedback based on blockchain in internet of vehicles. *IEEE Transactions on Intelligent Transportation Systems*, Vol. 23, no. 2, pp. 1639–1648, Feb. 2022, https://doi.org/10.1109/TITS.2021.3100103

[32] G. Chen, J. Wu, W. Yang, A. K. Bashir, G. Li, M. Hammoudeh, Leveraging graph convolutional-LSTM for energy-efficient caching in blockchain-based green IoT. *IEEE Transactions on Green Communications and Networking*, Vol. 5, no. 3, pp. 1154–1164, Sept. 2021, https://doi.org/10.1109/TGCN.2021.3069395

[33] Yulei Wu, Zehua Wang, Yuxiang Ma, Victor C. M. Leung, Deep reinforcement learning for blockchain in industrial IoT: A survey. *Computer Networks*, Vol. 191, p. 108004, 2021, https://doi.org/10.1016/j.comnet.2021.108004

[34] Djallel Hamouda, Mohamed Amine Ferrag, Nadjette Benhamida, Hamid Seridi, PPSS: A privacy-preserving secure framework using blockchain-enabled federated deep learning for Industrial IoTs. *Pervasive and Mobile Computing*, Vol. 88, p. 101738, 2023, https://doi.org/10.1016/j.pmcj.2022.101738

[35] A. I. Torre-Bastida, J. Díaz-de-Arcaya, E. Osaba et al., Bio-inspired computation for big data fusion, storage, processing, learning and visualization: State of the art and future directions. *Neural Computing and Applications*, 2021, https://doi.org/10.1007/s00521-021-06332-9

[36] J. Xu, J. Lin, W. Liang, et al., Privacy preserving personalized blockchain reliability prediction via federated learning in IoT environments. *Cluster Computing*, Vol. 25, pp. 2515–2526, 2022, https://doi.org/10.1007/s10586-021-03399-w

[37] Y. Liu, J. Zhang, J. Zhan, Privacy protection for fog computing and the internet of things data based on blockchain. *Cluster Computing*, Vol. 24, pp. 1331–1345, 2021, https://doi.org/10.1007/s10586-020-03190-3

[38] M. Loporchio, A. Bernasconi, D. D. F. Maesa, L. Ricci, Authenticating spatial queries on blockchain systems. *IEEE Access*, Vol. 9, pp. 163363–163378, 2021, https://doi.org/10.1109/ACCESS.2021.3132990

[39] M. A. Rahman, E. Hassanain, M. M. Rashid, S. J. Barnes, M. S. Hossain, Spatial blockchain-based Secure mass screening framework for children with dyslexia. *IEEE Access*, Vol. 6, pp. 61876–61885, 2018, https://doi.org/10.1109/ACCESS.2018.2875242

Chapter 4

Mining intelligence hierarchical feature for malware detection over 5G network

Chaitanya Kulkarni
VPKBIET, Baramati, India

Zekrifa Djabeur Mohamed Seifeddine
Centre of Excellence for Quantum Computation and
Communication Technology, Australia

Manvitha Gali
University of the Cumberlands, Williamsburg, Kentucky

Sheshang Degadwala
Sigma University, Vadodara, India

4.1 INTRODUCTION

Mining malware has emerged as a novel and concerning type of malware [1]. Its extensive and persistent computing nature imposes significant energy losses on computer users [2], resulting in substantial business losses for victims [3]. Existing approaches for static detection of mining malware mainly rely on standard malware detection methods, such as employing opcode features [4], grayscale images [5], other static characteristics, and classifier models. Research indicates that mining malware shares shallow knowledge of bytecode and PE (Portable Executable) structures with common malware [2], but it also possesses specialized expertise related to blockchain computing [6] over 5G network. Based on the varying levels of expert knowledge involved in threat intelligence features, the features of mining malware can be categorized into three layers. First, the bytecode of binary samples serves as a fundamental intelligence feature, which can be transformed into grayscale image features through dimensionality reduction and other techniques [7–9], or the entropy feature can be utilized to extract classification patterns. Deep learning technology can also eliminate classification patterns from the original byte [10, 11]. Second, the PE file structure information of malicious PE files exhibits distinct intelligence characteristics [12, 13], including abnormal segment structures, file headers, and other details [14], which can

DOI: 10.1201/9781003470281-4

be extracted as feature vectors to train classification models for malware identification. Lastly, mining operations involve intricate blockchain calculations that require substantial expert knowledge [1] to connect with cryptocurrency infrastructure and generate revenue.

Additionally, malicious behaviors such as system environment detection [15] are crucial in facilitating mining operations. These factors are captured in the static analysis of binary files and can be transformed into matching analyses of specific patterns. These three features represent a progression from shallow to deep regarding the depth of threat intelligence knowledge.

This study develops a viable method for identifying 5G mining malware. Long-term and large-scale mining malware causes energy losses and commercial implications, which the study addresses. First, distinguish mining malware from other malware. This includes its limited understanding of bytecode and PE structures and its deep blockchain computing capabilities. The second goal is to evaluate static malware mining approaches that use opcode characteristics, grayscale photos, and classifier models. The goal is to evaluate these technologies and find ways to enhance mining malware detection. Third, offer hierarchical feature mining for mining malware detection. This method analyzes bytecode properties, PE file structure information, and mining process characteristics. Dimensionality reduction, entropy features, and deep learning help extract and assess these characteristics. Fourth, create a classification model using extracted characteristics to properly detect mining malware. The article matches binary file static analysis patterns. Finally, using relevant datasets and performance indicators, assess the suggested strategy. This assessment tests the suggested method for mining malware detection via 5G networks. The suggested method will be compared against current approaches to prove its superiority. This article attempts to improve malware detection, particularly mining malware, and mitigate energy and commercial losses caused by such malware in 5G networks.

The contribution of this work lies in developing an effective approach for detecting mining malware over 5G networks. The key contributions can be summarized as follows:

[1] Enhanced understanding of mining malware: The research provides a comprehensive analysis of the characteristics of mining malware, highlighting its distinct features compared to common malware. This deeper understanding helps identify the specific challenges associated with mining malware detection.

[2] Hierarchical feature mining approach: The proposed approach introduces a novel hierarchical feature mining technique that considers three layers of features: bytecode features, PE file structure information, and mining operation characteristics. This approach enables more comprehensive and accurate mining malware detection by capturing shallow and deep threat intelligence knowledge.

4.2 DESCRIPTION OF THREAT INTELLIGENCE HIERARCHY

Classifiers trained with different static features have specific preferences for malware classification. In addition, these static features can model other malware characteristics to achieve the purpose of malware classification. As shown in Figure 4.1, threat Intelligence extraction is divided into layers according to mining malware. In this paper, threat intelligence information is divided into three layers: binary file bytecode, PE structure information, and mining operation information. The three layers of threat intelligence information are converted into byte features, PE structure features, mining my operation features, the analysis depth of three-level features, and feature engineering design knowledge from shallow to profound, and feature dimensions are becoming more and more sparse. When feature description dimensions are too high, feature extraction relies on high-dimensional machine learning and deep learning data processing capabilities. This section will introduce the extraction methods for these types of features.

4.2.1 Bytecode feature layer

Each byte of a PE file represents a specific meaning, and the byte feature is the essential feature of a binary file. This paper uses feature engineering and deep learning technology to obtain the classification mode of the bytecode feature level; these features include grayscale images, raw byte features, and entropy features. Table 4.1 lists the main parameters of the three bytecode features used in this paper.

Two mathematical vector modes can represent the entropy histogram features in Table 4.1. In essence, the elements in the bytecode layer mainly

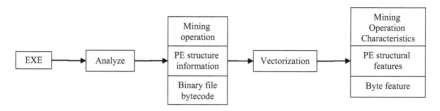

Figure 4.1 Hierarchical feature extraction of mining malware.

Table 4.1 Feature categories of byte code feature layer

Feature class	Characteristic mathematical form	Feature dimension
Raw Bytes	One-dimensional matrix	1000 kB
Grayscale Image	Two-dimensional matrix	163 pixels × 65 pixels
Entropy Histogram	1D/2D matrix	512/16 × 32

Table 4.2 Composition of PE structure information

Feature	Feature dimension
General document information	10
PE header information	62
Node features	255
Function export table	128
PE file entropy characteristics	256
PE file byte statistics characteristic	256

describe the similarity of mining malware binary files. Whether it is image or entropy features, both aim to obtain the similarity measurement results between samples and discover their category classification patterns.

4.2.2 PE structure information

The PE structure also contains a lot of threat information, and the abnormality of some PE information represents the means malware uses to attack or evade detection. Referring to the feature extraction method of the EMBER malware dataset [17], the format features of PE files are extracted as the classification basis of mining malware. Table 4.2 shows the preliminary information about these features. The PE structure information can be converted into a feature vector through vectorization and character hashing. The PE structure information used in this paper is transformed into a 967-dimensional feature vector.

4.2.3 Mining operation execution feature layer

The mining operation execution feature layer describes the characteristics of mining malware in four aspects, mining action features, malware essential attributes, character rule features, and avoidance features. These features are vectorized as training samples for mining malware detection models.

The characteristics of mining actions mainly relate to the specific execution characteristics of the software participating in the blockchain calculation process. For example, encryption calculations have opcode execution characteristics and function call characteristics. So, if the target software contains encryption function names and specific opcode distributions, it will indicate that it is classified as a Possibility of malicious mining software. Blockchain computing requires a lot of computing resources, and Bitcoin mining relies heavily on GPU computing equipment. Mining pool settings, wallet addresses, etc. are also important parameters for cryptocurrency revenue acquisition, and this characteristic information can indicate the degree of suspicion of mining malware to be tested.

The primary attributes of malware are the file information contained in the malware. These essential characteristics of the software can describe the suspiciousness of the malware. For example, the number of resource sections may indicate malicious behavior, such as file release, and the abnormal section data can also mean the binary file's suspicion of maliciousness.

The character rule feature extracts unique strings of binary files as feature vectors, and individual strings are also important indicators of mining malware. Mining malware relies heavily on strings such as file paths and URLs when performing resident and command control operations, mining malware is malware with specific actions, and its string distribution will differ from other types of samples. This article analyzes these unique characters using the YaraRule Gen tool (https://github.com/Neo23x0/yarGen). String rules are mined, Yara rules are generated to match the pieces to be tested, and feature dimensions are designed according to the number of matches. These feature dimensions can effectively extract high-level semantic features of character rules.

The avoidance feature is a common feature of malware. To resist debugging analysis and anti-virus software, malware often uses the detection system environment information to avoid them. By matching the avoidance feature string contained in the malware binary file, the number of matches will be a detection signature for mining malware.

4.3 MACHINE LEARNING METHODS AND MODEL INTEGRATION

This section introduces the machine learning method used for mining malware features in this paper and then describes their ensemble learning method. The two-stage learning task is shown in Figure 4.2. In addition, this paper uses labeled data training for recognition tasks. The machine learning model and the machine learning methods involved are all supervised machine learning methods.

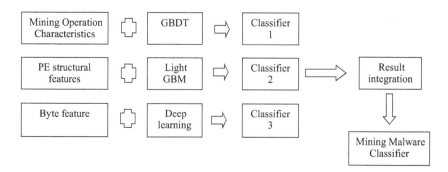

Figure 4.2 Machine learning method and its integrated learning.

4.3.1 Task model using machine learning techniques

Traditional shallow machine learning methods and deep machine learning methods are examples of machine learning methods. By increasing the network level, deep learning compresses feature vectors adaptively in end-to-end learning tasks [16]. In contrast, shallow machine learning techniques rely on the feature engineering method to achieve accurate feature extraction. Still, manual feature reduction will inevitably remove the feature's valuable dimension for classification. Shallow machine learning technology and deep learning technology meet the task model specified in Formula (4.1).

$$f_\phi\left(x_i^\theta\right) = y \tag{4.1}$$

The vector y is the classification result of the machine learning output, and the work is the discriminative result of positive (+) or negative (−). In this paper, mining malware is represented as a positive case, and non-mining malware is defined as a negative case. The malware characteristics described in the previous section have their vector characteristics. For example, grayscale images are typical two-dimensional matrix features, while opcodes are sequence features. Because of their inherent characteristics, each part has a machine-learning model suitable for its calculation characteristics. Table 4.4 lists the elements involved in this paper and the training models they use.

As shown in Table 4.3, the model and its parameters of the machine learning method elaborate in this paper are listed in the table, where Conv represents the convolution layer, followed by an integer representing the numeral of convolution kernels, and a two-dimensional integer defining the size of the convolution kernel. The Dense layer represents the fully connected layer, and the numbers in parentheses represent the number of neurons in the current layer. Among them, the entropy statistical histogram feature (Entropy Histogram, EH) in this paper uses two deep learning models for training in the two mathematical vector modes. Grayscale Image features (Grayscale Image, GI) are trained using convolutional neural

Table 4.3 Principal structure and parameters of machine learning models that correspond to various characteristics

Feature	Model structure
RB	Embedding layer+Conv1D(256)*λConv1D(256)
PF	LightGBM: model with100 trees and 31 leaves per tree
CF	GBDT method depth = 5 with # of leaves = 25
EH	Conv90*(3,3) + Conv200*(3,3) + Dense(500)
EH	Dense(1500) + Dense(1000) + Dense(500)
GI	2*[Conv32(3,3)] + 2*[Conv128(3,3)] + 2*[Conv256(3,3)]

networks, and byte-valued features (Raw Bytes, RB) are prepared using the original Malconv [18]. PE structural features (PE format features, PF) refer to EMBER [19] to choose the LightGBM (Light Gradient Boosting Machine) method for training. There is no correlation in each dimension in the mining malware operation execution features (Cryptojacking Features, CF), so the gradient boosting decision tree (Gradient Boosting Decision Tree, GBDT) is used) method for training.

As described earlier, in the actual method construction, different PE file features to be tested are trained under other machine learning models to obtain the classifier model. In the test, the likelihood estimation value of a single sample obtained will be in the next step input to the ensemble learning method to construct mining malicious.

4.3.2 Model integration

Different levels of features have different emphases on the description of mining malware, so this paper uses classifiers trained by various threat intelligence level features to build an integrated detection method for mining malware. The blended learning method consists of different layers of single machine learning detection. The technique is combined, and the mathematical description is as follows:

$$\Pi(f_1, f_2, f_3) = y \tag{4.2}$$

In Formula (4.2), Π represents the ensemble learning method, $f\phi$ represents the machine learning model trained with different features, the confidence scores output by the three models form a feature vector, and after the operation of the ensemble learning method, the final positive or negative example is output result of the judgment.

In theory, all models can calculate the ensemble learning model. But as mentioned earlier, different feature levels describe other malware characteristics, and these features pay attention to different knowledge levels of mining malware. So the ensemble learning method adopted in this paper uses the elements at the level of threat intelligence knowledge for training, uses the output results of the classifiers trained by these features as training samples, and then introduces the ensemble learning model to obtain the final mining malware classifier. This paper involves the report's three-layer threat intelligence features, including six machine learning models, and 20 combinations can be obtained when the three models are combined. According to the threat intelligence layered feature combination method proposed in this paper, four combination models are accepted, and the remaining 16 combinations are random. In selecting ensemble learning methods, this paper aims to choose a simple linear model as the ensemble learning method, making the learned model more interpretable and facilitating the deployment of

Table 4.4 The number of dominant random forest (RF) and logistic regression (LR) combinations

Combined category	Integration method	Leading combination
Layered composition of threat intelligence	LR	4
	RF	0
other combinations	LR	12
	RF	4

classification models in real-world scenarios. Standard linear model methods include support Vector Machine (SVM), Random Forest (RF), and Logistic Regression (LR). For Support Vector Machine, its output is 0 or 1, and its output cannot indicate the maliciousness of malware Probability; only qualitative classification can be made. At the same time, the support vector machine model does not have good interpretability [20], which is weakly persuasive for such security concerns of malware, which is not conducive to the actual deployment of the model. For logistic regression compared with the random forest method, both have good interpretability and linear classification performance. This paper compares the performance difference between the two in the ensemble learning task through experiments.

Experiments tested the performance of two machine learning classifiers under different ensemble learning combinations and found that logistic regression had a clear advantage over the random forest. As shown in Table 4.4, under the setting of three model ensembles, the six single machine learning models can be integrated into twenty combinations, four of which are the three-level threat intelligence feature combinations proposed in this paper. After testing, the logistic regression method has achieved a leading position. When comparing all four combinations of three-level threat intelligence, random forest was used. Among the remaining 16 combinations, logistic regression demonstrated the highest detection performance. This performance comparison is consistent with the existing research conclusions [21]. Finally, logistic regression was chosen as the ensemble learning method.

4.4 EXPERIMENTAL EVALUATION AND ANALYSIS

This section first introduces the datasets used and the evaluation methods of model performance. Then it tests the presentation of the machine learning methods elaborate in this paper and their integrated learning models in the simulated laboratory datasets and simulated real-world datasets. At the same time, to illustrate the necessity of the three-level combination, a comparative experiment is set up to analyze the performance difference between the two-level integration method and the three-level integration method.

4.4.1 Dataset

This paper selects two datasets as the performance testing environment for machine learning models and ensemble learning methods. Among them is the training. The dataset is published in the preliminary stage of the competition, and the test dataset is released by the competition organizer after the match. These two datasets are recorded as datasets A and B, as shown in Table 4.5.

CMal in the table represents a positive sample, whereas Not CMal represents a negative sample, since the goal of this article is to advance a mining malware detector. Table 4.6 demonstrates that the proportion is around one to three. Furthermore, there is about a 1:2 ratio of good to negative cases across the two datasets. Datasets A and B are employed as test beds to model the real-world detection challenge of mining malware. Tests of how well machine learning algorithms function are conducted using real-world datasets. The same principle applies to the creation of malware detectors in the real world. In contrast to the large data sizes often seen in detection situations, the developed plans are commonly trained and adjusted on relatively small datasets. This kind of test paradigm is more similar to the detection impact of machine learning techniques in mining malware detection in the real world, and it may effectively relieve the local optimum that may be generated by tiny data test sets.

The competition organizer calibrates all labels of the Datacon2020 dataset, and the non-mining malicious sample dataset contains other types of malware and benign software. The competition organizer deleted the flag bits

Table 4.5 Quantity distribution of Datacon 2020 datasets

Experiment	Dataset A		Dataset B	
	CMal	Not	CMal	Not
Original	02000	04000	05898	11759
Opcode	01885	03699	05823	11120

Table 4.6 Results of the model method performing cross-validation tests on the training dataset

Model	Accuracy	Precision	Recall	F-score
EH with MLP [22]	0.989	0.990	0.945	93.650
EH with CNN [23]	0.987	0.986	0.945	93.231
GI with CNN [24]	0.963	0.980	0.909	89.130
RB with Malconv [25]	0.978	0.996	0.937	93.330
OP with LSTM [26]	0.966	0.967	0.932	90.210
PF with LGB [27]	0.987	0.989	0.973	96.290
CF with GBDT	0.986	0.993	0.964	95.750

and function import tables in the PE structure of all samples. For the feature categories that need to use the analysis software to analyze the PE structure, the experiment first completes the PE and MZ flags so that the disassembly software can perform feature extraction. In Table 4.6, due to the failure of the analysis, the opcode features are relative. Therefore, there is a certain amount of reduction in the original dataset.

4.4.2 Evaluation indicators

Malware detection experiments can use accuracy (accuracy), precision (precision), and recall (recall) as the comparison standard of model performance, among which recall rate index and precision rate index are essential performance metrics; the former describes the detector. The sensor's detection ability measures the sensor's user experiential applications. This paper is oriented to practical applications. In addition to comparing the accuracy, precision, and recall of different methods in the results, the performance index calculation method of Datacon2020 is used for reference. The experiment introduces F-score as the fourth detection performance measurement index. F-score mainly measures the total recall and precision rate score and uses the weighted penalty method to calculate the detection performance of mining malware. The calculation method is as follows:

$$D - score = Rec \times 100 - 0.9(1 - Pre) \times 100 \tag{4.3}$$

The timeliness of the model is also an essential indicator of the classifier. Therefore, the experiment also tested the punctuality of all methods. The timeliness mainly includes three indicators: the time consumption of the feature extraction phase, the time consumption of the model training phase, and the time ingesting of the sample after the model is deployed—the time consumption of feature vector calculation. In the ensemble learning method, in addition to the time consumption required by the single model, the training time and inference time of the ensemble learning model are additionally increased.

4.4.3 Effect of simulated laboratory dataset

Experimentations on the mock lab dataset use cross-validation to avoid the randomness of small datasets. The 6,000 samples in the simulated lab dataset are randomly divided into five parts; one is used as the test for each test dataset, and the other four are used as training datasets. In the result display, the accuracy results of five averages are taken as the comparison data of the detection performance on the simulated laboratory dataset. The test of the ensemble learning method is the same as the single machine learning method's test, using the fivefold cross-validation method to measure the performance index. For ensemble learning, the experiments use the performance

Table 4.7 Test results of partial hierarchical integration combination model in simulated
laboratory dataset

Combination of features	Accuracy	Precision	Recall	F-score
CF with PF, and EHm	0.989	0.995	0.973	96.890
CF with PF, and RB	0.982	0.994	0.973	96.851
CF with PF and GI	0.981	0.993	0.973	96.800
CF with PF and EHc	0.987	0.994	0.972	96.791
RB with EHm and GI	0.981	0.993	0.951	94.491

and part of the single machine learning model; the test results of the integrated learning combination model on the simulated laboratory dataset are
shown in Tables 4.6 and 4.7, respectively.

As exposed in Table 4.6, the single machine learning methods listed are all
mining malware detection methods involved in this paper. Among them, OP
represents the opcode method, EH represents the entropy histogram feature
method, GI represents the grayscale image method, RB represents the original byte method [28], PF is the PE structural feature, and CF is the mining
operation feature. OP is the baseline method of this paper [29], which uses
the opcode sequence as the feature and the bidirectional LSTM model as the
classification model to build a mining malware classifier. It can be understood
from Table 4.6 that in the single-model method, the PE structural features
and mining operation features have achieved good results, occupying the first
and second positions, respectively. Among the bytecode features, the original
byte feature of the model also achieved good results and obtained the highest precision rate among all models. Furthermore, the PE structural feature
performed best in the F-score and recall rate. On the other hand, in Table 4.6,
the baseline method, the opcode feature [29], obtained poor results.

The single-model method constitutes a hierarchical feature integration
method. Among the three feature levels, there are four feature types in the
bytecode feature layer, and there is only one feature in the PE structure layer
and mining operation layer. For different feature levels in the experiment the
combination was tested. As shown in Table 4.7, EHc represents the entropy
histogram feature classifier trained by the CNN model, and EHm represents
the entropy histogram feature classifier trained by the MLP model. The table
lists the F-score of the three combination methods. Among the top four
combinations, CF+PF+EHm achieved the best results. Compared with the
baseline method opcode [4], the combination method obtained an F-score
improvement of 6.67, and it was also better than all single machine learning
methods. The model, particularly the general malware detection technique
Malconv [11], exhibits a significant increase of 3.56 in its F-score score. It is
also the integration of three types of features. The detection performance of
the RB+EHm+GI combination method in the fifth row is low because this
feature combination does not select the feature types of different threat intelligence feature levels. Due to the small scale of the test sample, the results on

the simulated laboratory dataset are not precisely the same as those in the simulated real-world dataset scenario.

4.4.4 Simulating the effect of real-world datasets

The test environment that simulates the real-world dataset is closer to the data processed after the machine learning model is deployed. Therefore, compared to the effect of the simulated laboratory dataset, the test on the simulated real-world dataset adopts the same model and result-processing method. Like the previous experiment, the five models in the cross-validation were used as classification models to test the simulated real-world datasets, and the obtained performance indicators were averaged as the model evaluation indicators. This can ensure that the simulation experiments are compared on a unified scale. Table 4.9 displays the detection performance of all individual machine learning models on the simulated real-world dataset, as well as the experimental findings of the models on the laboratory dataset and the simulated real-world dataset.

Compared with Tables 4.8 and 4.6, the machine learning model's performance on the simulated real-world dataset has been significantly degraded. However, the mining operation and PE structure characteristics remain leading performance indicators. This demonstrates that the feature hierarchy employed in this paper is capable of the data regularity of mining malware can be precisely characterized. The machine learning model also achieved good results on the four bytecode features. However, a significant performance decline was compared to the simulated laboratory dataset. The generalization performance of elements is not enough for large-scale mining malware datasets. The detection method of mining malware can be better constructed using ensemble learning methods, as shown in Figure 4.3.

Table 4.9 lists the integrated learning effects of different threat intelligence-level features. The bold fonts are the top four methods in the three feature integrations. It can be seen that these four combinations are the three threat intelligence feature-level integration methods. The four combinations of such

Table 4.8 Single machine learning model method on the simulated natural environment dataset

Feature (Model)	Accuracy	Precision	Recall	F-Score
EH and MLP	94.4	95.8	87.3	83.520
EH and CNN	94.3	95.5	87.2	83.201
GI and CNN	92.1	95.3	80.4	76.291
RB with Malconv [10]	94.6	97.2	86.5	83.970
OP and LSTM [4]	90.8	93.1	79.2	73.071
PF and LGB	96.4	96.2	92.8	89.500
CF and GBDT	96.7	97.9	92.1	90.320

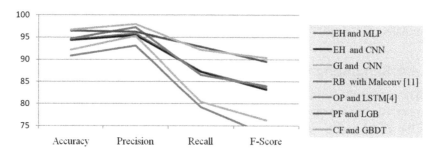

Figure 4.3 Results of the single machine learning model method.

Table 4.9 Hierarchical feature integration method on the simulated real-world dataset

Combination of Features	Accuracy	Precision	Recall	F-Score
CF with PF and RB	97	97.6	93.3	91.191
CF with PF and GI	97	97.5	93.3	91.150
CF with PF and EH	96.9	97.5	93.2	90.970
CF with PF and EHm	96.9	97.2	93.5	90.891
CF with EHc and EHm	96.4	97.1	92.2	89.580
PF with EHm and GI	96.3	96.2	92.8	89.330
EHc with EHm and GI	94.5	95.2	88.2	83.881

result rankings are similar to the ensemble learning test results on the simulated laboratory dataset. Among the four optimal combinations, the detection of the combination of the original byte method, the grayscale mode, and the entropy histogram feature is selected. The effects are in descending order. This performance ranking is different from the detection performance ranking of the single model on the simulated real-world dataset in Table 4.9, indicating that GI features have higher feature integration performance. This shows from the side that by simply stacking the optimal test, as shown in Figure 4.4.

As a result, better results may not necessarily be obtained in ensemble learning, and the ensemble's focus lies in selecting feature combinations. In addition to listing the first four feature combinations with the best performance, Table 4.9 lists the three for comparison. It can be seen that the combined performance of the same feature level drops significantly. The combined performance of multiple bytecode features is weaker than that of three different levels of combination integration methods. Compared with the best score of 90.32 for a single model, the integration learning method achieved an F-score of 91.19. Compared with the opcode baseline method [4], the ensemble learning method proposed in this paper has achieved better performance, with a maximum accuracy of 6.13% and an F-score of 18.12.

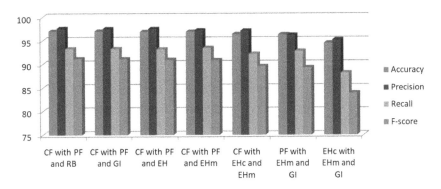

Figure 4.4 Hierarchical feature integration method on the simulated real-world dataset.

It can be seen from Table 4.9 that the performance of the integration method composed of the same original byte-type features is relatively poor compared with the integration between different parts. It can be seen that the combined effects of CF+EHc+EHm and PF+EHm+GI are even lower than those of CF and PF alone. The impact of the model fully shows that in the integrated learning method, the type of single feature should be selected reasonably; otherwise, it may have side effects on the classification performance. The above performance verifies the assumption at the beginning of the performance evaluation in this section, with different threat intelligence feature levels. The integrated detection method of mining malware can achieve better detection results.

Combining feature levels significantly improves performance for a single machine learning model, and some features slightly improve for a three-level feature combination. To prove the necessity of these features, the variety of two machine learning models is listed in Table 4.10. Simulated test results on real-world datasetsare as shown in Figure 4.5.

Table 4.11 lists the performance of the ensemble learning model of some two-class features, where CF+PF is the two-class combination in the best three-class hierarchical combination. In Table 4.9, D, the CF+PF+RB combination demonstrates superior performance compared to the CF+PF combination. Still, after adding the entropy histogram feature and grayscale feature

Table 4.10 Feature levels on the simulated real-world dataset

Integration method	Accuracy	Precision	recall	F-score
CF with PF and EHm	97	97.3	93	91.181
CF with PF and RB	97.6	96.8	92.3	89.990
CF with PF and GI	96.8	98.7	93.3	90.681
CF with PF and EHc	95.3	93.9	88.4	83.280

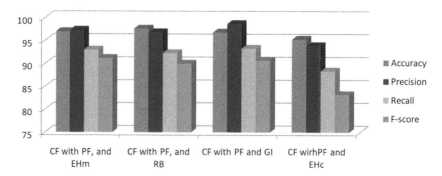

Figure 4.5 Feature levels on the simulated real-world dataset.

Table 4.11 Comparison of machine learning model time consumption

Model	Feature extraction	Model training	Model reasoning
EH and MLP method	39	117.0	17.95
EH andCNN method	39	193.8	19.35
GI and CNN method	08	89.64	17.48
RB (Malconv) [10]	00	1435	1032
OP and LSTM [4]	3740	10016	4906
PF and LGB method	0118	11.94	0082
CF and GBDT method	0630	02.40	63.41

training, the classifier performance of the three-level combination formed is weaker than that of the two-type variety, indicating that these features are in the integrated learning model of the three-type combination. The effect is small, which hinders the original feature combination classifier in the mix. And comparing Tables 4.8 and 4.10, it can be found that in the binary classification experiment, the performance of the combination feature is also weaker than that of the single machine learning model. EHm+ The combination of EHc is more vulnerable than their single model performance, and the implementation of EHm+GI is also lower than that of the EHm single model. This strengthens the conclusion that feature selection plays a vital role in model integration.

Based on the above experimental results analysis, the feature-level combination based on threat intelligence has achieved a substantial performance improvement compared to the baseline mining malware detection method based on opcode features [4].

4.4.5 Timeliness analysis

All machine learning models' consumption times are summarized in Table 4.11. All the time, tests are performed in a single-threaded manner. To compare the time consumption of the feature extraction stage, the "Feature Extraction" column shows that each feature extraction method processes 1,000 times the required for each sample. In the model training phase, results are obtained by multiplying the training rounds by the single training. In the model inference phase, the table lists the machine learning on the replicated real-world dataset. Table 4.11 displays the time efficiency of various machine learning algorithms. From Table 4.11, we can see the time efficiency of different machine learning. The baseline method of op-code [4] is affected by the vast computing network of BiLSTM and the disassembly and analysis time of IDA Pro, and its timeliness is much weaker than other machine learning methods.

In the training and testing of ensemble learning, three kinds of machine learning models are selected as the ensemble objects. At the same time, the shallow model used in the ensemble method has the characteristics of simple calculation, so the training and detection time consumed by different ensemble learning methods are the same. After testing the logic the training time of the ensemble learning model for regression is 0.51705 s, and the test time of simulating the real-world dataset is 89.29s. In practical applications, the multilevel feature ensemble learning method proposed in this paper will not consume more. The three models' primary consumption of time lies in the calculation time. Taking the CF+PF+GI combination method in Table 4.10 as an example, the total time consumption is still far better than the opcode baseline method [4], and compared with the original word, the section method [10] still has an advantage (1448 s VS. 2467 s).

Furthermore, according to the ecological survey of mining malware, packed malware only accounts for 30% of the existing mining malware [19]; the superposition of these two factors makes the influence of shelling technology on the static analysis method adopted in this paper limited in reality. Instead, the machine learning classification model trained in this paper also faces problems such as model aging [20] and adversarial attacks [21], which may lead to the continuous decline in the performance of the machine learning model. Aging brings a specific performance loss, but the integrated learning model is based on the performance combination of the model. This principle determines that it has better balance and robustness than the single-model method. The impact on ensemble learning is also smaller than that of single machine learning models.

4.5 CONCLUSIONS

The current detection of mining malware mainly refers to the feature design method of joint malware detection. Such a feature design method will quickly lead to a significant decline in the model's performance in the natural environment. This paper uses the threat intelligence characteristics of mining malware. Through the bytecode feature layer, PE structure feature layer, and mining operation execution feature layer, integrated learning designed a mining malware detection method. The investigational results show that the proposed method outperforms the baseline method by a large margin on simulated real-world datasets.

REFERENCES

[1] Daniel Gibert, Carles Mateu, Jordi Planes, HYDRA: A multimodal deep learning framework for malware classification, *Computers & Security*, vol. 95, 2020, p. 101873, ISSN 0167-4048, https://doi.org/10.1016/j.cose.2020.101873

[2] Daniel Gibert, Jordi Planes, Carles Mateu, Quan Le, Fusing feature engineering and deep learning: A case study for malware classification, *Expert Systems with Applications*, vol. 207, 2022, p. 117957, ISSN 0957-4174, https://doi.org/10.1016/j.eswa.2022.117957

[3] H. Darabian, S. Homayounoot, A. Dehghantanha et al. Detecting cryptomining malware: A deep learning approach for static and dynamic analysis, *Journal of Grid Computing*, vol. 18, 2020, pp. 293–303, https://doi.org/10.1007/s10723-020-09510-6

[4] D. T. Uysal, P. D. Yoo, K. Taha, Data-driven malware detection for 6G networks: A survey from the perspective of continuous learning and explainability via visualisation, *IEEE Open Journal of Vehicular Technology*, vol. 4, 2023, pp. 61–71, https://doi.org/10.1109/OJVT.2022.3219898

[5] N. Martins, J. M. Cruz, T. Cruz, P. Henriques Abreu, Adversarial machine learning applied to intrusion and malware scenarios: A systematic review, *IEEE Access*, vol. 8, 2020, pp. 35403–35419, https://doi.org/10.1109/ACCESS.2020.2974752

[6] E. S. Parildi, D. Hatzinakos, Y. Lawryshyn, Deep learning-aided runtime opcode-based windows malware detection, *Neural Comput & Applic*, vol. 33, 2021, pp. 11963–11983, https://doi.org/10.1007/s00521-021-05861-7

[7] V. Ravi, R. Chaganti, EfficientNet deep learning meta-classifier approach for image-based android malware detection, *Multimedia Tools and Applications*, 2022, https://doi.org/10.1007/s11042-022-14236-6

[8] Tal Tsafrir, Aviad Cohen, Etay Nir, Nir Nissim, Efficient feature extraction methodologies for unknown MP4-Malware detection using Machine learning algorithms, *Expert Systems with Applications*, vol. 219, 2023, p. 119615, ISSN 0957-4174, https://doi.org/10.1016/j.eswa.2023.119615

[9] Vinayakumar Ravi, Mamoun Alazab, Shymalagowri Selvaganapathy, Rajasekhar Chaganti, A Multi-View attention-based deep learning framework for malware detection in smart healthcare systems, *Computer Communications*, vol. 195, 2022, pp. 73–81, ISSN 0140-3664, https://doi.org/10.1016/j.comcom.2022.08.015

[10] Tom Landman, Nir Nissim, Deep-Hook: A trusted deep learning-based framework for unknown malware detection and classification in Linux cloud environments, *Neural Networks*, vol. 144, 2021, pp. 648–685, ISSN 0893-6080, https://doi.org/10.1016/j.neunet.2021.09.019

[11] A. Abusnaina, et al., DL-FHMC: Deep learning-based fine-grained hierarchical learning approach for robust malware classification, *IEEE Transactions on Dependable and Secure Computing*, vol. 19, no. 5, 1 Sept.-Oct. 2022, pp. 3432–3447, https://doi.org/10.1109/TDSC.2021.3097296

[12] R. Vinayakumar, M. Alazab, K. P. Soman, P. Poornachandran, S. Venkatraman, Robust intelligent malware detection using deep learning, *IEEE Access*, vol. 7, 2019, pp. 46717–46738. https://doi.org/10.1109/ACCESS.2019.2906934

[13] D. Ö. Şahın, S. Akleylek, E. Kiliç, Lin RegDroid: Detection of android malware using multiple linear regression models-based classifiers, *IEEE Access*, vol. 10, 2022, pp. 14246–14259, https://doi.org/10.1109/ACCESS.2022.3146363

[14] C. S. Yadav, S. Gupta, A review on malware analysis for IoT and android system, *SN Computer Science*, vol. 4, 2023, p. 118, https://doi.org/10.1007/s42979-022-01543-w

[15] Y. Ye, T. Li, K. Huang, et al., Hierarchical associative classifier (HAC) for malware detection from the large and imbalanced gray list, *Journal of Intelligent Information Systems*, vol. 35, 2010, pp. 1–20, https://doi.org/10.1007/s10844-009-0086-7

[16] F. Shahzad, M. Farooq, ELF-Miner: Using structural knowledge and data mining methods to detect new (Linux) malicious executables, *Knowledge and Information Systems*, vol. 30, 2012, pp. 589–612, https://doi.org/10.1007/s10115-011-0393-5

[17] Manel Jerbi, Zaineb Chelly Dagdia, Slim Bechikh, Lamjed Ben Said, Android malware detection as a Bi-level problem, *Computers & Security*, vol. 121, 2022, p. 102825, ISSN 0167-4048, https://doi.org/10.1016/j.cose.2022.102825

[18] P. K. Mvula, P. Branco, G. V. Jourdan, et al., A systematic literature review of cyber-security data repositories and performance assessment metrics for semi-supervised learning, *Discover Data*, vol. 1, 2023, p. 4, https://doi.org/10.1007/s44248-023-00003-x

[19] A. Boukhtouta, S. A. Mokhov, N. E. Lakhdari, et al., Network malware classification comparison using DPI and flow packet headers, *Journal of Computer Virology and Hacking Techniques*, vol. 12, 2016, 69–100, https://doi.org/10.1007/s11416-015-0247-x

[20] B. Urooj, M. A. Shah, C. Maple, M. K. Abbasi, S. Riasat, Malware detection: A framework for reverse engineered android applications through machine learning algorithms, *IEEE Access*, vol. 10, 2022, pp. 89031–89050, https://doi.org/10.1109/ACCESS.2022.3149053

[21] S. A. Roseline, S. Geetha, S. Kadry, Y. Nam, Intelligent vision-based malware detection and classification using deep random forest paradigm, *IEEE Access*, vol. 8, 2020, pp. 206303–206324, https://doi.org/10.1109/ACCESS.2020.3036491

[22] Ning Lu, Dan Li, Wenbo Shi, Pandi Vijayakumar, Francesco Piccialli, Victor Chang, An efficient combined deep neural network based malware detection framework in 5G environment, *Computer Networks*, vol. 189, 2021, p. 107932, ISSN 1389-1286.

[23] Valerian Rey, Pedro Miguel Sánchez Sánchez, Alberto Huertas Celdrán, Gérôme Bovet, Federated learning for malware detection in IoT devices, *Computer Networks*, vol. 204, 2022, p. 108693, ISSN 1389-1286.

[24] Chuanchang Liu, Jianyun Lu, Wendi Feng, Enbo Du, Luyang Di, Zhen Song, MobiPCR: Efficient, accurate, and strict ML-based mobile malware detection, *Future Generation Computer Systems*, vol. 144, 2023, pp. 140–150, ISSN 0167-739X.

[25] M. Grace, M. Sughasiny, Behaviour analysis of inter-app communication using a lightweight monitoring app for malware detection, *Expert Systems with Applications*, vol. 210, 2022, p. 118404, ISSN 0957-4174.

[26] Furqan Rustam, Imran Ashraf, Anca Delia Jurcut, Ali Kashif Bashir, Yousaf Bin Zikria, Malware detection using image representation of malware data and transfer learning, *Journal of Parallel and Distributed Computing*, vol. 172, 2023, pp. 32–50, ISSN 0743-7315.

[27] Lihua Yin, Muyijie Zhu, Wenxin Liu, Xi Luo, Chonghua Wang, Yangyang Li, WaterPurifier: A scalable system to prevent the DNS water torture attack in 5G-enabled SIoT network, *Computer Communications*, vol. 199, 2023, pp. 186–195, ISSN 0140-3664.

[28] Vasileios Syrris, Dimitris Geneiatakis, On machine learning effectiveness for malware detection in Android OS using static analysis data, *Journal of Information Security and Applications*, vol. 59, 2021, p. 102794, ISSN 2214-2126.

[29] Himanshu Sharma, Neeraj Kumar, Deep learning based physical layer security for terrestrial communications in 5G and beyond networks: A survey, *Physical Communication*, vol. 57, 2023, p. 102002, ISSN 1874-4907.

Chapter 5

Enhancing reliability and security of power monitoring systems in the era of 5G networks

Jitendra Kumar Chaudhary
Graphic Era Hill University, Bhimtal Campus, Dehradun, India

Saurabh Kumar
Teerthankar Mahaveer University, Moradabad, India

S. A. Sivasankari
Technology & Research (Deemed to be University), Guntur, India

Vibhor Kumar Vishnoi
Teerthanker Mahaveer University, VIBHU, Moradabad, India

5.1 INTRODUCTION

The power industry has always been an essential part of the national economic production and operation. The normal and sustainable operation of power equipment is the minimum guarantee for system security. Diversity and real-time capability are the current development directions of power system operations, but they also result in the generation of massive amounts of data from multiple sources [1]. The timely control of risks becomes more urgent due to the continuous occurrence of network attacks, which inevitably leads to vulnerabilities in the network [2]. The existence of these vulnerabilities inevitably causes uncertain losses to the power grid, making risk assessment of significant importance [3]. Researchers both domestically and internationally have conducted comprehensive and in-depth studies on how to describe the risks associated with various uncertainties in power system operations [4]. Reliability analysis primarily focuses on identifying existing network risks, analysing and evaluating the robustness of power monitoring systems, and achieving real-time risk control management and assessment [5]. This paper specifically analyses the risk level of power monitoring systems by adopting an attack graph–based approach combined with analytic hierarchy process (AHP) and fuzzy evaluation. Currently, the accuracy of power system risk assessment is relatively low, and the assessment duration is long [6]. Reliability models are an effective method for conducting network security assessments of power monitoring systems [7]. Effective security risk

DOI: 10.1201/9781003470281-5

assessments can guide the allocation of security protection resources and fill in the gaps [8–10]. Network reliability assessment can be achieved through the assessment of network security risks and the use of vulnerability scanning tools to discover weak points in the network [11–14]. However, reliability calculations have high time complexity [15–19]. There are generally two forms of assessment: qualitative assessment and quantitative assessment. Qualitative assessment is more convenient in terms of evaluation operations but lacks the ability to objectively analyse the losses that security attacks may cause. Quantitative security assessment techniques and methods can objectively describe the risk level of the system being tested. In particular, research on quantitative methods is the main direction of industrial control system information security assessment at present.

The reference [18–20] uses a probabilistic neural network to assess the riskiness of wind power situations. This method gives a reasonable assessment of the condition of wind turbines as well as dependable references for maintenance staff. Reference [21–26] gives a framework for calculating assets and quantifying aspects such as risks and vulnerabilities. Yang et al. suggested a host importance–based network host node risk assessment method [27, 28], which examines the risk of host nodes in a network environment completely and obtains more reasonable hazards. However, additional optimization is required to adapt this strategy to the network dangers associated with power monitoring systems.

The goal of this work is to create a method for assessing the dependability and reliability of power monitoring systems on a network. In order to maintain the normal and long-term operation of power equipment, which is essential for system security, the power industry must play a significant role in the production and operation of the national economy. However, as power system operations become more diverse and real-time, enormous amounts of data from several sources are generated, creating dangers and network vulnerabilities.

The contribution of this work is the creation of a thorough assessment system that incorporates communication pathways, network structure, and the main functions of the devices in the power monitoring system. Based on these variables, the researchers develop relevant reliability evaluation indicators and develop a hierarchical analysis structure model using the analytic hierarchy process and fuzzy comprehensive assessment. With the help of this model, it is possible to evaluate power monitoring systems' dependability in great detail.

The work addresses the shortcomings of current methods for assessing the risk of the power system, namely their poor accuracy and protracted evaluation times. The suggested mechanism delivers objective assessments of the risk level associated with power monitoring systems by using an attack graph–based approach and adding quantitative evaluation approaches. The evaluation's findings can be helpful resources and recommendations for network security administrators in the power sector.

In this paper, related reliability evaluation indicators are constructed based on the network topology of the power monitoring system and integrating the primary business activities of the devices in the power monitoring system and the communication paths. To build a hierarchical analysis structure model, the analytic hierarchy process is employed, and fuzzy comprehensive evaluation is performed, taking into account the evaluation indicator system and expert opinions. Finally, a mechanism for evaluating the network dependability of power monitoring systems is established. This assessment system can thoroughly assess the reliability of power monitoring systems based on the network topology of the systems, reflecting the dependability level of the systems and giving objective references and suggestions for network security managers.

5.2 RELIABILITY ASSESSMENT FRAMEWORK FOR POWER MONITORING SYSTEMS

In the reliability analysis and evaluation model for power monitoring systems, the weights assigned to each evaluation factor play a crucial role in the final reliability assessment. The methods for assigning weights to indicators mainly fall into two categories: objective weighting and subjective weighting. Subjective weighting relies too heavily on experiential judgement and lacks objectivity, while objective weighting lacks support from historical experience and also has limitations [29–33]. In this paper, an improved analytic hierarchy process is used to solve the weighting problem. The analytic hierarchy process has objectivity in evaluating the comprehensive impact of multiple factors. By determining weights using the analytic hierarchy process and then determining reliability using state attack graphs and fuzzy evaluation methods, the comprehensive indicator weights are combined, incorporating both subjective and objective aspects, resulting in more reasonable and comprehensive reliability assessment results for power monitoring systems.

5.2.1 Analytic hierarchy process

5.2.1.1 Hierarchical structure model

The decision objective is represented at the top level, the decision factors are represented at the intermediate level, and the solution alternatives are represented at the bottom level in the hierarchical structure model. In this study, a two-level hierarchical structure is built utilizing the analytical hierarchy approach to get the weights of each choice element as parameters for the reliability analysis framework and to provide weight analysis data for subsequent evaluations. The bottom level is the factor level, while the two top levels are the objective levels. The weights for each choice element are divided using the bottom-level structure.

5.2.1.2 Construction of judgement matrices

After determining the hierarchical structure, this paper uses pair-wise comparisons of indicators to select the final solution, aiming to analyse the weight of bottom-level factors on the upper levels [34–39]. By using a proportional scale table for judgement, the pair-wise comparison results of each factor are obtained to form the judgement matrix. Table 5.1 shows the importance level determination for pair-wise comparisons. The judgement matrix is represented by Equation 5.1.

$$b_{ij} = \frac{1}{b_{ij}} \qquad\qquad (5.1)$$

5.2.1.3 Hierarchical single ranking and consistency check

Hierarchical single ranking is done after the judgement matrix is constructed. The judgement matrix's characteristic value is denoted by the symbol, while its maximal characteristic value is denoted by the symbol λ, and λ_{max}. The normalized eigenvector X is used. The components of W stand for the rankings of the factors' relative weights in relation to the reliability assessment aim.

The sum of the elements in X is 1, i.e., $\sum_{i=1}^{n} X_i = 1, X_i$, where X_i represents the weight of the i-th factor in the lower level on a certain factor in the upper level. This method of determining the weight vector is known as the eigenvalue method. Additionally, according to the theorem of matrices, it is known that the unique nonzero eigenvalue of an n-order consistent matrix is n.

For an n-order reciprocal matrix $N(b_{ij} > 0, b_{ij} = 1/b_{ij}, b_{ij} = 1)$, the maximum eigenvalue $\lambda_{max} \geq n$ if and only if $\lambda = n$, indicating that N is a consistent matrix. Therefore, the magnitude of $\lambda_{max} - n$ is used to measure the inconsistency of matrix N the greater the difference between λ_{max} and n, the more severe the inconsistency of N, resulting in larger judgement errors.

For the results of hierarchical single ranking, a consistency check is performed. The consistency index is represented by DI, and its calculation

Table 5.1 Proportional scale table

Factor i vs Factor j	Quantized value
equally important	1
Slightly important	2
Strong and important	5
Strongly important	7
extremely important	9
The median value of two adjacent judgements	2,4,6,8

formula is shown in Equation 5.2. A smaller value of the consistency index indicates higher consistency. The consistency index is defined as:

$$DI = \frac{\lambda_{max} - n}{n - 1} \tag{5.2}$$

The consistency index DI equals 0 indicates complete consistency in the results of hierarchical single ranking. If it approaches 0, it indicates acceptable consistency in the results. The larger the value, the more inconsistent it is.

To evaluate the results of DI, the random consistency index SI is used for judgement.

$$SI = \frac{DI_2 + DI_2 + ... + DI_n}{n} \tag{5.3}$$

Based on the formula for calculating the SI index, multiple experiments are conducted by randomly generating judgement matrices. The DI values are calculated for each experiment, and then the square root of the arithmetic mean is taken to obtain the RI value. The corresponding relationship between different orders of SI values and the order of the matrix is shown in Table 5.2.

The consistency of the matrix is tested using the consistency ratio DR to avoid errors caused by random factors. The test coefficient is calculated as follows:

$$DR = \frac{DI}{SI} \tag{5.4}$$

If DR < 0.1, it indicates that the matrix passes the consistency test; otherwise, it does not pass.

5.2.1.4 Hierarchical overall ranking and consistency check

All factors are ranked in terms of their weights on the objective level, starting from the highest level and proceeding downward, while conducting consistency checks at each level.

Table 5.2 Corresponding matrix order

Order of the matrix	N
1	0
2	0
3	0.6
4	0.9
5	1.1
6	1.2
7	1.3
8	1.4

5.2.2 Fuzzy comprehensive evaluation method

When evaluating the reliability of the power monitoring system, some ambiguous and challenging-to-quantify parameters are quantified using the fuzzy comprehensive evaluation method. Multiple layers and influencing factors make up the power monitoring system, and these components are frequently both numerous and complex. It makes more sense to examine the reliability of the power monitoring system from a variety of angles rather than just one. To reflect the entire status of the evaluated object, the numerous power monitoring system indicators are therefore compiled and merged. A membership matrix (fuzzy relation matrix) is built by choosing the weights for each choice element in Section 5.2.1. The membership vector is then calculated to give the whole evaluation result, indicating the power monitoring system's reliability level objectively.

5.2.3 Attribute attack graph

Based on distinct search orientations, the attack graph construction technique may be divided into two types: forward attack graph generation algorithm and reverse attack graph generation algorithm. The forward attack graph generating technique takes the attacker's viewpoint into account. It can be seen that the attacker forward searches the network for weak hosts in order to target the objective. To produce the final links, the outcome of the network state must contain the previous network states. The target of the assault need not be identified for the forward attack graph generating technique to work. It starts at the first node and looks for all possible attack routes through the system. The reverse attack graph generation technique, on the other hand, seeks out all attack paths that potentially lead to the target by going backwards from the target node. In this procedure, useless pathways are eliminated. When the target is precisely defined, the algorithm for creating the reverse attack graph is appropriate. Thus, the construction of attack graphs uses this technique. The attack graph creation framework is shown in Figure 5.1.

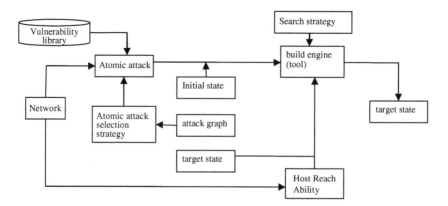

Figure 5.1 Attack graph generation framework.

5.2.4 Grey wolf optimization algorithms

The grey wolf optimization (GWO) algorithm replicates wolf packs with four forms of leadership: alpha (α), beta (β), delta (δ), and omega (ω). The three processes of wolf hunting that the GWO algorithm mimics are finding the target, encircling the target, and attacking the target. The second and third best solutions are given as α, and β and δ respectively, and the remaining candidate solutions are given as ω using the GWO method. The following are examples of how wolves behave when hunting prey:

$$E = \left| D.Y_Q(t) - Y(u) \right| \tag{5.5}$$

$$Y(u+1) = Y_Q(t) - B \cdot E \tag{5.6}$$

The distance between a wolf and its target is represented by Equation (5.5), while the wolf's position update rule is represented by Equation (5.6). In these equations, t stands for the number of iterations, A and C are coefficients, XP stands for the target location, and X stands for the wolf's position. The following are the expressions for A and C:

$$B = 2b \cdot s_1 - a \tag{5.7}$$

$$D = 2 \cdot s_2 \tag{5.8}$$

where B is the convergence factor, its value decreases linearly with the increase of iteration number. s_1 and s_2 are random numbers with values between 0 and 1.

When a grey wolf locates the position of the target, β and δ guide the wolf pack under the leadership of α to surround the target. The surrounding behaviour is modelled as:

$$\begin{aligned} E_\alpha &= \left| D_1 \cdot Y_\alpha - Y \right| \\ E_\beta &= \left| D_2 \cdot Y_\beta - Y \right| \\ E_\delta &= \left| D_3 \cdot Y_\delta - Y \right| \end{aligned} \tag{5.9}$$

where E_α, E_β, and E_δ stand for the separations between α, β, and δ and other people. The current positions of α, β, and δ are denoted by Y_α, Y_β, and Y_δ respectively. D1, D2, and D3 are random vectors, and Y shows where the grey wolf is right now.

$$\begin{aligned} Y_1 &= Y_\alpha - B_1 \cdot \left(E_\alpha \right) \\ Y_2 &= Y_\beta - B_1 \cdot \left(E_\beta \right) \\ Y_3 &= Y_\delta - B_1 \cdot \left(E_\delta \right) \end{aligned} \tag{5.10}$$

$$Y(u+1) = \frac{Y_1 + Y_2 + Y_3}{3} \tag{5.11}$$

Equation (5.10) represents the distance of the ω individual to the updated positions of α, β, and δ, and the final position is determined by Equation (5.11).

5.3 RELIABILITY ANALYSIS FRAMEWORK

5.3.1 Establishment of indicator set and evaluation set

The application of reliability theory to system analysis yields reliability indicators, which form the basis for quantifying system reliability. The three pillars of modern network security are unified in the power monitoring system's network risk evaluation index. It takes into account all aspects of a thorough security evaluation, including the physical environment, communications networks, boundaries between zones, computer environments, and construction management. Communication risk, business risk, and system risk are summed up, and the security evaluation of expanding businesses is also incorporated. This becomes the basis for the power monitoring system's network risk evaluation index. Please see Figure 5.2 for clarification.

The establishment of the indicator set is divided into three major indicators and 11 detailed indicators, where $U = \{U_1, U_2, U_3\} = \{$communication risk,

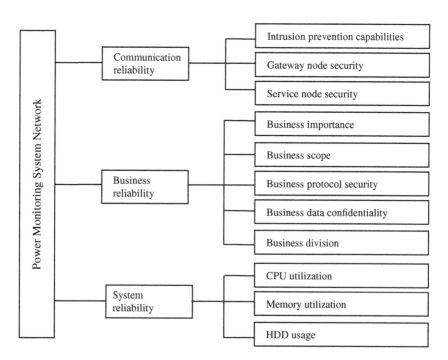

Figure 5.2 Network risk evaluation index system of power monitoring system.

Table 5.3 Evaluation indicators

Grade	Explain	Score
Health V1	low risk	Less than or equal to 0.1
Normal V2	lower risk	0.1–0.3
Note V3	medium risk	0.3–0.6
Abnormal V4	higher risk	0.6–0.8
Severe V5	high risk	greater than or equal to 0.8

business risk, system risk}. The detailed indicators include $U_1 = \{U_{11}, U_{12}, U_{13}\} =$ {intrusion prevention capability, gateway node security, perception node security}; $U_2 = \{U_{21}, U_{22}, U_{23}, U_{24}, U_{25}\}$ = {business importance, business scope, business protocol security, business data confidentiality, business partition}; $U_3 = \{U_{31}, U_{32}, U_{33}\}$ = {CPU utilization, memory utilization, disk usage}.

The establishment of the evaluation set includes five evaluation indicators: healthy, normal, caution, abnormal, and critical, as shown in Table 5.3.

5.3.2 Improving grey wolf optimization algorithm for analytic hierarchy processsweighting

The analytic hierarchy process is widely used to assign relative importance to various aspects of the power monitoring system reliability evaluation. Final weights of each evaluative component are acquired by optimization utilizing the enhanced GWO method. The results of the power monitoring system's reliability analysis are then provided, with the help of the judgement matrix constructed with the help of the fuzzy evaluation approach (Figure 5.3).

A GWO model is constructed by optimizing the GWO model using the Cuckoo Search algorithm, and an AHP fitness function is created. The judgement matrix of each feasible solution is obtained from Equation

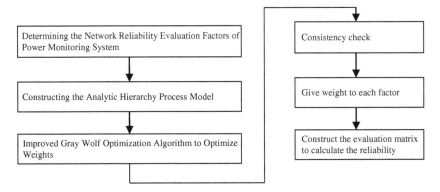

Figure 5.3 Optimization model for AHP weighting using grey wolf optimization algorithm [23].

(5.1). Equations (5.2) and (5.4) are used as constraints and as termination conditions for the optimization algorithm. The optimal eigenvalue and eigen-vector are searched through the algorithm to construct the judgement matrix for each indicator.

The risk assessment scores are presented in Table 5.4.

The judgement scores for communication risk indicators are shown in Table 5.5.

The weight results for business risk indicators are shown in Table 5.9.

The weight results for system risk indicators are shown in Table 5.10.

The weight results for the factor layer indicators are shown in Table 5.11.

Table 5.4 Risk indicator judgement matrix

Risk	Communication risk	Business risk	Systemic risk
communication risk	1	1/9	1
business risk	9	1	5
systemic risk	1	1/5	1

Notes: DI = 0.0194, DR = 0.0216, DR < 0.1, passing the consistency test.

Table 5.5 Judgement matrix for communication risk indicators

U_1	U_{11}	U_{12}	U_{13}
U_{11}	1	3	3
U_{12}	1/3	1	1
U_{13}	1/3	1	1

Notes: CI = 2.2 × 10^{-16}, DR = 2.4 × 10^{-16}, DR < 0.1, passing the consis-tency test. The judgement scores for business risk indicators are shown in Table 5.6. $U_2 = \{U_{21}, U_{22}, U_{23}, U_{24}, U_{25}\}$

Table 5.6 Judgement matrix for business risk indicators

U_2	U_{21}	U_{22}	U_{23}	U_{24}	U_{25}
U_{21}	1	9	5	5	9
U_{22}	1/9	1	1/7	1/7	1
U_{23}	1/5	7	1	3	7
U_{24}	1/5	7	1/3	1	7
U_{25}	1/9	1	1/7	1/7	1

Notes: DI = 0.117, DR = 0.094, DR < 0.1, passing the consistency test. The judgement scores for system risk indicators are shown in Table 5.7.

Table 5.7 Judgement matrix for system risk indicators

U_3	U_{31}	U_{32}	U_{33}
U_{31}	1	3	3
U_{32}	1/3	1	1
U_{33}	1/3	1	1

Notes: DI = 2.2 × 10⁻¹⁶, DR = 2.4 × 10⁻¹⁶, DR < 0.1, passing the consistency test. The weight results for communication risk indicators are shown in Table 5.8.

Table 5.8 Weight results for communication risk indicators

U_1	U_{11}	U_{12}	U_{13}
X_1	0.6	0.2	0.2

Table 5.9 Weight results for business risk indicators

U_2	U_{21}	U_{22}	U_{23}	U_{24}	U_{25}
X_2	0.5261	0.0371	0.2315	0.1683	0.0371

Table 5.10 Weight results for system risk indicators

U_3	U_{31}	U_{32}	U_{33}
X_3	0.6	0.2	0.2

Table 5.11 Weight results for factor layer indicators

U	U_1	U_2	U_3
X	0.1062	0.7651	0.1288

The optimized weight results using the improved grey wolf optimization algorithm are shown in Figure 5.4 and 5.5.

$X_1 = \{0.6, 0.2, 0.2\}$
$X_2 = \{0.5261, 0.0371, 0.2315, 0.1683, 0.0371\}$
$X_3 = \{0.6, 0.2, 0.2\}$
$X = \{0.10620, 0.76510, 0.1288\}$

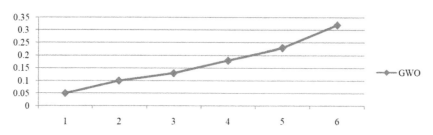

Figure 5.4 Convergence results of the improved grey wolf optimization algorithm.

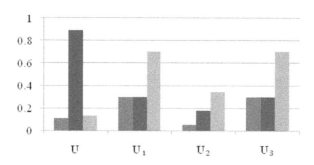

Figure 5.5 Illustration of weight results.

5.3.3 Establishing a fuzzy evaluation model

(1) Establishing the factor set U

The main factor set $U = \{U_1, U_2, U_3\}$ = {communication risk, business risk, system risk};

The minor factor set $U_1 = \{U_{11}, U_{12}, U_{13}\}$ = {intrusion prevention capability, gateway node security, perception node security};

$U_2 = \{U_{21}, U_{22}, U_{23}, U_{24}, U_{25}\}$ = {business importance, business scope, business protocol security, business data confidentiality, business partitioning};

$U_3 = \{U_{31}, U_{32}, U_{33}\}$ = {CPU utilization, memory utilization, disk usage}.

(2) Constructing the relevant risk evaluation set $A = \{A_1, A_2, A_3, A_4, A_5\}$ = {healthy, normal, attention, abnormal, severe}, with different indicators normalized.

(3) Determining the fuzzy relation matrix S

The scores given to each component make up the evaluations in the fuzzy relation matrix. Si = (si1, si2, si3, si4, si5) is the evaluation result for the i-th factor if the i-th factor in factor set U is a member of the risk evaluation set A with degree si1. The fuzzy relation matrix S is the product of all 11 U evaluations. In this study, we use expert reviews from the field of power system security to determine membership degree, with the average value of these reviews serving as the final conclusion.

(4) Establishing a comprehensive evaluation model

After determining the fuzzy relation matrix S and the weight values X of each factor, the comprehensive evaluation result B can be represented as $C = X \circ S$, where the comprehensive evaluation synthesis algorithm adopts the weighted average type.

5.4 EXPERIMENTAL SIMULATION AND ANALYSIS

5.4.1 Introduction to experimental simulation environment

5.4.1.1 Simulation Scenario of Thermal Power Plant

The simulation scenario simulates the relevant processes of boilers, steam turbines, and generators in a thermal power plant. It demonstrates the power generation of the thermal power generator and its input to the high-voltage grid through the step-up station. The simulation scenario uses virtual machines to simulate the auxiliary control system, SIS system, production MIS system, and engineer operation and maintenance workstation in the thermal power plant. Multiple sets of PLC devices are used to simulate data collection of pressure, temperature, and other parameters, as well as generator control processes. The business topology of the scenario is shown in Figure 5.6.

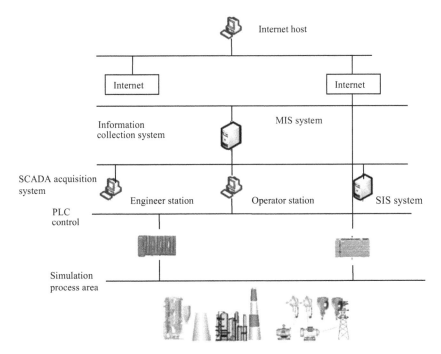

Figure 5.6 Topology of thermal power generation simulation scenario.

The simulation scenario consists of the auxiliary control system, SIS system, production MIS system, engineer station, PLC devices, sensors, and the thermal power generation model. The data transmission flow within the system is as follows: The auxiliary control system monitors the real-time operation of the generator and uses PLC devices for sensor data collection and generator control. The engineer station is used to configure the parameters of the PLC devices. The auxiliary control system forwards real-time data to the SIS system. The SIS system deploys interface servers to facilitate the transmission of production control zone data and management information zone data. Real-time data from the generator and the step-up station is transmitted to the production MIS system through the SIS system. Tables 5.12 and 5.13 list the IP addresses and existing vulnerabilities in the thermal power generation scenario.

Based on the business topology and vulnerabilities discovered through scanners, an attribute attack graph is constructed, as shown in Figure 5.7. Rectangles represent the used attack attributes, while ellipses represent nodes. Each system in the thermal power plant scenario is assigned a number: MIS system (1), SIS system (2), engineer station (3), operator station (4), and node 0 represent the attack node. "MS17-010(0,1)" represents an attack from node 0 to node 1 using the MS17-010 vulnerability to obtain user privileges.

Table 5.12 IP addresses in thermal power generation scenario

System	Uplink IP	Downlink IP
MIS system	192.168.3.11	192.168.4.101
SIS system	192.168.4.114	192.168.5.102
Engineer Station	192.168.5.112	192.168.100.100
Operator Station	192.168.5.113	192.168.100.101
PLC (left)	192.168.100.201	
PLC (right)	192.168.100.202	

Table 5.13 Vulnerability points in thermal power generation scenario

Business system	Operating system	Vulnerability point
MIS system	WIN7SP1	.MS17-010 PHPStuday Backdoor File Upload Vulnerability
SIS system	WIN7SP1	MS17-010 VNC weak password
engineer station	WIN7SP1	MS17-010 VNC weak password
operator station	WIN7SP1	MS17-010 VNC weak password
PLC (left)	S7-300	1. Flame indicator light in boiler goes out
PLC (right)	S7-1200	2. Generator stops running
		3. Tampering with the temperature and pressure values on the SCADA host computer remains unchanged

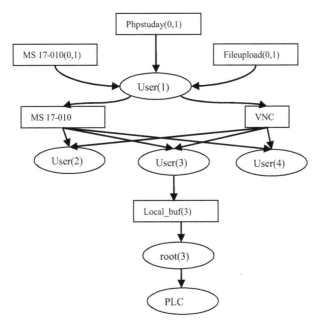

Figure 5.7 Attribute attack graph.

Table 5.14 Single-factor scores for thermal power generation

	U_1	U_2	U_3	U_4	U_5
U_{11}	0.3	0.3	0.3	0.4	0.2
U_{12}	0.3	0.3	0.3	0.35	0.2
U_{13}	0.2	0.3	0.3	0.25	0.2
U_{21}	0.4	0.4	0.5	0.35	0.2
U_{22}	0.8	0.8	0.85	0.3	0.2
U_{23}	0.3	0.45	0.5	0.3	0.3
U_{24}	0.3	0.4	0.4	0.3	0.3
U_{25}	0.7	0.8	0.85	0.2	0.2
U_{31}	0.2	0.4	0.6	0.3	0.1
U_{32}	0.3	0.4	0.4	0.3	0.1
U_{33}	0.4	0.5	0.5	0.4	0.2

Determining the fuzzy matrix S, Table 5.14 presents the single-factor scores for thermal power generation.

Based on the evaluation results, a comprehensive evaluation of the scores is conducted using grey correlation analysis combined with the TOPSIS method. The evaluation results are shown in Figure 5.8.

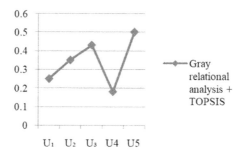

Figure 5.8 Comprehensive evaluation results using grey correlation analysis.

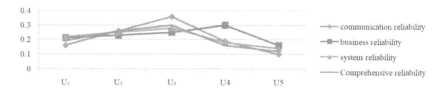

Figure 5.9 Evaluation results.

By combining the hierarchical weights determined earlier with the fuzzy evaluation method, the evaluation results of the scores are obtained, as shown in Figure 5.9.

Specific evaluation results:
    Communication Reliability: {0.194, 0.208, 0.208, 0.25, 0.139}
    Business Reliability: {0.203, 0.232, 0.268, 0.17, 0.126}
    System Reliability: {0.157, 0.253, 0.325, 0.193, 0.072}
    Reliability: {0.194, 0.229, 0.262, 0.181, 0.116}

Based on the data presented earlier, it is clear that the thermal power generating system is in a "normal" dependable state in terms of communication reliability, as determined by the reliability assessment. In terms of system and business reliability, however, it is currently in an"attention" condition. This assessment suggests that there is a moderate risk in the system, and failure to address it will result in a further decline in the reliability of the system. As a result, the "attention" level is likewise within the scope of the method's thorough reliability. Both sets of data show that the status of the thermal power generating scenario is "attention" according to the results produced from grey correlation analysis. The approach provided in this study, on the other hand, provides a more thorough and reasonable explanation of the power monitoring system's dependability status and clearly calls out areas of concern within the power monitoring system's network space. This helps the network security and operations team have a more complete and fair picture of the power monitoring system's dependability status.

5.5 CONCLUSION

This study suggests an enhanced fuzzy analytic hierarchy process–based model for network reliability analysis of power monitoring systems. To determine reliability factors in power monitoring systems, the model incorporates network tier protection techniques. It employs the improved grey wolf optimization algorithm in combination with the optimized analytic hierarchy process to calculate the weights of each factor using the analytic hierarchy method. In order to provide the reliability results of the power monitoring system to network security and operations employees, a fuzzy evaluation matrix is lastly created to determine the degree of membership of the reliability results to the evaluation set. The proposed technique has practical relevance in real-world applications and may depict the reliability level of the power monitoring system in a granular and comprehensive manner through comparison with grey correlation analysis paired with the TOPSIS method.

Additionally, the reliability evaluation approach proposed in the research relies on expert judgement to build the indicator system and choose weights, which has clear limits due to the shortcomings of the algorithm model used. It is advised that future research employ large data mining and analytic tools to identify the initial collection of indicators and their weights, assess their dangers, and achieve dynamic weight parameter adjustment. The risk level of the power monitoring system will be more precisely reflected by such a reliability assessment approach.

REFERENCES

[1] Abdul Ahad, Zahra Ali, Abdul Mateen, Mohammad Tahir, Abdul Hannan, Nuno M. Garcia, Ivan Miguel Pires, A comprehensive review on 5G-based smart healthcare network security: Taxonomy, issues, solutions and future research directions, *Array*, Volume 18, 2023, 100290, ISSN 2590-0056, https://doi.org/10.1016/j.array.2023.100290

[2] Himanshu Sharma, Neeraj Kumar, Deep learning based physical layer security for terrestrial communications in 5G and beyond networks: A survey, *Physical Communication*, Volume 57, 2023, 102002, ISSN 1874-4907, https://doi.org/10.1016/j.phycom.2023.102002

[3] Sabrina Sicari, Alessandra Rizzardi, Alberto Coen-Porisini, 5G in the internet of things era: An overview on security and privacy challenges, *Computer Networks*, Volume 179, 2020, 107345, ISSN 1389-1286, https://doi.org/10.1016/j.comnet.2020.107345

[4] Fauzia Irram, Mudassar Ali, Muhammad Naeem, Shahid Mumtaz, Physical layer security for beyond 5G/6G networks: Emerging technologies and future directions, *Journal of Network and Computer Applications*, Volume 206, 2022, 103431, https://doi.org/10.1016/j.jnca.2022.103431

[5] Saqib Hakak, Thippa Reddy Gadekallu, Praveen Kumar Reddy Maddikunta, Swarna Priya Ramu, Parimala M, Chamitha De Alwis, Madhusanka Liyanage,

Autonomous vehicles in 5G and beyond: A survey, *Vehicular Communications*, Volume 39, 2023, 100551, ISSN 2214-2096, https://doi.org/10.1016/j.vehcom.2022.100551

[6] Cherry Mangla, Shalli Rani, Nawab Muhammad Faseeh Qureshi, Aman Singh, Mitigating 5G security challenges for next-gen industry using quantum computing, *Journal of King Saud University-Computer and Information Sciences*, Volume 35, Issue 6, 2023, 101334, ISSN 1319-1578, https://doi.org/10.1016/j.jksuci.2022.07.009

[7] Amir Afaq, Noman Haider, Muhammad Zeeshan Baig, Komal S. Khan, Muhammad Imran, Imran Razzak, Machine learning for 5G security: Architecture, recent advances, and challenges, *Ad Hoc Networks*, Volume 123, 2021, 102667, ISSN 1570-8705, https://doi.org/10.1016/j.adhoc.2021.102667

[8] Charles Rajesh Kumar J., Ahmed Almasarani, M.A. Majid, 5G-wireless sensor networks for smart grid-accelerating technology's progress and innovation in the Kingdom of Saudi Arabia, *Procedia Computer Science*, Volume 182, 2021, 46–55, ISSN 1877-0509, https://doi.org/10.1016/j.procs.2021.02.007

[9] K. Raghavendra, Deepti Kakkar, 14- Reliability of 5G in human health monitoring using blockchain technology, Editor(s): Sudeep Tanwar, *Blockchain applications for healthcare informatics*, Academic Press, 2022, 313–326, ISBN 9780323906159, https://doi.org/10.1016/B978-0-323-90615-9.00012-8

[10] Md Mijanur Rahman, Fatema Khatun, Sadia Islam Sami, Ashik Uzzaman, The evolving roles and impacts of 5G enabled technologies in healthcare: The world epidemic COVID-19 issues, *Array*, Volume 14, 2022, 100178, ISSN 2590-0056, https://doi.org/10.1016/j.array.2022.100178

[11] M. Kumaresan, R. Gopal, M. Mathivanan, T. Poongodi, 13- Amalgamation of blockchain, IoT, and 5G to improve security and privacy of smart healthcare systems, Editor(s): Sudeep Tanwar, *Blockchain applications for healthcare informatics*, Academic Press, 2022, 283–312, ISBN 9780323906159, https://doi.org/10.1016/B978-0-323-90615-9.00015-3

[12] Xun Zhao, Hassan Askari, Jun Chen, Nanogenerators for smart cities in the era of 5G and Internet of Things, *Joule*, Volume 5, Issue 6, 2021, 1391–1431, ISSN 2542-4351, https://doi.org/10.1016/j.joule.2021.03.013

[13] Umar Ghafoor, Mudassar Ali, Humayun Zubair Khan, Adil Masood Siddiqui, Muhammad Naeem, NOMA and future 5G & B5G wireless networks: A paradigm, *Journal of Network and Computer Applications*, Volume 204, 2022, 103413, ISSN 1084-8045, https://doi.org/10.1016/j.jnca.2022.103413

[14] Ali Hassan Sodhro, Ali Ismail Awad, Jaap van de Beek, George Nikolakopoulos, Intelligent authentication of 5G healthcare devices: A survey, *Internet of Things*, Volume 20, 2022, 100610, ISSN 2542-6605, https://doi.org/10.1016/j.iot.2022.100610

[15] Kai Zhan, Sports and health big data system based on 5G network and Internet of Things system, *Microprocessors and Microsystems*, Volume 80, 2021, 103363, ISSN 0141-9331, https://doi.org/10.1016/j.micpro.2020.103363

[16] Long Liu, Xinge Guo, Chengkuo Lee, Promoting smart cities into the 5G era with multi-field Internet of Things (IoT) applications powered with advanced mechanical energy harvesters, *Nano Energy*, Volume 88, 2021, 106304, ISSN 2211-2855, https://doi.org/10.1016/j.nanoen.2021.106304

[17] Dinh C. Nguyen, Pubudu N. Pathirana, Ming Ding, Aruna Seneviratne, Blockchain for 5G and beyond networks: A state of the art survey, *Journal of Network and*

Computer Applications, Volume 166, 2020, 102693, ISSN 1084-8045, https://doi.org/10.1016/j.jnca.2020.102693

[18] Huimin Chen, Jiajia Liu, Jiadai Wang, Yijie Xun, Towards secure intra-vehicle communications in 5G advanced and beyond: Vulnerabilities, attacks and countermeasures, *Vehicular Communications*, Volume 39, 2023, 100548, ISSN 2214-2096, https://doi.org/10.1016/j.vehcom.2022.100548

[19] Dimitris Mourtzis, Smart manufacturing and tactile internet powered by 5G: Investigation of current developments, challenges, and future trends, *Procedia CIRP*, Volume 104, 2021, 1960–1969, ISSN 2212-8271, https://doi.org/10.1016/j.procir.2021.11.331

[20] Bismi B. S., Saniya Azeem, A survey on increasing the capacity of 5G Fronthaul systems using RoF, *Optical Fiber Technology*, Volume 74, 2022, 103078, ISSN 1068-5200, https://doi.org/10.1016/j.yofte.2022.103078

[21] Sulaiman Khan, Anwar Hussain, Shah Nazir, Fazlullah Khan, Ammar Oad, Mohammad Dahman Alshehri, Efficient and reliable hybrid deep learning-enabled model for congestion control in 5G/6G networks, *Computer Communications*, Volume 182, 31–40, 2022, ISSN 0140-3664, https://doi.org/10.1016/j.comcom.2021.11.001

[22] Misbah Shafi, Rakesh Kumar Jha, Manish Sabraj, A survey on security issues of 5G NR: Perspective of artificial dust and artificial rain, *Journal of Network and Computer Applications*, Volume 160, 2020, 102597, ISSN 1084-8045, https://doi.org/10.1016/j.jnca.2020.102597

[23] Sangeeta Bhattacharjee, Tamaghna Acharya, Uma Bhattacharya, Cognitive radio based spectrum sharing models for multicasting in 5G cellular networks: A survey, *Computer Networks*, Volume 208, 2022, 108870, ISSN 1389-1286, https://doi.org/10.1016/j.comnet.2022.108870

[24] Fadi Al-Turjman, Intelligence and security in big 5G-oriented IoNT: An overview, *Future Generation Computer Systems, Volume* 102, 2020, 357–368, ISSN 0167-739X, https://doi.org/10.1016/j.future.2019.08.009

[25] Ahmed Slalmi, Hasna Chaibi, Abdellah Chehri, Rachid Saadane, Gwanggil Jeon, Nadir Hakem, On the ultra-reliable and low-latency communications for tactile internet in 5G era, *Procedia Computer Science*, Volume 176, 2020, 3853–3862, ISSN 1877-0509, https://doi.org/10.1016/j.procs.2020.09.003

[26] Yulei Wu, Yuxiang Ma, Hong-Ning Dai, Hao Wang, Deep learning for privacy preservation in autonomous moving platforms enhanced 5G heterogeneous networks, *Computer Networks*, Volume 185, 2021, 107743, ISSN 1389-1286, https://doi.org/10.1016/j.comnet.2020.107743

[27] Arzoo Miglani, Neeraj Kumar, Blockchain management and machine learning adaptation for IoT environment in 5G and beyond networks: A systematic review, *Computer Communications*, Volume 178, 2021, 37–63, ISSN 0140-3664, https://doi.org/10.1016/j.comcom.2021.07.009

[28] Jan Mertes, Daniel Lindenschmitt, Masoud Amirrezai, Nima Tashakor, Moritz Glatt, Christian Schellenberger, Swati Matwankar Shah, Ali Karnoub, Christopher Hobelsberger, Li Yi, Stefan Götz, Jan C. Aurich, Hans D. Schotten, Evaluation of 5G-capable framework for highly mobile, scalable human-machine interfaces in cyber-physical production systems, *Journal of Manufacturing Systems*, Volume 64, 2022, 578–593, ISSN 0278-6125, https://doi.org/10.1016/j.jmsy.2022.08.009

[29] Hasna Fourati, Rihab Maaloul, Lamia Chaari, Mohamed Jmaiel, Comprehensive survey on self-organizing cellular network approaches applied to 5G networks, *Computer Networks*, Volume 199, 2021, 108435, ISSN 1389-1286, https://doi.org/10.1016/j.comnet.2021.108435

[30] K.F. Muteba, K Djouani, T. Olwal, 5G NB-IoT: Design, considerations, solutions and challenges, *Procedia Computer Science*, Volume 198, 2022, 86–93, ISSN 1877-509, https://doi.org/10.1016/j.procs.2021.12.214

[31] Shunliang Zhang, Dali Zhu, Yongming Wang, A survey on space-aerial-terrestrial integrated 5G networks, *Computer Networks*, Volume 174, 2020, 107212, ISSN 1389-1286, https://doi.org/10.1016/j.comnet.2020.107212

[32] Anjali Vaghani, Keshav Sood, Shui Yu, Security and QoS issues in blockchain enabled next-generation smart logistic networks: A tutorial, *Blockchain: Research and Applications*, Volume 3, Issue 3, 2022, 100082, ISSN 2096-7209, https://doi.org/10.1016/j.bcra.2022.100082

[33] İbrahim Yazici, Ibraheem Shayea, Jafri Din, A survey of applications of artificial intelligence and machine learning in future mobile networks-enabled systems, *Engineering Science and Technology, an International Journal*, Volume 44, 2023, 101455, ISSN 2215-0986, https://doi.org/10.1016/j.jestch.2023.101455

[34] Tolulope T. Oladimeji, Pradeep Kumar, Nicholas O. Oyie, Propagation path loss prediction modelling in enclosed environments for 5G networks: A review, *Heliyon*, Volume 8, Issue 11, 2022, e11581, ISSN 2405-8440, https://doi.org/10.1016/j.heliyon.2022.e11581

[35] Yan Zhou, Liyuan Li, The 5G communication technology-oriented intelligent building system planning and design, *Computer Communications*, Volume 160, 2020, 402–410, ISSN 0140-3664, https://doi.org/10.1016/j.comcom.2020.06.022

[36] Rizwana Shahzadi, Mudassar Ali, Humayun Zubair Khan, Muhammad Naeem, UAV assisted 5G and beyond wireless networks: A survey, *Journal of Network and Computer Applications*, Volume 189, 2021, 103114, ISSN 1084-8045, https://doi.org/10.1016/j.jnca.2021.103114

[37] José María Jorquera Valero, Pedro Miguel Sánchez Sánchez, Manuel Gil Pérez, Alberto Huertas Celdrán, Gregorio Martínez Pérez, Toward pre-standardization of reputation-based trust models beyond 5G, *Computer Standards & Interfaces*, Volume 81, 2022, 103596, ISSN 0920-5489, https://doi.org/10.1016/j.csi.2021.103596

[38] Mohamed Amine Ferrag, Leandros Maglaras, Antonios Argyriou, Dimitrios Kosmanos, Helge Janicke, Security for 4G and 5G cellular networks: A survey of existing authentication and privacy-preserving schemes, *Journal of Network and Computer Applications*, Volume 101, 2018, 55–82, ISSN 1084-8045, https://doi.org/10.1016/j.jnca.2017.10.017

[39] Dudu Mimran, Ron Bitton, Yehonatan Kfir, Eitan Klevansky, Oleg Brodt, Heiko Lehmann, Yuval Elovici, Asaf Shabtai, Security of open radio access networks, *Computers & Security*, Volume 122, 2022, 102890, ISSN 0167-4048, https://doi.org/10.1016/j.cose.2022.102890

Chapter 6

Passive voice in 5G mobile edge computing

Optimizing energy efficiency and resource utilization

Arijeet Chandra Sen
BITS Pilani, Pilani, India

Ihtiram Raza Khan
Jamia Hamdard, Delhi, India

Ajeet Kumar Srivastava
C S J M University, Kanpur, India

Sujeet More
Trinity College of Engineering and Research, Pune, India

6.1 INTRODUCTION

The rapid advancement of mobile intelligent technology has led to a significant increase in data volume, driven by computing-intensive applications like smart classrooms, online gaming, and 3D modeling. However, the limited computational resources of existing mobile devices pose challenges in meeting user demands for low latency, energy efficiency, and reliability [1]. These challenges have given rise to critical issues in mobile networks [2, 3].

Cloud computing offers powerful storage and computing capabilities to handle high-energy and complex tasks, but the distance between cloud servers and users results in unnecessary energy consumption and latency in data transmission. To address the challenges of low latency, high load, and mobility faced by future networks and reconcile the limitations of device resources with intelligent applications, mobile edge computing (MEC) has emerged as a promising computing paradigm [4]. MEC allows mobile devices to offload compute-intensive tasks to the edge, reducing the need for remote data transmission and significantly enhancing the network's bandwidth and transmission latency, ultimately improving user experience.

DOI: 10.1201/9781003470281-6

In the context of mobile edge computing, large-scale computing tasks may exceed the capabilities of edge nodes, while users might be situated beyond the coverage area of MEC servers with sufficient computing resources. To address these challenges, a relay-assisted MEC system model has been proposed, which utilizes neighboring edge nodes as relays to assist in forwarding tasks and extending the communication range, improving link transmission capacity, and reducing signal interruption probability [5, 6]. This model has garnered widespread attention in recent research.

Several studies have explored different aspects of the relay-assisted MEC system. Some focus on optimizing computing and communication resource allocation for energy consumption minimization under various constraints [7, 8]. Others have investigated relay selection schemes considering communication and computation capabilities [9–11]. To enhance resource utilization and network capacity, researchers have utilized Wireless Access Points (WAP) as relays to offload computing tasks to MEC servers [11–15].

However, existing research overlooks the randomness of real-time tasks and the need to minimize long-term average energy consumption while ensuring the stability of each edge node in the MEC system. Previous works have primarily concentrated on source and destination subsystems, disregarding the critical role of relay subsystems in terms of communication distance and limited computing resources [16, 17]. Therefore, this paper aims to comprehensively consider relay selection and relay offloading decisions while ensuring task buffer queue stability, addressing the issue of minimizing long-term average energy consumption in the relay-assisted MEC system.

The main objective of this research paper is to propose a novel approach for optimizing energy efficiency in a relay-assisted MEC system that includes multiple users and relay nodes. The paper establishes a long-term average energy consumption minimization problem by considering relay selection and buffer queue stability. The problem is formulated as a mixed-integer stochastic optimization problem, divided into two stages: relay selection and relay decision-making. The proposed method introduces user energy consumption and buffer queue weight parameter V_1, MEC energy consumption and queue weight parameter V_2, dynamically adjusting the emphasis on different factors at each stage. This method of optimization converges on the optimal solution via exhaustive search and effectively modifies the trade-off between energy consumption and latency based on the requirements at hand.

The results demonstrate that the proposed optimization method modifies the emphasis on user energy consumption, system queues, and MEC energy consumption effectively, validating its efficacy in improving energy efficiency and resource utilization in relay-assisted MEC systems. This work contributes to the larger field of 5G mobile edge computing by providing valuable insights into optimizing energy efficiency and a comprehensive comprehension of the performance of the relay-assisted MEC system.

6.2 SYSTEM MODEL AND PROBLEM FORMULATION

This section presents the energy and task buffer queue formulations for local computation, relay computation, and remote computation after introducing the system model.

6.2.1 System model

As seen in Figure 6.1, the relay-assisted MEC system under consideration in this research comprises of several users, numerous relay nodes (RN), and a remote server (RS).

Let $V = \{v_i \mid i = 1, 2, \ldots, n\}$ represent the set of users, and $S = \{s_j \mid j = 1, 2, \ldots, m\}$ represent the set of relay nodes. In this paper, i and j are used to denote the indices of users and relay nodes, respectively. Due to the random arrival of tasks, users need to make decisions between local computation and task offloading. RN provides a shared task buffer queue for the users requesting service, where tasks that have arrived at RN but have not been executed yet are stored. Therefore, when multiple users select the same RN, tasks enter the buffer queue in the order of arrival, forming a queue.

Users evaluate the channel conditions, computation capabilities, and task buffer queue lengths of the RNs. If they choose task offloading, they select the optimal relay node from the set of RNs to perform the task. In practical applications, different RN nodes receive different task volumes, leading to varying queue lengths. During the relay selection stage, to balance the queue pressure on each RN, the queue length needs to be taken

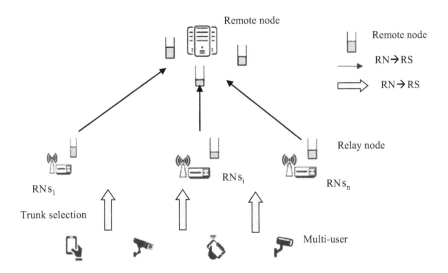

Figure 6.1 MEC system with multiple users and multiple relay servers.

into account. On the other hand, as the RN buffer queue becomes longer with increasing task volume, it becomes crucial to mitigate the queue pressure on the relay nodes.

To alleviate the queue pressure while meeting the stability constraint of the MEC server's task buffer queue, this paper further considers offloading tasks to an RS auxiliary server as shown in Figure 6.1. Each RN is provided with an independent buffer queue. The system is assumed to operate on a timeline, which is discredited into each time slot $u \in U = \{0, 1, 2,..., U\}$. At each time slot $s = \tau_{ms}$, users need to make decisions within each time frame τ based on channel conditions, computation capabilities, and task buffer queue lengths for the RNs in the set. They decide whether to place tasks for local computation or perform offloading. Similarly, the RNs also need to make decisions within each time frame τ on whether to keep tasks in the buffer queue or upload them to the RS. Therefore, the joint optimization algorithm proposed in this paper for minimizing average energy consumption mainly includes relay node selection and relay offloading decisions. The detailed process for user u_i can be divided into the following five stages:

Stage 1: Generate random tasks at the current time slot and select a relay node from the set of relay nodes. If no suitable RN is available, proceed to Stage 2. If there is an available RN, make the optimal offloading decision and proceed to Stage 3.

Stage 2: Perform local computation for the tasks generated at the current time slot and move to time slot u+1, then restart Stage 1.

Stage 3: Fully offload the tasks to the RN's buffer queue for processing and proceed to Stage 4.

Stage 4: Based on the optimization algorithm, each RN makes an offloading decision, whether to keep the computing tasks in the RN's buffer queue for processing or continue uploading them to the RS. Proceed to Stage 5.

Stage 5: Update the buffer queue length for each relay node and restart Stage 1.

6.2.2 Problem formulation

1) Local Computation Model: This paper considers a complete offloading model; where when performing relay offloading, users need to select an RN from the set of relay nodes to completely offload the tasks to the RN. Conversely, when the workload on a relay node is heavy or the buffer queue is too long, tasks need to be computed locally. To model this, a binary variable $y_{ij}(u)$ is introduced to describe whether the user offloads data with the help of an RN. $y_{ij}(u) = 1$ indicates that user v_i offloads tasks to s_j at time t, otherwise $y_{ij}(u) = 0$. Additionally, an extra state $y_{i0}(u) = 1$ is introduced to represent the scenario when user v_i cannot find a suitable

RN and must perform local computation [18–21]. Therefore, the selection of RN servers can be represented as follows:

$$\sum_{j=0}^{m} y_{ij}(u) = 1, y_{ij}(u) \in \{0,1\}, u \in U \tag{6.1}$$

Let $B_i(u)$ represent the random task quantity generated by user v_i at time u, where random tasks are uniformly distributed in the interval $[B_{i,\min}, B_{i,\max}]$ (independent and identically distributed, iid). M_i represents the effective switch capacitance dependency on the chip architecture for user v_i, D_0 denotes the local computation frequency, and g_i indicates the number of CPU cycles required for user v_i to perform 1 bit [22–24]. When tasks can only be computed locally, the computation energy consumption can be represented as:

$$\varepsilon_{\mathrm{wer},i}(u) = m_i D_0^2 h_i B_i(u) \tag{6.2}$$

2) RN Computation Model: When user v_i selects relay node s_j as an auxiliary node, tasks need to be offloaded and executed on s_j. The energy consumption of relay node s_j mainly includes: (1) energy consumed in data transmission from user v_i to relay node s_j, and (2) energy consumed in task execution on s_j. Let e_{ij} represent the distance between user v_i and s_j, and the path loss coefficient is given by $1/(1+e_{ij}^f)$, where α is a constant [25–27] representing the path loss exponent ($\alpha > 2$). According to Shannon's formula, the energy consumed in transmitting data from v_i to s_j can be represented as:

$$F_{ij}^{\mathrm{tran}}(u) = p_{i0} \frac{B_i(u)}{x \log_2 \left(1 + \dfrac{q_{i0}|g_{ij}|^2}{(1+e_{ij}^a)\sigma^2}\right)} \tag{6.3}$$

where x is the channel bandwidth, p_{i0} is the fixed transmission power for each user v_i, σ^2 is the variance of the additive white Gaussian noise (AWGN), and g_{ij} represents the channel fading coefficient for the transmission from v_i to s_j.

Let $D_j(u)$ represent the CPU cycle frequency of relay node s_j, and this frequency cannot exceed the maximum value $D_j^{\max}$. For simplicity in analysis, this paper assumes that all m relay nodes have the same $F_j^{\mathrm{cal}}(u)$. Therefore, the computable task quantity $F_{j,\max}^{\mathrm{cal}}$ for s_j has a maximum value [28].

Let g_j represent the number of CPU cycles required for s_j to perform 1 bit, and m_j represents the effective switch capacitance dependency on the chip architecture for s_j. The computable task quantity $F_j^{\text{cal}}(u)$ at time t and the energy consumption to complete the computing task can be respectively represented as:

$$\mathcal{F}_j^{\text{cal}}(u) = uh_j^{-1}D_j(u) \tag{6.4}$$

$$\varepsilon_j^{\text{cal}}(u) = M_i D_j^3(u)\tau \tag{6.5}$$

At time u, the total energy consumption of relay node s_j can be represented as:

$$\varepsilon_{\text{relay},j}(u) = \sum_{i=1}^{n} \varepsilon_{ij}^{\text{tran}}(u) + \varepsilon_j^{\text{cal}}(u) \tag{6.6}$$

3) RS Computation Model: When the buffer queue of the relay node becomes too long, tasks can be further uploaded and executed on the remote server (RS). In this case, the energy consumption also includes both transmission and computation energy consumption [29–31]. According to Shannon's formula, the task transmission quantity $F_{r,j}(t)$ and transmission energy consumption at time t can be represented as:

$$\mathcal{F}_{r,j}(u) = x\tau \log_2\left(1 + \frac{q_{ux,j}(u)|g_j|^2}{(1 + e_j^a)\sigma^2}\right) \tag{6.7}$$

$$\varepsilon_{tx,j}(u) = q_{ux,j}(u)\tau \tag{6.8}$$

Where $q_{ux,j}(u)$ represents the transmission power of relay node s_j, g_j is the channel fading coefficient between relay node s_j and RS, and e_j is the distance between relay node s_j and RS. At each time slot, the task transmission quantity $\mathcal{F}_{r,j}(u)$ has a maximum value $F_{r,j,\max}$. Assuming that at time t, the CPU cycle frequency of RS is $D_e(u)$, this frequency cannot exceed the maximum value $D_e^{\max}$. Therefore, the computable task quantity $\mathcal{F}_e(u)$ for RS has a maximum value $\mathcal{F}_{j,\max}^{\text{cal}}$. Let h_d represent the number of CPU cycles required for RS to complete 1 bit of task, and M_e represents the effective switch capacitance dependency on the chip $C_d^{\max}$ architecture for RS [32–35]. The computable task quantity $F_e^{\text{cal}}(u)$ at time t and the energy consumption to complete the computing task can be respectively represented as:

$$\mathcal{F}_e^{\text{cal}}(u) = \tau g_d^{-1} D_d(u) \tag{6.9}$$

$$\varepsilon_d(u) = k_d D_e^3(u)\tau \tag{6.10}$$

At time t, the total energy consumption of RS is:

$$\varepsilon_{\text{remote}}(u) = \sum_{j=1}^{m} \varepsilon_{tx,j}(u) + \varepsilon_e(u) \tag{6.11}$$

4) Queue Model: After users complete relay selection and make optimal offloading decisions, they offload the computing tasks to the selected relay node s_j. The tasks that have arrived at r_j but have not been executed will be queued in a task buffer area with sufficient capacity. After relay selection, the task quantity arriving at RN, $C_j(u)$, can be represented as:

$$C_j(u) = \sum_{i=1}^{n} y_{ij}(u) B_i(u) \tag{6.12}$$

where the task quantity arriving at RN, $C_j(u)$, has a maximum value $C_{j,\max}$. When the arriving task quantity, $C_j(u)$, exceeds $C_{j,\max}$, the relay node r_j will reject task offloading. Assuming that the queue length of relay node s_j at time u is $\zeta(u) = [\zeta_1(u), \zeta_2(u), \ldots, \zeta_m(u)]$ where $\zeta_j(u)$ represents the queue length of relay node s_j. Based on the arrivals and departures from the queue at time u, the queue length of node s_j at time $u + 1$ can be represented as:

$$\zeta_j(u+1) = \max\{\zeta_j(u) - \mathcal{F}_j^{\text{cal}}(u) - \mathcal{F}_{r,j}(u), 0\} + C_j(u), u \in \Gamma \tag{6.13}$$

The remote server RS maintains an independent task buffer for each relay node with task requests. Assuming that at time u, RS provides a queue length for the buffer of m relay nodes, denoted as $\eta(u) = [\eta_1(u), \eta_2(u), \ldots, \eta_m(u)]$. Based on the arrivals and departures from the queue at time u, the queue length of the corresponding buffer for relay node s_j at time $u + 1$ can be represented as:

$$\eta_j(u+1) = \max\{\eta_j(t) - \mathcal{F}_j^{\text{cal}}(u), 0\}$$
$$+ \min\{\max\{\zeta_j(u) - \mathcal{F}_j^{\text{cal}}(u), 0\}, F_{r,j}(u)\}, u \in \Gamma \tag{6.14}$$

6.2.3 Performance metrics

This paper mainly considers the minimization of energy consumption during the task execution process for users, relay nodes, and the RS server, subject to relay selection and task buffer queue length constraints. The energy consumption is considered within a single time slot τ, and as the total timeline U approaches positive infinity, the total system energy consumption can be represented as:

$$\varepsilon = \lim_{U \to \infty} \frac{1}{U} \sum_{t=0}^{U-1} F\left[\varepsilon \Sigma(u)\right] \tag{6.15}$$

where $\varepsilon \sum (u)$ is defined as:

$$\varepsilon_\Sigma(u) = \sum_{j=0}^{m}(1-y_{i0})\left[\varepsilon_{\text{relay},j}(u)+\varepsilon_{\text{remote},j}(u)\right]+\sum_{i=1}^{n}y_{i0}\,\varepsilon_{\text{user},i}(u) \tag{6.16}$$

According to Little's law [36–39], the average execution delay experienced by each relay node RN and the RS server is directly proportional to the number of tasks waiting in their respective MEC system queues, i.e., it is proportional to the total length of the task buffer queues on the RN and RS. Therefore, the total length of the task buffer queues on all RNs and RS in the system can be considered as a measure of execution delay, denoted as:

$$R = \lim_{U \to \infty} \frac{1}{U} \sum_{u=0}^{U-1} \sum_{j=1}^{m} E\left[\zeta_j(u)+\eta_j(u)\right] \tag{6.17}$$

In this system, each user needs to make offloading decisions at each time slot $u \in \Gamma = \{0, 1, 2,..., U\}$. Due to differences in performance among different relay nodes (RN), users need to make optimal choices to minimize energy consumption. User v_i needs to make a relay selection decision $y_{ij}(u)$ based on channel conditions, computing capabilities, and the task buffer queue length $[\zeta_j(u), g_{ij}, e_{ij}]$ at time u. Additionally, to relieve the queue pressure on relay nodes, tasks can be offloaded to the remote RS server when the relay node's buffer queue becomes too long. To minimize the system's energy consumption, the relay node needs to determine the optimal relay computation frequency, transmission power, and the computation frequency required from the remote RS server, denoted as $X(u) = [D_j(u), q_{ux,j}(u), D_e(u)]$. Therefore, the proposed average energy minimization problem based on relay selection and queue stability can be formulated as:

$$Q_{1\,\{yij(u),X(u)\}} \quad \min \varepsilon \tag{6.18}$$

$$\text{s.t.} 0 \leq q_{ux,j}(u) \leq q_{ux,\max} 1 \leq j \leq m \tag{6.19}$$

$$0 \leq D_j(u) \leq D_{j,\max}, 1 \leq j \leq m \tag{6.20}$$

$$0 \leq D_e(u) \leq D_{e,\max} \tag{6.21}$$

$$\sum_{j=0}^{m} y_{ij}(u) = 1, y_{ij}(u) \in \{0,1\}, 1 \leq i \leq n \tag{6.22}$$

$$\lim_{U \to \infty} \frac{E\left[|\varsigma_j(u)|\right]}{U} = 0, 1 \leq j \leq m \tag{6.23}$$

$$\lim_{U \to \infty} \frac{F\left[|\eta_j(U)|\right]}{U} = 0, 1 \leq j \leq m \tag{6.24}$$

where constraint (6.19) represents the transmission power range of relay node s_j, constraints (6.20) and (6.21) represent the computation frequency range of RN and RS respectively, constraint (6.22) represents the user's full offloading strategy, and constraints (6.23) and (6.24) represent the queue length stability constraints of RN and RS respectively.

6.3 ALGORITHM DESIGN

Problem Q_1 is a mixed-integer nonlinear programming problem containing four sets of decision variables, $[y_{ij}(u), D_j(u), q_{ux,j}(u), D_e(u)]$. Since $y_{ij}(u)$ is related to the user's relay selection results and $[D_j(u), q_{ux,j}(u), D_e(u)]$ is related to the relay's offloading decision, solving this problem can be done in two stages. This paper decomposes Q_1 into two stages: first, determining the optimal relay selection decision $y_{ij}(u)$ by minimizing the weighted sum of transmission energy consumption and buffer queue length; second, using the Lyapunov optimization algorithm to obtain the relay offloading decision is $X(u) = [D_j(u), q_{ux,j}(u), D_e(u)]$.

6.3.1 User's optimal relay selection

When there are available relay nodes in the set, each user needs to select one RN from the set to execute task offloading. This selection strategy needs to consider both the channel conditions between the user and the relay node and the task buffer queue length of the relay node. Different types of users have different preferences for transmission energy consumption and waiting time for computation after task offloading (i.e., buffer queue length). To address this, we introduce W_1 (bits·X^{-1}) as a weight parameter for the optimal relay selection stage to adjust the importance of these two metrics. Therefore, the optimal relay selection stage uses the weighted sum of transmission energy consumption and buffer queue length as the basis for selection, as shown below:

$$T_{ij}(u) = W_1 \varepsilon_{ij}^{tran}(u) + \zeta_j(u) \tag{6.25}$$

The relay selection strategy for user v_i can be represented as:

$$\phi_i(u) = \{y_{i1}(u), y_{i2}(u), \dots, y_{im}(u)\} \tag{6.26}$$

In summary, the relay selection strategy that balances transmission energy consumption and waiting time for computation can be expressed as:

$$\phi_i^*(u) = \underset{\phi_i(u)}{\arg\min} T_{ij}(u) \tag{6.27}$$

6.3.2 Optimal relay offloading

After completing the relay selection in stage 1, users offload tasks to the buffer queue of the relay node. When the buffer queue becomes too long, tasks will continue to be offloaded to the remote RS. The relay offloading stage needs to determine the computation frequency and transmission power of the RN, as well as the computation frequency of the remote RS. This section will use the Lyapunov optimization algorithm to solve Q_1 after relay selection, and at each time slot, it converts the stochastic optimization problem into a deterministic problem. Let $\Theta(t) = [\zeta(t), \eta(t)]$ represent the set of RN and RS task buffer queue lengths at time t, then the quadratic Lyapunov function and Lyapunov drift function can be defined as follows [17]:

$$K(\Theta(u)) = \frac{1}{2} \sum_{j=1}^{m} \left[\zeta_j^2(u) + \eta_j^2(u) \right] \tag{6.28}$$

$$\Delta(\Theta(u)) = E[K(\Theta(u+1)) - K(\Theta(u+1)) \mid \Theta(u)] \tag{6.29}$$

Furthermore, the Lyapunov drift plus penalty function can be expressed as:

$$\Delta_v(\Theta(u)) = \Delta(\Theta(u)) + W_2 \cdot F[\varepsilon_\Sigma(u) \mid \Theta(u)] \tag{6.30}$$

where W_2 (bits². X^{-1}) is the weight coefficient introduced in the optimal relay offloading decision stage.

Lemma 1

There exists an upper bound for all parameters in the range of $X(u)$ in Equation (6.30).

Proof: By squaring the RN task buffer queue length and using Equations (6.13) and (6.14), we obtain:

$$
\begin{aligned}
\zeta_j^2(u+1) &= C_j^2(u) + \left(\max\left\{ \zeta_j(u) - \mathcal{F}_j^{\text{cal}}(u) - \mathcal{F}_{r,j}(u), 0 \right\} \right)^2 \\
&\quad + 2C_j(t) \max\left\{ \zeta_j(u) - \mathcal{F}_j^{\text{cal}}(u) - \mathcal{F}_{r,j}(u), 0 \right\} \\
&\leq \left(\zeta_j(u) - \mathcal{F}_j^{\text{cal}}(u) - \mathcal{F}_{r,j}(u) \right)^2 + C_j^2(u) + 2C_j(u)\zeta_j(u) \quad (6.31) \\
&= \zeta_j^2(u) + \left(\mathcal{F}_j^{\text{cal}}(u) + \mathcal{F}_{r,j}(u) \right)^2 + C_j^2(u) \\
&\quad - 2\zeta_j(u)\left(\mathcal{F}_j^{\text{cal}}(u) + \mathcal{F}_{r,j}(u) - C_j(u) \right)
\end{aligned}
$$

Similarly, by performing the same operation on the task buffer queue in RS, we get:

$$
\begin{aligned}
\eta_j^2(u+1) &\leq \left(\max\left\{ \eta_j(u) - \mathcal{F}_e^{\text{cal}}(u), 0 \right\} + \mathcal{F}_{r,j}(u) \right)^2 \\
&= \left(\max\left\{ \eta_j(u) - \mathcal{F}_e^{\text{cal}}(u), 0 \right\} \right)^2 + \mathcal{F}_{r,j}^2(u) + \quad (6.32) \\
&\leq \left(\eta_j(u) - \mathcal{F}_e^{\text{cal}}(u) \right)^2 + \mathcal{F}_{r,j}^2(u) + 2\mathcal{F}_{r,j}(u)\eta_j(u) 2\mathcal{F}_{r,j}(u)\max\left\{ \eta_j(u) - \mathcal{F}_e^{\text{cal}}(u), 0 \right\} \\
&= \eta_j^2(u) - 2\eta_j(u)\left(\mathcal{F}_e^{\text{cal}}(u) - \mathcal{F}_{r,j}(u) + \left(\mathcal{F}_{r,j}^2(u) \right) \right) + \left(\mathcal{F}_e^{\text{cal}}(t) \right)^2
\end{aligned}
$$

Since $C_d^{\max}$, we can deduce from Equations (6.31) and (6.32):

$$
\begin{aligned}
\Delta\left(\Theta(u)\right) &\leq \frac{1}{2}\sum_{j=1}^{m}\left[\left(\mathcal{F}_{j,\max}^{\text{cal}} - \mathcal{F}_{r,j,\max} \right)^2 \right] + \frac{1}{2}\sum_{j=1}^{m}\left[\left(\mathcal{F}_{e,\max}^{\text{cal}} \right)^2 + \mathcal{F}_{r,j,\max}^2 + C_{j,\max}^2 \right] \\
&\quad - F\left[\sum_{j=1}^{m}\zeta_j(u)\left(\mathcal{F}_j^{\text{cal}}(u) + \mathcal{F}_{r,j}(u) - C_j(t) \right) | \Theta(u) \right] \\
&\quad - E\left[\sum_{j=1}^{m}\eta_j(u)\left(\mathcal{F}_e^{\text{cal}}(u) - \mathcal{F}_{r,j}(u) \right) | \Theta(u) \right] \quad (6.33)
\end{aligned}
$$

Thus, the expression for the constant upper bound E is:

$$
\begin{aligned}
E &= \frac{1}{2}\sum_{j=1}^{m}\left[\left(\mathcal{F}_{j,\max}^{\text{cal}} - F_{s,j,\max} \right)^2 + F_{s,j,\max}^2 \right] \\
&\quad + \frac{1}{2}\sum_{j=1}^{m}\left[\left(\mathcal{F}_{e,\max}^{\text{cal}} \right)^2 + C_{j,\max}^2 \right]
\end{aligned}
\quad (6.34)
$$

Using Lyapunov optimization, we approximate the optimal solution for Q_1 by minimizing the upper bound of the drift plus penalty function $\Delta(\Theta(u)) + W_2 \cdot F[\varepsilon_\Sigma(u)|\Theta(u)]$ at each time slot, yielding:

$$
\begin{aligned}
\Delta_v\left(\Theta(u)\right) \leq{}& F + W_2 \cdot F[\varepsilon_\Sigma(u) | \Theta(u)] \\
&- F\left[\sum_{j=1}^{m} \varsigma_j(u)\left(\mathcal{F}_j^{\mathrm{cal}}(u) + F_{r,j}(u) - C_j(u)\right) | \Theta(u)\right] \\
&- F\left[\sum_{j=1}^{m} \eta_j(u)\left(\mathcal{F}_e^{\mathrm{cal}}(u) - F_{r,j}(t)\right) | \Theta(t)\right]
\end{aligned}
\tag{6.35}
$$

Based on the above analysis, the deterministic optimization problem can be formulated as:

$$
Q_2 : \min - \sum_{j=1}^{m} \varsigma_j(u)\left(\mathcal{F}_j^{\mathrm{cal}}(u) + F_{s,j}(u)\right) - \sum_{j=1}^{m} \eta_j(u)\left(\mathcal{F}_e^{\mathrm{cal}}(u) - F_{r,j}(u)\right) + W_2 \varepsilon_\Sigma(u)
\tag{6.36}
$$

$$
\text{s.t.} (19) - (24)
$$

To obtain the solution for the deterministic optimization problem Q_2, we further decompose Q_2 into three subproblems: optimal relay transmission power, optimal relay computation frequency, and optimal RS computation frequency.

1) Optimal relay transmission power: At time t, the optimal relay offloading transmission power $ptx,j(t)$ can be obtained by solving the subproblem TP_1:

$$
\begin{aligned}
UQ_1 : \min - {}& \sum_{j=1}^{m}\left(\varsigma_j(u) - \eta_j(u)\right) F_{s,j}(u) + V_2 \varepsilon_{tx,j}(u) \\
&- \sum_{j=1}^{m}\left(\varsigma_j(u) - \eta_j(u)\right) x\tau \log_2\left(1 + \frac{q_{ux,j}(u)\left|g_j\right|^2}{\left(1 + e_j^r\right)\sigma^2}\right) \\
&- \sum_{j=1}^{m} W_2 q_{ux,j}(u)\tau
\end{aligned}
\tag{6.37}
$$

By taking the derivative of Equation (6.37) the extremum of $q_{ux,j}(u)$ is given by:

$$q_{ux,j}(t) = \max\left\{\min\left[\frac{X\left(\zeta_j(u)-\eta_j(u)\right)}{W_2 \ln 2} - \frac{\left(1+e_j^f\right)\sigma^2}{\left|g_j\right|^2}, q_{ux,\max}\right], 0\right\} \quad (6.38)$$

2) Optimal relay computation frequency: At time u, the optimal relay computation frequency $D_j(u)$ can be obtained by solving the sub-problem UQ_2:

$$UQ_2 : \min - \sum_{j=1}^{m} \zeta_j(u)\mathcal{F}_j^{\mathrm{cal}}(u) + W_2 \varepsilon_j^{\mathrm{cal}}(u)$$

$$= -\sum_{j=1}^{m} \zeta_j(u)\tau g_j^{-1} D_j(u) + W_2 m_j D_j^3(u), \qquad (6.39)$$

$$\mathrm{s.t.}(20)$$

By taking the derivative of Equation (6.39) the extreme of $D_j(u)$ is given by:

$$D_j(u) = \min\left\{\sqrt{\frac{\zeta_j(u)}{3W_2 m_j h_j}}, D_{j,\max}\right\} \qquad (6.40)$$

3) Optimal RS computation frequency: At time t, the optimal RS computation frequency $D_e(u)$ can be obtained by solving the sub problem UQ_3:

$$QU : \min - \sum_{j=1}^{m} \eta_j(u)\mathcal{F}_j^{\mathrm{cal}}(u) + W_2 \varepsilon_e(u)$$

$$= -\sum_{j=1}^{m} \eta_j(u)\tau h_e^{-1} D_e(u) + W_{2kd} D_e^3(u)\tau \qquad (6.41)$$

$$\mathrm{s.t.}(21)$$

By taking the derivative of Equation (6.41) the extreme of $D_e(u)$ is given by:

$$D_e(u) = \min\left\{\sqrt{\frac{\eta_j(u)}{3W_2 m_e h}}, D_{e,\max}\right\} \qquad (6.42)$$

In summary, the proposed average energy minimization optimization algorithm based on relay selection and buffer queue stability involves making relay selection and offloading decisions at each time slot.

6.3.3 Algorithm description

The average energy minimization optimization algorithm based on relay selection and buffer queue stability is described in Algorithm 1.

ALGORITHM 1 UQ$_x$

1. Obtain the channel conditions between each node.

2. for u = 0 to U

3. Input: Random tasks generated by each user and the buffer queue lengths from the previous time slot.

4. for i = 1 to n

5. if there are currently no available relay nodes in the set

6. Compute the generated tasks locally at the current time.

7. else

8. The user selects the relay node according to the channel condition and the length of the task queue, and transmits the task to the RN;

9. Endif

10. end for

11. for j = 1:m

12. Offload the task to the remote RS, and obtain the optimal transmission power of the relay, the optimal calculation frequency of the relay and the optimal calculation frequency of the RS according to UQ$_1$, UQ$_2$, and UQ$_3$;

13. Update the buffer queues of RN and RS, and move to time $u+1$.

14. end for

15. end for

6.4 SIMULATION RESULTS ANALYSIS

The simulation experiments were conducted in an environment with an AMD R7, 16GB memory, and 3.6 GHz CPU, using Python as the design language. To simulate the heterogeneous nature of the computing and communication environments, the channel gains, distances, and computation capacities are assumed to be random numbers within the intervals $[2.5 \times 10^{-4}, 7.5 \times 10^{-4}]$, [200, 800] meters, and [0, 10] GHz, respectively. During the experiments, time is mainly used as the horizontal axis to analyze the total system energy consumption and queue stability in both the user relay selection and relay offloading decision-making stages.

6.4.1 Performance analysis of optimal user relay selection

To evaluate the relay selection strategy proposed in Stage 1, Weighted Transmission Energy and Buffer Queue Minimization (WTBM), this section compares WTBM with two other selection strategies: Transmission Energy Consumption Minimization (TECM) and Task Buffer Queue Minimization (TBQM).

Transmission Energy Consumption Minimization (TECM): In Equation (6.25), as W_1 approaches infinity, $T_{ij}(u) \approx W_1 \varepsilon_{ij}^{\mathrm{tan}}(u), T_{ij}(u)$, where the size of $T_{ij}(u)$ depends only on $\varepsilon_{ij}^{\mathrm{tran}}(u)$. This means that at each time slot, users ignore the task buffer queue and select a relay node from the available set that minimizes the transmission energy consumption.

Task Buffer Queue Minimization (TBQM): In Equation (6.25), as W_1 approaches zero, $T_{ij}(u) \approx \zeta_j(u)$, where the size of $T_{ij}(u)$ depends only on $\zeta_j(u)$. This means that at each time slot, users consider only the minimization of the task buffer queue when making relay selections.

Figures 6.2–6.4 compare the three strategies in terms of total energy consumption, total buffer queue length, and average user energy consumption, respectively. From Figure 6.2, it can be observed that the total energy consumption of the proposed algorithm is superior to the other two algorithms at each time slot, and it stabilizes and converges after a certain period of time. Figure 6.3 illustrates the variation of the total buffer queue length over time. It can be seen that at each time slot, the total buffer queue length of the proposed algorithm is close to the optimal buffer queue selection method and much better than the minimum user energy consumption selection method. Additionally, in Figure 6.4, it can be seen that at each time slot, the average user energy consumption obtained by the proposed algorithm is close to the

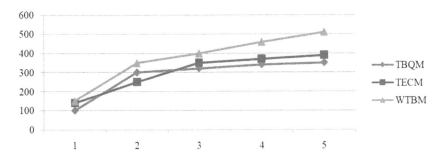

Figure 6.2 Overall power consumption with time change comparison.

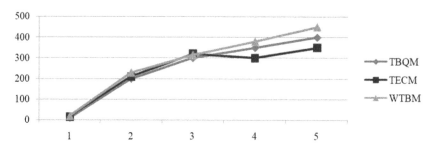

Figure 6.3 General buffer queue as a result of time change comparison.

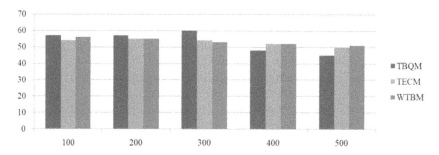

Figure 6.4 User average power consumption changes over time comparison.

minimum user average energy consumption selection method and much better than the optimal buffer queue selection method.

In conclusion, the relay selection algorithm proposed in this paper not only reduces the total energy consumption compared to the other two algorithms but also approaches the optimal buffer queue selection method and minimum user energy consumption selection method in terms of total buffer queue length and average user energy consumption. The reason for this is that the proposed algorithm considers both user transmission energy consumption and task buffer queue during the relay selection stage and uses W_1 as the weighting coefficient for these two factors, which helps minimize system energy consumption.

To analyze the effect of W_1 in the user relay selection stage, Tables 6.1 and 6.2 analyze the changes in user total energy consumption and system total buffer queue with respect to time. A smaller W_1 value indicates a higher importance on user energy consumption, resulting in a decrease in energy consumption as W_1 increases. Conversely, the total buffer queue increases with an increase in W_1, indicating a decrease in the importance of user energy consumption.

Tables 6.3 and 6.4 show the effects of varying W_1 on transmission energy consumption and buffer queue over time. As shown in Table 6.3,

Table 6.1 Analysis of average energy consumption of users under different W_1

Time/plus	$W_1 = 10$ bits $* x^{-1}$	$W_1 = 30$ bits $* x^{-1}$	$W_1 = 100$ bits $* x^{-1}$
100	55.3	54.5	54.1
200	55.4	54.6	54.2
300	55.5	54.7	54.3
400	55.6	54.8	54.4
500	55.6	54.9	54.5

Table 6.2 Analysis of the total buffer queue under different W_1

Time/plus	$W_1 = 10$ bits $* x^{-1}$	$W_1 = 30$ bits $* x^{-1}$	$W_1 = 100$ bits $* x^{-1}$
100	50	50	50
200	180	186	190
300	259	262	268
400	310	315	320
500	440	446	452

Table 6.3 The influence of the adjustment of different users W_1 on the transmission energy consumption of users

User $G1\ W_1: 10=>100$	User $G_2\ W_1: 100=>10$
54.9	55.1
54.95	55.12
54.5	55.13
55	55.1

Table 6.4 The effect of the adjustment of all users W_1 on the total buffer queue

$W_1: 10->100$	$W_1: 100=>10$
0	0
250	255
300	332
350	333
421	389

user G_1 experiences a rapid decrease in transmission energy consumption as V_1 increases, while user G_2 experiences an increase in transmission energy consumption as W_1 decreases. Since user selection of relay nodes is dynamic, the change in W_1 for a single user may not be directly reflected in the total buffer queue. However, Table 6.4 presents the impact of varying W_1 for all users on the total buffer queue, demonstrating that

W_1 adjustment has a certain regulatory effect on transmission energy consumption and buffer queue for different users.

6.4.2 Performance analysis of relay offloading

This section analyzes the system's total energy consumption and the buffer queue change over time by adjusting the weight coefficient W_2 of the relay unloading decision-making stage. For the convenience of analysis, let the buffer queue of a relay node and the buffer queue provided by the remote RS node be a group of relay pairs when the initial value of the task queue is 0. It can be seen from the figure that within a certain period, under different weight coefficients W_2, the performance of the relay pair, The speed at which the energy consumption and the buffer queue reach the convergence point is different, and the energy consumption value and the length of the buffer queue are also other. According to the size of the energy consumption and the length of the buffer queue, it can be found that there is a trade-off between energy consumption and the length of the buffer queue.

Tables 6.5 and 6.6 analyze the variation of total energy consumption and total buffer queue length with respect to the number of users under different weight parameters W_2, while keeping other parameters constant. From the graphs, it can be observed that as the number of user's increases, both total energy consumption and total buffer queue length also increase. Additionally, the impact of the weight parameter W_2 on total

Table 6.5 Energy consumption analysis for a set of relay pairs under different W_2 values

Time/plus	$W_2 = 10$ bits $* x^{-1}$	$W_2 = 30$ bits $* x^{-1}$	$W_2 = 100$ bits $* x^{-1}$
0	0	0	0
5000	18	19	20
10,000	21	25	29
15,000	56	60	63
20,000	66	69	72
25,000	82	86	89

Table 6.6 Buffer queue analysis for a set of relay pairs under different W_2 values

Time/plus	$W_2 = 10$ bits $* x^{-1}$	$W_2 = 30$ bits $* x^{-1}$	$W_2 = 100$ bits $* x^{-1}$
0	0	0	0
5000	1800	1900	2000
10,000	2100	2500	2900
15,000	5600	6000	6300
20,000	6600	6900	7200
25,000	8200	8600	8900

energy consumption and total buffer queue length also increases with an increase in the number of users. Therefore, when the number of users is larger, the adjustment of the weight parameter W_2 has a greater influence on the emphasis given to energy consumption and buffer queue length. It is essential to adjust W_2 based on the actual importance of energy consumption and buffer queue length.

6.4.3 Algorithm effectiveness analysis

In this section, under the premise that the task queue is stable, the results obtained by the proposed energy optimization algorithm are compared with those obtained by an exhaustive search. The thorough search method also uses $\Delta_W(\Theta(u))$ as the target value. When the task queue's initial value is 220, the obtained results are shown in Tables 6.7 and 6.8.

It can be seen from Figure 6.5 that as time goes by; the energy consumption obtained by the optimization algorithm can converge to the minimum value received by an exhaustive search. In addition, the task buffer queue is also approaching the result obtained by comprehensive search, as shown in Figure 6.6. Therefore, the energy optimization strategy proposed in this paper can get the effect of an approximate exhaustive search with less complexity.

Table 6.7 Comparison of total energy consumption between the proposed method and exhaustive search

Time/plus	$W_2 = 1$ bits^2 * x^{-1}	$W_2 = 10$ bits^2 * x^{-1}	$W_2 = 50$ bits^2 * x^{-1}
3	475	489	499
6	599	612	630
9	648	660	680
12	733	745	766
15	896	900	912

Table 6.8 Comparison of total buffer queue length between the proposed method and exhaustive search

Time/plus	$W_2 = 1$ bits^2 * x^{-1}	$W_2 = 10$ bits^2 * x^{-1}	$W_2 = 50$ bits^2 * x^{-1}
3	100	115	123
6	124	135	148
9	148	152	159
12	169	178	182
15	180	194	198

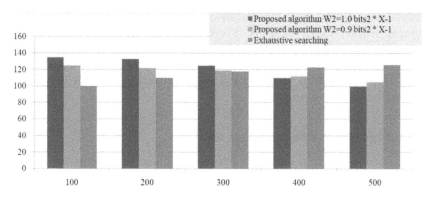

Figure 6.5 Comparison of energy consumption between the method in this paper and the exhaustive search method.

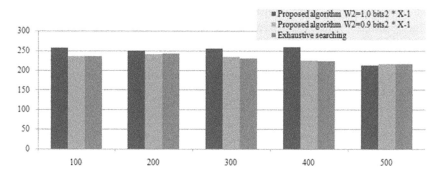

Figure 6.6 Comparison of task queues between the method in this paper and the exhaustive search method.

6.5 CONCLUSION

The traditional relay-assisted MEC system only considers deterministic tasks and cannot adapt to the randomness of real-time tasks in complex MEC environments. Therefore, this paper proposes an energy model for relay selection and relay offloading under task buffer queue stability constraints. It optimizes the relay computation frequency, relay transmission power, and remote node computation frequency to minimize the long-term average energy consumption of the system. Simulation results show that the proposed joint optimization algorithm effectively reduces system energy consumption under the queue stability constraint. However, the transmission power of relay nodes in this paper is fixed when transmitting tasks, whereas it can change over time and have an impact on energy consumption. Dynamic adjustment is required. Additionally, the current experiments are mainly based on Python simulations, and real-world deployments are lacking. Future work will focus on applying the proposed energy optimization strategy to specific scenarios.

REFERENCE

[1] Anita Sethi, Shelendra Kumar Jain, Sandip Vijay, Secure self optimizing software defined framework for NB-IoT towards 5G, *Procedia Computer Science*, Volume 171, 2020, 2740–2749, ISSN 1877-0509, https://doi.org/10.1016/j.procs.2020.04.298

[2] B.S. Bismi, Saniya Azeem, A survey on increasing the capacity of 5G fronthaul systems using RoF, *Optical Fiber Technology*, Volume 74, 2022, 103078, ISSN 1068-5200, https://doi.org/10.1016/j.yofte.2022.103078

[3] Umar Ghafoor, Mudassar Ali, Humayun Zubair Khan, Adil Masood Siddiqui, Muhammad Naeem, NOMA and future 5G & B5G wireless networks: A paradigm, *Journal of Network and Computer Applications*, Volume 204, 2022, 103413, ISSN 1084-8045, https://doi.org/10.1016/j.jnca.2022.103413

[4] Adil Israr, Qiang Yang, Wei Li, Albert Y. Zomaya, Renewable energy powered sustainable 5G network infrastructure: Opportunities, challenges and perspectives, *Journal of Network and Computer Applications*, Volume 175, 2021, 102910, ISSN 1084-8045, https://doi.org/10.1016/j.jnca.2020.102910

[5] Xiang Liu, Chapter 2 - 5G Wireless technologies, Editor(s): Xiang Liu, *Optical Communications in the 5G Era*, Academic Press, 2022, 29–47, ISBN 9780128216279, https://doi.org/10.1016/B978-0-12-821627-9.00013-9

[6] Sandeep K. Sood, Kiran Deep Singh, SNA based resource optimization in optical network using fog and cloud computing, *Optical Switching and Networking*, Volume 33, 2019, 114–121, ISSN 1573-4277, https://doi.org/10.1016/j.osn.2017.12.007

[7] Ishfaq Bashir Sofi, Akhil Gupta, A survey on energy efficient 5G green network with a planned multi-tier architecture, *Journal of Network and Computer Applications*, Volume 118, 2018, 1–28, ISSN 1084-8045, https://doi.org/10.1016/j.jnca.2018.06.002

[8] William Lehr, Fabian Queder, Justus Haucap, 5G: A new future for mobile network operators, or not?, *Telecommunications Policy*, Volume 45, Issue 3, 2021, 102086, ISSN 0308-5961, https://doi.org/10.1016/j.telpol.2020.102086

[9] Kibeom Park, Sangmo Sung, Hokeun Kim, Jae-il Jung, Technology trends and challenges in SDN and service assurance for end-to-end network slicing, *Computer Networks*, Volume 234, 2023, 109908, ISSN 1389-1286, https://doi.org/10.1016/j.comnet.2023.109908

[10] Paola Vargas, Iris Tien, Impacts of 5G on cyber-physical risks for interdependent connected smart critical infrastructure systems, *International Journal of Critical Infrastructure Protection*, Volume 42, 2023, 100617, ISSN 1874-5482, https://doi.org/10.1016/j.ijcip.2023.100617

[11] Mohammed Banafaa, Ibraheem Shayea, Jafri Din, Marwan Hadri Azmi, Abdulaziz Alashbi, Yousef Ibrahim Daradkeh, Abdulraqeb Alhammadi, 6G Mobile Communication Technology: Requirements, Targets, Applications, Challenges, Advantages, and Opportunities, *Alexandria Engineering Journal*, Volume 64, 2023, 245–274, ISSN 1110-0168, https://doi.org/10.1016/j.aej.2022.08.017

[12] Massimo Condoluci, Toktam Mahmoodi, Softwarization and virtualization in 5G mobile networks: Benefits, trends and challenges, *Computer Networks*, Volume 146, 2018, 65–84, ISSN 1389-1286, https://doi.org/10.1016/j.comnet.2018.09.005

[13] Rajni Gupta, Juhi Gupta, Future generation communications with game strategies: A comprehensive survey, *Computer Communications*, Volume 192, 2022, 1–32, ISSN 0140-3664, https://doi.org/10.1016/j.comcom.2022.05.024

[14] Nisha Panwar, Shantanu Sharma, Awadhesh Kumar Singh, A survey on 5G: The next generation of mobile communication, *Physical Communication*, Volume 18, Part 2, 2016, 64–84, ISSN 1874-4907, https://doi.org/10.1016/j.phycom.2015.10.006

[15] Shunliang Zhang, Dali Zhu, Yongming Wang, A survey on space-aerial-terrestrial integrated 5G networks, *Computer Networks*, Volume 174, 2020, 107212, ISSN 1389-1286, https://doi.org/10.1016/j.comnet.2020.107212

[16] Chuan Yu, Shuhui Chen, Fei Wang, Ziling Wei, Improving 4G/5G air interface security: A survey of existing attacks on different LTE layers, *Computer Networks*, Volume 201, 2021, 108532, ISSN 1389-1286, https://doi.org/10.1016/j.comnet.2021.108532

[17] Himanshu Sharma, Neeraj Kumar, Rajkumar Tekchandani, Physical layer security using beamforming techniques for 5G and beyond networks: A systematic review, *Physical Communication*, Volume 54, 2022, 101791, ISSN 1874-4907, https://doi.org/10.1016/j.phycom.2022.101791

[18] Ajay Kakkar, A survey on secure communication techniques for 5G wireless heterogeneous networks, *Information Fusion*, Volume 62, 2020, 89–109, ISSN 1566-535, https://doi.org/10.1016/j.inffus.2020.04.009

[19] Yasser Narimani, Esmaeil Zeinali, A. Mirzaei, QoS-aware resource allocation and fault tolerant operation in hybrid SDN using stochastic network calculus, *Physical Communication*, Volume 53, 2022, 101709, ISSN 1874-4907, https://doi.org/10.1016/j.phycom.2022.101709

[20] Parjanay Sharma, Siddhant Jain, Shashank Gupta, Vinay Chamola, Role of machine learning and deep learning in securing 5G-driven industrial IoT applications, *Ad Hoc Networks*, Volume 123, 2021, 102685, ISSN 1570-8705, https://doi.org/10.1016/j.adhoc.2021.102685

[21] Dinesh Soni, Neetesh Kumar, Machine learning techniques in emerging cloud computing integrated paradigms: A survey and taxonomy, *Journal of Network and Computer Applications*, Volume 205, 2022, 103419, ISSN 1084-8045, https://doi.org/10.1016/j.jnca.2022.103419

[22] Sergio Martiradonna, Alessandro Grassi, Giuseppe Piro, Gennaro Boggia, Understanding the 5G-air-simulator: A tutorial on design criteria, technical components, and reference use cases, *Computer Networks*, Volume 177, 2020, 107314, ISSN 1389-1286, https://doi.org/10.1016/j.comnet.2020.107314

[23] Puja Singh, Shashi Prakash, Optical network unit placement in Fiber-Wireless (FiWi) access network by Whale optimization algorithm, *Optical Fiber Technology*, Volume 52, 2019, 101965, ISSN 1068-5200, https://doi.org/10.1016/j.yofte.2019.101965

[24] Preksha Jain, Akhil Gupta, Neeraj Kumar, A vision towards integrated 6G communication networks: Promising technologies, architecture, and use-cases, *Physical Communication*, Volume 55, 2022, 101917, ISSN 1874-4907, https://doi.org/10.1016/j.phycom.2022.101917

[25] Huimin Chen, Jiajia Liu, Jiadai Wang, Yijie Xun, Towards secure intra-vehicle communications in 5G advanced and beyond: Vulnerabilities, attacks and countermeasures, *Vehicular Communications*, Volume 39, 2023, 100548, ISSN 2214-2096, https://doi.org/10.1016/j.vehcom.2022.100548

[26] Hanan Elazhary, Internet of Things (IoT), mobile cloud, cloudlet, mobile IoT, IoT cloud, fog, mobile edge, and edge emerging computing paradigms: Disambiguation and research directions, *Journal of Network and Computer Applications*, Volume 128, 2019, 105–140, ISSN 1084-8045, https://doi.org/10.1016/j.jnca.2018.10.021

[27] Nicola Piovesan, Angel Fernandez Gambin, Marco Miozzo, Michele Rossi, Paolo Dini, Energy sustainable paradigms and methods for future mobile networks: A survey, *Computer Communications*, Volume 119, 2018, 101–117, ISSN 0140-3664, https://doi.org/10.1016/j.comcom.2018.01.005

[28] Hongzhi Guo, Xiaoyi Zhou, Jiajia Liu, Yanning Zhang, Vehicular intelligence in 6G: Networking, communications, and computing, *Vehicular Communications*, Volume 33, 2022, 100399, ISSN 2214-2096, https://doi.org/10.1016/j.vehcom.2021.100399

[29] Shimaa A. Abdel Hakeem, Hanan H. Hussein, Hyung Won Kim, Vision and research directions of 6G technologies and applications, *Journal of King Saud University-Computer and Information Sciences*, Volume 34, Issue 6, Part A, 2022, 2419–2442, ISSN 1319-1578, https://doi.org/10.1016/j.jksuci.2022.03.019

[30] Sami Ben Slama, Prosumer in smart grids based on intelligent edge computing: A review on Artificial Intelligence Scheduling Techniques, *Ain Shams Engineering Journal*, Volume 13, Issue 1, 2022, 101504, ISSN 2090-4479, https://doi.org/10.1016/j.asej.2021.05.018

[31] Shunliang Zhang, Dali Zhu, Towards artificial intelligence enabled 6G: State of the art, challenges, and opportunities, *Computer Networks*, Volume 183, 2020, 107556, ISSN 1389-1286, https://doi.org/10.1016/j.comnet.2020.107556

[32] Rasheed Hussain, Fatima Hussain, Sherali Zeadally, Integration of VANET and 5G Security: A review of design and implementation issues, *Future Generation Computer Systems*, Volume 101, 2019, 843–864, ISSN 0167-739X, https://doi.org/10.1016/j.future.2019.07.006

[33] Ertugrul Basar, Huseyin Arslan, Yue Xiao, Editorial on Special Issue "Radio Access Technologies for Beyond 5G Wireless Networks", *Physical Communication*, Volume 38, 2020, 100967, ISSN 1874-4907, https://doi.org/10.1016/j.phycom.2019.100967

[34] Xiang Liu, Chapter 11 - The fifth generation fixed network (F5G), Editor(s): Xiang Liu, *Optical Communications in the 5G Era*, Academic Press, 2022, 317–342, ISBN 9780128216279, https://doi.org/10.1016/B978-0-12-821627-9.00002-4

[35] Mittal K. Pedhadiya, Rakesh Kumar Jha, Hetal G. Bhatt, Device to device communication: A survey, *Journal of Network and Computer Applications*, Volume 129, 2019, 71–89, ISSN 1084-8045, https://doi.org/10.1016/j.jnca.2018.10.012

[36] Anshuman Kalla, Chamitha de Alwis, Pawani Porambage, Gürkan Gür, Madhusanka Liyanage, A survey on the use of blockchain for future 6G: Technical aspects, use cases, challenges and research directions, *Journal of Industrial Information Integration*, Volume 30, 2022, 100404, ISSN 2452-414X, https://doi.org/10.1016/j.jii.2022.100404

[37] Dawit Hadush Hailu, Berihu G. Gebrehaweria, Samrawit H. Kebede, Gebrehiwot G. Lema, Gebremichael T. Tesfamariam, Mobile fronthaul transport options in C-RAN and emerging research directions: A comprehensive study, *Optical Switching and Networking*, Volume 30, 2018, 40–52, ISSN 1573-4277, https://doi.org/10.1016/j.osn.2018.06.003

[38] Marja Matinmikko, Matti Latva-aho, Petri Ahokangas, Veikko Seppänen, On regulations for 5G: Micro licensing for locally operated networks, *Telecommunications Policy*, Volume 42, Issue 8, 2018, 622–635, ISSN 0308-5961, https://doi.org/10.1016/j.telpol.2017.09.004

[39] Partha Pratim Ray, A perspective on 6G: Requirement, technology, enablers, challenges and future road map, *Journal of Systems Architecture*, Volume 118, 2021, 102180, ISSN 1383-7621, https://doi.org/10.1016/j.sysarc.2021.102180

Chapter 7

Exchange matching algorithm for low-complexity traffic scheduling for 5G fronthaul networks

V. Mahalakshmi, Rajan John, and
Betty Elezebeth Samuel
Jazan University, Jazan, Kingdom of Saudi Arabia

M. Ramkumar Raja
King Khalid University, Abha, Saudi Arabia

7.1 INTRODUCTION

With the widespread application of advanced information and communication technology in the power system, the explosive growth of data collection terminals for power business presents a significant challenge to the access capability of the power communication network [1–4]. The increasing contradiction between the strict requirements of the power grid for real-time scheduling and precise control, and the limited business-bearing capacity of the power communication access network, have garnered widespread attention in the industry to address issues arising from massive concurrent data access such as network congestion and overload [5–7]. In this context, 5G technology, characterized by its high bandwidth, extensive connectivity, and low latency, offers a feasible solution for the deployment of power communication access networks.

In the context of a 5G power communication access network, the fronthaul network, which serves as the link between base stations and comprehensive access equipment rooms, plays a crucial role in determining the network access capacity. Traditional fronthaul network technologies are inadequate to meet the demands of the power control domain shifting toward deterministic services [8–12]. Time-Sensitive Networking (TSN) offers advantages such as ultra-low latency, controllable transmission, and flexible scalability. It demonstrates good compatibility with existing fronthaul network technologies, and its integration can effectively enhance the business-bearing capacity of the power + 5G fronthaul network [13–16].

In order to achieve efficient utilization of network resources in complex power communication scenarios, traffic scheduling mechanisms have become a research focus due to their ability to coordinate and control the transmission of multiple service flows. Traditional traffic scheduling algorithms for fronthaul networks, such as Fast Flow Scheduling (FFS), which caters to

DOI: 10.1201/9781003470281-7

rapidly arriving random service data, struggle to adapt to the current complex and dynamic business scenarios due to the lack of effective control mechanisms [17–22]. As a result, research on traffic scheduling algorithms based on a unified scheduling cycle has gained widespread attention [23]. Reference [24] introduces a Strict Priority Flow Scheduling (SPFS) algorithm that prioritizes high-priority business data by classifying services into different levels. Literature [25] presents a Higher Rate Flow Scheduled Later (HRSL) algorithm, which reduces fronthaul network congestion by prioritizing the transmission of smaller data volume service flows. Literature [26] utilizes Monte Carlo Simulation (MCS) to optimize data flow scheduling, enhancing network resource utilization through extensive random experiments.

However, existing research mostly focuses on scheduling single-type data flows in public network scenarios, demonstrating poor compatibility with power communication scenarios and struggling to achieve real-time perception of differentiated business demands and dynamic adjustment of traffic scheduling strategies [26]. Moreover, the preemptive access of power communication business data with large-scale concurrency can impair the performance of other services or the overall network. With the continuous expansion of power communication access network scale, coordinating the forwarding of various data flows from the perspectives of overall network performance improvement and individual performance assurance has become an urgent problem. Addressing the aforementioned issues, this paper proposes a Matching-based QoS-aware Flow Scheduling (MQFS) algorithm based on exchange matching and Quality of Service (QoS) awareness.

7.2 SYSTEM MODEL

7.2.1 Network model

It needs to be emphasized that the described network is exclusively used for power system communication and is primarily based on network slicing technology. It utilizes user plane functionality for traffic diversion, directly transmitting industry user data to the internal network.

The currently mature 5G fronthaul network technology, such as the enhanced Common Public Radio Interface (eCPRI) specification, forms the technical foundation for the integration of TSN and 5G fronthaul networks [27]. The integrated power + 5G fronthaul network model with TSN is shown in Figure 7.1, where the Centralized User Configuration (CUC) unit is responsible for perceiving the QoS requirements of power communication services and relaying them to the Central Network Control (CNC) unit. The CNC unit manages functions like traffic scheduling and issues configuration information such as admission control lists to TSN switches based on feedback on service performance.

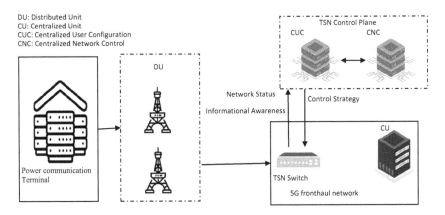

DU: Distributed Unit
CU: Centralized Unit
CUC: Centralized User Configuration
CNC: Centralized Network Control

Figure 7.1 Fusion TSN's power+5G pre-internet architecture.

7.2.2 Latency analysis

Referring to the 5G TSN bridge architecture defined by 3GPP R16 and the TSN control architecture in the IEEE 802.1 Qcc protocol [28], a traffic scheduling model based on transmission gate control is illustrated in Figure 7.2. At the beginning of a single scheduling cycle, a total of M service packets arrive at TSN switch ports simultaneously, represented as the set $S = \{1, 2, ..., m, M\}$. After scheduling, these packets are transmitted through the fronthaul network in a sequential manner. Once all the service packets have been forwarded, the next scheduling cycle begins. The service packets entering the fronthaul network establish a new order. This paper introduces the concept of Virtual Transmission Position (VTP), denoted as the set $P = \{1, 2, ..., n, N\}$, where $N = M$.

The forwarding latency of power communication service packets consists of three components: buffering latency, transmission latency, and queuing latency [29]. Packet m first arrives at the buffer, and considering that buffering latency is relatively small compared to queuing and transmission latency, the model simplifies this latency by setting it uniformly as τ^{Sto}. To avoid conflicts during scheduling, only one gate can be opened at a time, and there is an inherent time interval between the opening of two gates for non-service information-bearing protection band data to pass through. This protection latency is denoted as τ^{Pro}. The packet size of m is defined as D_m, and the transmission rate supported by the fronthaul network is λ. Therefore, the transmission latency is calculated as follows:

$$\tau_m^{\text{Tra}} = \frac{D_m}{\lambda} \tag{7.1}$$

Furthermore, $\phi_{m,n}$ is used to represent the relationship between the positions of the data packet before and after scheduling, where $\phi_{m,n} = 1$ indicates that data packet m at the nth VTP on the fronthaul network is the packet before

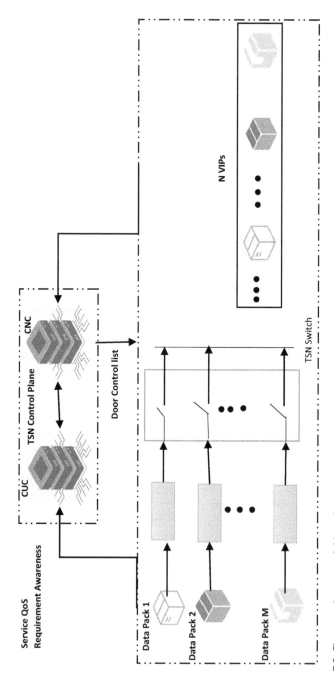

Figure 7.2 Flow regulation model based on transport gate control.

scheduling, otherwise $\phi_{m,n} = 0$. Considering the stringent packet loss rate requirements of power communication services and the inherent advantages of 5G networks, the traffic scheduling model studied in this paper is lossless and does not experience overlap phenomena [5, 17], i.e.,

$$\sum_{n=1}^{N} \phi_{m,n} = 1, \sum_{m=1}^{M} \phi_{m,n} = 1 \tag{7.2}$$

For a power communication service data packet m located at the nth VTP, its queuing latency is given by:

$$\tau_{m,n}^{Que} = (n-1)\tau^{Pro} + \sum_{v=1}^{M} \sum_{l=1}^{n-1} \phi_{v,l}\tau_v^{Tra} \tag{7.3}$$

Therefore, the total forwarding latency for a data packet from its arrival at the TSN switch until the completion of transmission is:

$$\tau_{m,n} = \tau^{Sto} + \tau_{m,n}^{Que} + \tau_m^{Tra} \tag{7.4}$$

Additionally, in consideration of various requirements for latency in different power business scenarios [17], the forwarding latency constraint for packet m is expressed as:

$$\sum_{n=1}^{N} \phi_{m,n}\tau_{m,n} \leq \tau_{m,\max} \tag{7.5}$$

Here, $\tau_{m,\max}$ represents the maximum allowable latency.

7.2.3 Problem modeling

The network utility is modeled as the ratio between power business priorities and the total forwarding latency. This paper aims to maximize the overall utility of the fronthaul network, which can be expressed as:

$$\max_{\{\phi_{m,n}\}} \sum_{m=1}^{M} \sum_{n=1}^{N} \phi_{m,n}\alpha_m / \tau_{m,n}$$

$$s.t. C_1 : \sum_{n=1}^{N} \phi_{m,n} = 1$$

$$C_2 : \sum_{m=1}^{M} \phi_{m,n} = 1 \tag{7.6}$$

$$C_3 : \sum_{n=1}^{N} \phi_{m,n}\tau_{m,n} \leq \tau_{m,\max}$$

where α_m represents the priority of different power business data packets, C_1 indicates lossless operation, C_2 indicates no overlap phenomena, and C_3 represents the total forwarding latency constraint.

7.3 ALGORITHM DESIGN

7.3.1 Problem transformation

Based on Equation (7.6), the utility of different data packets is related not only to their own characteristics but also to other packets and their relative positions. To solve this problem, all possible permutations of M data packets should be determined, and the solution that maximizes network utility while satisfying the total forwarding latency constraint should be found. However, such an exhaustive traffic scheduling algorithm has a high complexity of M factorial.

Therefore, this paper transforms the optimization problem into a one-to-one matching problem. Due to the coupling of matching decisions for different business data packets, the algorithm continuously exchanges and iteratively maximizes the optimization objective. However, the complexity of the traditional full-exchange matching algorithm is $O(M^2)$ [30], which is still unsuitable for the massive concurrent data access scenario in power communication. This paper further improves the algorithm while reducing complexity with minor performance loss, as follows:

1. Establish utility functions from both individual and network-wide perspectives for different matching relationships during the exchange iteration process, ensuring the cumulative utility values of both parties involved in the exchange and the overall network utility are improved simultaneously.
2. Considering the specific characteristics of fronthaul network traffic scheduling, where a higher VTP achieves better network utility, limit the exchanges to forward-only and within a range of J.

7.3.2 Problem transformation

The two parties involved in the matching are the M power communication business data packets and the N VTPs, and the controlling entity of the algorithm is the control plane. A set of one-to-one matching relationships is defined as $\theta = \{(m, n)\}$, where its elements satisfy $\phi_{m,n}=$, indicating a unique correspondence between different data packets and VTPs. The TSN control plane establishes a preference list for data packets based on the VTP position relationship, where a higher-ranked VTP is favored. $\gamma_m(n)$ and $\gamma_{\text{total}}(\theta)$ represent the individual network utility obtained by data packet m and the overall network utility under the current matching relationship, respectively, and their values are consistent with the optimization objective of this paper:

$$\gamma_m(n) = \alpha_m / \tau_{m,n} \tag{7.7}$$

$$\gamma_{\text{total}}(\theta) = \sum_{m=1}^{M} \sum_{n=1}^{N} \phi_{m,n} \alpha_m / \tau_{m,n} \tag{7.8}$$

For ease of algorithm expression, the following definitions are provided:

Definition 1: Exchange Operation

Given two sets of matching relationships for data packets and VTPs, (m, n) and $(v, 1) \in \theta$, satisfying $m, v \in S$, $n, l \in P$, and $m \neq v$, $n \neq 1$, the exchange operation involves swapping the matching partners of data packets m and v in the original matching relationship, represented as:

$$\theta_{mv}^{nl} = \{\theta \setminus (m,n), (v,l)\} \cup \{(m,l), (v,n)\} \tag{7.9}$$

where $\theta \setminus \{(m, n), (v, l)\setminus\}$ represents the removal of the matching relationships between data packet m and VTP nth, and data packet v and VTP l in the original matching relationship set.

Definition 2: Swappable Matching and Bilateral Stable Matching

When $|m - v| \leq J$, after performing an exchange operation for the given two sets of data packets and VTPs, if:

$$\gamma_m(l) + \gamma_v(n) > \gamma_m(n) + \gamma_v(l) \tag{7.10}$$

$$\gamma_{\text{total}}(\theta_{mv}^{nl}) > \gamma_{\text{total}}(\theta) \tag{7.11}$$

Then the matching relationship at this point is swappable, denoted as $\theta_{mv}^{nl} > \theta$; otherwise, it is a bilaterally stable match.

As shown in Algorithm 1 in Chapter 6, the MQFS algorithm can be divided into three stages: initialization, exchange matching, and matching result transformation:

1. In the initialization stage, a random matching relationship θ is established between data packets and VTPs as long as it satisfies all constraints in Equation (7.6).
2. In the exchange matching stage, the TSN control plane controls each data packet m currently matched with the nth VTP to initiate a matching request to the lth VTP, which is the highest-ranked one in its preference list. If $\theta_{mv}^{nl} > \theta$, then replace the original matching θ with

θ_{mv}^{nl}; otherwise, keep θ unchanged, and remove the lth VTP from the preference list of data packet m. Repeat this process until no further exchange operations can be performed, and the exchange matching process terminates.

3. In the matching result transformation stage, the TSN control plane opens transmission gates according to the matching results, allowing all data packets to pass through in sequence and complete forwarding. After that, the system enters the next scheduling cycle.

7.3.3 Algorithm analysis

Based on the execution process of exchange matching described earlier, the MQFS algorithm can converge to a unique bilateral stable matching relationship, similar to the proof process described in reference [31].

Regarding algorithm complexity, the maximum number of exchange operations performed in the full-exchange matching algorithm proposed in reference [32] is $M(M - 1)$, while the method proposed in this paper requires

$$(M - J) \times J + \sum_{j=1}^{J-1} j \text{ operations.}$$

7.4 SIMULATION ANALYSIS

7.4.1 Simulation setup

The simulation is conducted on a 5G base station with eCPRI interfaces. Combining TSN data frame formats [33] and research on power business data collection and transmission [34–36], the size of a single data packet ranges from 8 to 12 Kb. In addition, the simulation includes four types of services: emergency control and protection information upload, energy management system, wide-area measurement system, and data collection and monitoring control system [37], with priorities of 7, 5, 5, and 2, and proportions of 2:10:5:10. The latency constraints are 20 μs, 50 μs, 70 μs, and 100 μs, respectively. The main simulation parameters are shown in Table 7.1.

Table 7.1 Simulation parameter setting

Parameters	Exchange rate	Parameter	Exchange value
M	100–500	τ^{Pro}	0.1 μs
J	M/2	D_m	8–12 Kb
α_m	1,2,5,7	λ	26 Gbps
τ^{Sto}	0.1 μs		

The following algorithms were compared in this paper:

1. SPFS Algorithm [38]: Data packets are transmitted in order of priority, with packets of the same priority transmitted in random order. The best-case exchange sorting operations are $M - 1$, and the worst case is $M(M - 1)/2$.
2. HRSL Algorithm [39]: The larger the data packet size, the later it is transmitted on the fronthaul network. The best-case comparison sorting operations are $M - 1$, and the worst case is $M(M - 1)/2$.
3. FFS Algorithm [37]: All data packets are sequentially transmitted by opening transmission control gates in random order. The number of sampling operations is M.
4. MCS Algorithm [36]: M^2 different traffic scheduling schemes are randomly generated, and the one with the maximum network utility is selected for traffic scheduling. The number of comparisons sorting operations is $M^2 - 1$.

For robustness, the following simulation results are averaged over 100 scheduling cycles.

7.4.2 Simulation results analysis

Figure 7.3 shows the impact of the number of business data packets on the overall network utility. As M increases, the overall network utility increases for all algorithms, but the average utility per individual business data packet decreases. The MQFS algorithm outperforms the other four algorithms in terms of both magnitude and growth. When $M = 300$, the overall network utility of the MQFS algorithm is improved by 20.44%, 25.45%, 37.87%, and

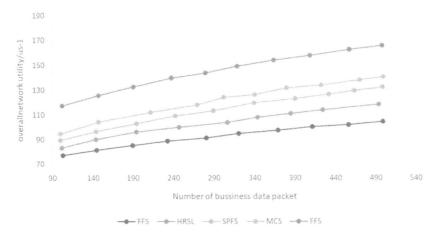

Figure 7.3 Impact of business data package volume on overall network performance.

53.01% compared to the MCS algorithm, SPFS algorithm, HRSL algorithm, and FFS algorithm, respectively. This is because the MQFS algorithm effectively considers different priority power communication business data packets, thereby enhancing the overall network utility. The SPFS algorithm is unable to effectively coordinate the forwarding schedule of business data packets with the same priority. The MCS, HRSL, and FFS algorithms can be considered as traffic scheduling algorithms based on randomness, where the MCS algorithm slightly outperforms the HRSL algorithm due to the larger sample size. The MCS algorithm prioritizes transmitting smaller data packets to reduce relative forwarding latency, making it slightly better than the FFS algorithm.

The box plot in Figure 7.4 illustrates the fluctuation in overall network utility obtained over multiple scheduling cycles when $M = 300$. The MQFS algorithm achieves smaller performance fluctuations in environments with high randomness in power communication networks because it can perform exchange iterations based on real-time awareness of business information. Notably, due to insufficient sampling in the MCS algorithm (even with a large sample size of M^2), network performance fluctuations remain relatively high.

Figure 7.5 demonstrates the impact of the number and priority of power communication business data packets on latency performance when using the MQFS algorithm. As M increases, the average and maximum forwarding latencies of different priority business data packets both increase, and higher-priority business data packets exhibit better latency performance. Additionally, the average latency performance of high-priority business data packets can remain at a lower level with a smaller increase compared to low-priority business data packets, which experience rapid latency rise.

Table 7.2 presents the impact of business priority on average latency performance when $M = 300$. The results of the MQFS, MCS, and SPFS algorithms are similar, showing that higher-priority business data packets have lower latencies. However, due to the random generation of scheduling plans

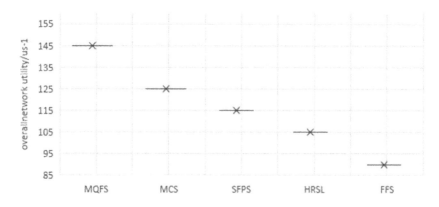

Figure 7.4 M = 300 times the overall performance of the network obtained by simulation.

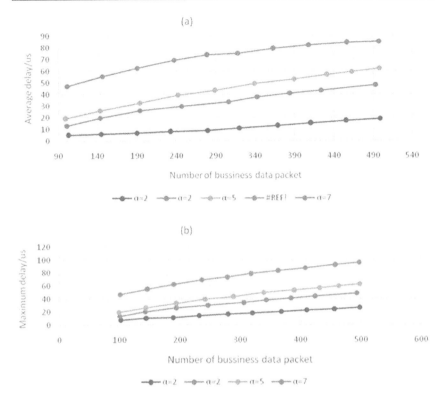

Figure 7.5 Impact of latency performance on business data package volume and business priority level. (a) Average delay. (b) Maximum delay.

Table 7.2 Impact of M = 300 time business priority on average time delay performance

Algorithm name	Business priority am			
	2	5	5	7
MQFS	50.27	33.99	17.21	3.68
MCS	40.85	25.76	25.51	7.96
SPFS	50.7	22.61	22.73	2.7
HRSL	31.28	31.27	31.48	31.26
FFS	31.55	31.54	31.41	31.17

by the MCS algorithm, higher-priority business packets may have larger average latencies. The SPFS algorithm considers only business priority as the sole criterion for traffic scheduling and cannot optimize for differentiated latency requirements of different types of business.

Figure 7.6 depicts the trade-off between the loss of overall network utility and the reduction in algorithm complexity for the MQFS algorithm

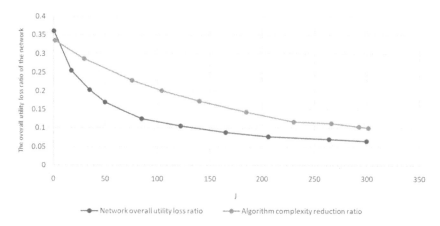

Figure 7.6 The impact of M = 300 J on network overall performance and algorithmic complexity.

compared to the full-exchange algorithm when $M = 300$. A larger range of exchange operations possible for the MQFS algorithm corresponds to higher-potential final network utility and increased algorithm complexity. When $J = 150$, corresponding to $M/2$, the overall network utility becomes relatively flat, and the algorithm complexity reduces by 62.46% compared to the full-exchange algorithm, while the performance loss ratio is only 8.76%.

7.5 CONCLUSION

In response to the challenges posed by the concurrent access of massive power communication business data, resulting in issues with deterministic latency and differentiated QoS requirements, this paper presents a novel scheduling model that integrates Time-Sensitive Networking (TSN) with power and 5G fronthaul networks. Furthermore, a low-complexity traffic scheduling algorithm based on exchange matching and QoS awareness is proposed. Simulation results demonstrate that the MQFS algorithm can effectively enhance overall network utility, reduce network performance fluctuations, and facilitate performance assurance for different categories of power communication services based on business priorities and differentiated QoS requirements. Future work will involve further integration of bandwidth allocation and frame preemption protocols to develop even more superior and lower-complexity traffic scheduling algorithms.

REFERENCES

[1] Y. Hao, F. Li, C. Zhao and S. Yang, "Delay-Oriented Scheduling in 5G Downlink Wireless Networks Based on Reinforcement Learning With Partial Observations," in *IEEE/ACM Transactions on Networking*, vol. 31, no. 1, pp. 380–394, Feb. 2023, doi: 10.1109/TNET.2022.3194953

[2] W. K. G. Seah, C.-H. Lee, Y. -D. Lin and Y. -C. Lai, "Combined Communication and Computing Resource Scheduling in Sliced 5G Multi-Access Edge Computing Systems," in *IEEE Transactions on Vehicular Technology*, vol. 71, no. 3, pp. 3144–3154, March 2022, doi: 10.1109/TVT.2021.3139026

[3] R. B. Abreu, G. Pocovi, T. H. Jacobsen, M. Centenaro, K. I. Pedersen and T. E. Kolding, "Scheduling Enhancements and Performance Evaluation of Downlink 5G Time-Sensitive Communications," in *IEEE Access*, vol. 8, pp. 128106–128115, 2020, doi: 10.1109/ACCESS.2020.3008598

[4] J. Li and X. Zhang, "Deep Reinforcement Learning-Based Joint Scheduling of eMBB and URLLC in 5G Networks," in *IEEE Wireless Communications Letters*, vol. 9, no. 9, pp. 1543–1546, Sept. 2020, doi: 10.1109/LWC.2020.2997036

[5] H. A. Alameddine, M. H. K. Tushar and C. Assi, "Scheduling of Low Latency Services in Softwarized Networks," in IEEE Transactions on Cloud *Computing*, vol. 9, no. 3, pp. 1220–1235, 1 July-Sept. 2021, doi: 10.1109/TCC.2019.2907949

[6] M. Yu, "Construction of Regional Intelligent Transportation System in Smart City Road Network via 5G Network," in *IEEE Transactions on Intelligent Transportation Systems*, vol. 24, no. 2, pp. 2208–2216, Feb. 2023, doi: 10.1109/TITS.2022.3141731

[7] A. Anand, G. de Veciana and S. Shakkottai, "Joint Scheduling of URLLC and eMBB Traffic in 5G Wireless Networks," in *IEEE/ACM Transactions on Networking*, vol. 28, no. 2, pp. 477–490, April 2020, doi: 10.1109/TNET.2020.2968373

[8] M. Maule, J. S. Vardakas and C. Verikoukis, "A Novel 5G-NR Resources Partitioning Framework Through Real-Time User-Provider Traffic Demand Analysis," in *IEEE Systems Journal*, vol. 16, no. 4, pp. 5317–5328, Dec. 2022, doi: 10.1109/JSYST.2021.3115896

[9] S. Kamath, S. Singh and M. S. Kumar, "Multiclass Queueing Network Modeling and Traffic Flow Analysis for SDN-Enabled Mobile Core Networks With Network Slicing," in *IEEE Access*, vol. 8, pp. 417–430, 2020, doi: 10.1109/ACCESS.2019.2959351

[10] I. -S. Comşa, R. Trestian, G. -M. Muntean and G. Ghinea, "5MART: A 5G SMART Scheduling Framework for Optimizing QoS Through Reinforcement Learning," in *IEEE Transactions on Network and Service Management*, vol. 17, no. 2, pp. 1110–1124, June 2020, doi: 10.1109/TNSM.2019.2960849

[11] K. Zhang, X. Xu, J. Zhang, B. Zhang, X. Tao and Y. Zhang, "Dynamic Multiconnectivity Based Joint Scheduling of eMBB and uRLLC in 5G Networks," in *IEEE Systems Journal*, vol. 15, no. 1, pp. 1333–1343, March 2021, doi: 10.1109/JSYST.2020.2977666

[12] K. Min, Y. Kim and H. -S. Lee, "Meta-Scheduling Framework With Cooperative Learning Toward Beyond 5G," in *IEEE Journal on Selected Areas in Communications*, vol. 41, no. 6, pp. 1810–1824, June 2023, doi: 10.1109/JSAC.2023.3273698

[13] H. Zhang, C. Huang, J. Zhou and L. Chen, "QoS-Aware Virtualization Resource Management Mechanism in 5G Backhaul Heterogeneous Networks," in *IEEE Access*, vol. 8, pp. 19479–19489, 2020, doi: 10.1109/ACCESS.2020.2967101

[14] L. Yang, J. Jia, H. Lin and J. Cao, "Reliable Dynamic Service Chain Scheduling in 5G Networks," in *IEEE Transactions on Mobile Computing*, vol. 22, no. 8, pp. 4898–4911, 1 Aug. 2023, doi: 10.1109/TMC.2022.3157312

[15] A. A. Z. Ibrahim, F. Hashim, N. K. Noordin, A. Sali, K. Navaie and S. M. E. Fadul, "Heuristic Resource Allocation Algorithm for Controller Placement in Multi-Control 5G Based on SDN/NFV Architecture," in *IEEE Access*, vol. 9, pp. 2602–2617, 2021, doi: 10.1109/ACCESS.2020.3047210

[16] M. C. Lucas-Estañ and J. Gozalvez, "Sensing-Based Grant-Free Scheduling for Ultra Reliable Low Latency and Deterministic Beyond 5G Networks," in *IEEE Transactions on Vehicular Technology*, vol. 71, no. 4, pp. 4171–4183, April 2022, doi: 10.1109/TVT.2021.3136725

[17] K. Qu, W. Zhuang, Q. Ye, X. Shen, X. Li and J. Rao, "Dynamic Flow Migration for Embedded Services in SDN/NFV-Enabled 5G Core Networks," in *IEEE Transactions on Communications*, vol. 68, no. 4, pp. 2394–2408, April 2020, doi: 10.1109/TCOMM.2020.2968907

[18] N. K. M. Madi, M. M. Nasralla and Z. M. Hanapi, "Delay-Based Resource Allocation With Fairness Guarantee and Minimal Loss for eMBB in 5G Heterogeneous Networks," in *IEEE Access*, vol. 10, pp. 75619–75636, 2022, doi: 10.1109/ACCESS.2022.3192450

[19] R. I. Rony, E. Lopez-Aguilera and E. Garcia-Villegas, "Dynamic Spectrum Allocation Following Machine Learning-Based Traffic Predictions in 5G," in *IEEE Access*, vol. 9, pp. 143458–143472, 2021, doi: 10.1109/ACCESS.2021.3122331

[20] Y. Cao, R. Wang, M. Chen and A. Barnawi, "AI Agent in Software-Defined Network: Agent-Based Network Service Prediction and Wireless Resource Scheduling Optimization," in *IEEE Internet of Things Journal*, vol. 7, no. 7, pp. 5816–5826, July 2020, doi: 10.1109/JIOT.2019.2950730

[21] M. Richart, J. Baliosian, J. Serrat, J. -L. Gorricho and R. Agüero, "Slicing With Guaranteed Quality of Service in WiFi Networks," in *IEEE Transactions on Network and Service Management*, vol. 17, no. 3, pp. 1822–1837, Sept. 2020, doi: 10.1109/TNSM.2020.3005594

[22] Xiang Liu, *Chapter 2 - 5G Wireless technologies, Editor(s): Xiang Liu, Optical Communications in the 5G Era*, Academic Press, 2022, pp. 29–47, ISBN 9780128216279, doi: 10.1016/B978-0-12-821627-9.00013-9

[23] Sandeep K. Sood, Kiran Deep Singh, "SNA Based Resource Optimization in Optical Network using Fog and Cloud Computing," in *Optical Switching and Networking*, vol. 33, 2019, pp. 114–121, ISSN 1573-4277, doi: 10.1016/j.osn.2017.12.007

[24] Kibeom Park, Sangmo Sung, Hokeun Kim, Jae-il Jung, "Technology Trends and Challenges in SDN and Service Assurance for End-to-End Network Slicing," in *Computer Networks*, vol. 234, 2023, p. 109908, ISSN 1389-1286, doi: 10.1016/j.comnet.2023.109908

[25] Paola Vargas, Iris Tien, "Impacts of 5G on Cyber-Physical Risks for Interdependent Connected Smart Critical Infrastructure Systems," in *International Journal of Critical Infrastructure Protection*, vol. 42, 2023, p. 100617, ISSN 1874-5482, doi: 10.1016/j.ijcip.2023.100617

[26] Mohammed Banafaa, Ibraheem Shayea, Jafri Din, Marwan Hadri Azmi, Abdulaziz Alashbi, Yousef Ibrahim Daradkeh, Abdulraqeb Alhammadi, Rajni Gupta, Juhi Gupta, "Future Generation Communications With Game Strategies: A Comprehensive Survey," in *Computer Communications*, vol. 192, 2022, pp. 1–32, ISSN 0140-3664, doi: 10.1016/j.comcom.2022.05.024

[27] Nisha Panwar, Shantanu Sharma, Awadhesh Kumar Singh, "A Survey on 5G: The Next Generation of Mobile Communication," in *Physical Communication*, vol. 18, Part 2, 2016, pp. 64–84, ISSN 1874-4907, doi: 10.1016/j.phycom.2015.10.006

[28] Shunliang Zhang, Dali Zhu, Yongming Wang, "A Survey on Space-Aerial-Terrestrial Integrated 5G Networks," in *Computer Networks*, vol. 174, 2020, p. 107212, ISSN 1389-1286, doi: 10.1016/j.comnet.2020.107212

[29] Ajay Kakkar, "A Survey on Secure Communication Techniques for 5G Wireless Heterogeneous Networks," in *Information Fusion*, vol. 62, 2020, pp. 89–109, ISSN 1566-535, doi: 10.1016/j.inffus.2020.04.009

[30] Yasser Narimani, Esmaeil Zeinali, A. Mirzaei, "QoS-Aware Resource Allocation and Fault Tolerant Operation in Hybrid SDN Using Stochastic Network Calculus," in *Physical Communication*, vol. 53, 2022, p. 101709, ISSN 1874-4907, doi: 10.1016/j.phycom.2022.101709

[31] Parjanay Sharma, Siddhant Jain, Shashank Gupta, Vinay Chamola, "Role of Machine Learning and Deep Learning in Securing 5G-Driven Industrial IoT Applications," in *Ad Hoc Networks*, vol. 123, 2021, p. 102685, ISSN 1570-8705, doi: 10.1016/j.adhoc.2021.102685

[32] Dinesh Soni, Neetesh Kumar, "Machine Learning Techniques in Emerging Cloud Computing Integrated Paradigms: A Survey and Taxonomy," in *Journal of Network and Computer Applications*, vol. 205, 2022, p. 103419, ISSN 1084-8045, doi: 10.1016/j.jnca.2022.103419

[33] Sergio Martiradonna, Alessandro Grassi, Giuseppe Piro, Gennaro Boggia, "Understanding the 5G-Air-Simulator: A Tutorial on Design Criteria, Technical Components, and Reference Use Cases," in *Computer Networks*, vol. 177, 2020, p. 107314, ISSN 1389-1286, doi: 10.1016/j.comnet.2020.107314

[34] Hanan Elazhary, "Internet of Things (IoT), Mobile Cloud, Cloudlet, Mobile IoT, IoT Cloud, Fog, Mobile Edge, and Edge Emerging Computing Paradigms: Disambiguation and Research Directions," in *Journal of Network and Computer Applications*, vol. 128, 2019, pp. 105–140, ISSN 1084-8045, doi: 10.1016/j.jnca.2018.10.021

[35] Nicola Piovesan, Angel Fernandez Gambin, Marco Miozzo, Michele Rossi, Paolo Dini, "Energy Sustainable Paradigms and Methods for Future Mobile Networks: A Survey," in *Computer Communications*, vol. 119, 2018, pp. 101–117, ISSN 0140-3664, doi: 10.1016/j.comcom.2018.01.005

[36] Sami Ben Slama, "Prosumer in Smart Grids based on Intelligent Edge Computing: A Review on Artificial Intelligence Scheduling Techniques," in *Ain Shams Engineering Journal*, vol. 13, Issue 1, 2022, p. 101504, ISSN 2090-4479, doi: 10.1016/j.asej.2021.05.018

[37] Shunliang Zhang, Dali Zhu, "Towards Artificial Intelligence Enabled 6G: State of the Art, Challenges, and Opportunities," in *Computer Networks*, vol. 183, 2020, p. 107556, ISSN 1389-1286, doi: 10.1016/j.comnet.2020.107556

[38] Rasheed Hussain, Fatima Hussain, Sherali Zeadally, "Integration of VANET and 5G Security: A Review of Design and Implementation Issues," in *Future*

Generation Computer Systems, vol. 101, 2019, pp. 843–864, ISSN 0167-739X, doi: 10.1016/j.future.2019.07.006

[39] Ertugrul Basar, Huseyin Arslan, Yue Xiao, Editorial on Special Issue "Radio Access Technologies for Beyond 5G Wireless Networks," in *Physical Communication*, vol. 38, 2020, p. 100967, ISSN 1874-4907, doi: 10.1016/j.phycom. 2019.100967

Chapter 8

Attack path discovery in dynamic network environments for automated penetration testing over 5G networks

Pramod Kumar
Ganga Institute of Technology and Management, Jhajjar, India

Rajiv Sharma
Baba Mastnath University Asthal Bohar, Rohtak, India

8.1 INTRODUCTION

With the expansion of network scale and the rapid development of technology, more and more security issues have emerged. As a controlled simulated intrusion, penetration testing can discover potential security flaws or system configuration issues. Traditional penetration testing is mainly performed manually by the penetration testing team, relying on the experience of experts in specific fields. When the network scale is large, it will consume a lot of manpower and time. Automated penetration testing can free users from the target network host selects the complex operation of the appropriate exploit program, and drives the exploit tools such as Metasploit through automated scripts, which can free users from relying on complex expert experience and improve the operability and test efficiency of penetration testing [1, 2]. Automated penetration testing has great practical significance.

Automated penetration testing mainly includes two stages: planning and moving. The planning stage usually needs to scan and analyse network and host configuration information, discover attack paths, and obtain attack paths composed of hosts and corresponding exploit actions. The moving stage is usually in the automation script, designates the attack path and vulnerability utilization information, drives the penetration testing tool to exploit the vulnerability, and then performs operations such as local privilege escalation to obtain the control of the host and uses this as a base to carry out the next round of attacks until reaching the target host [3, 4]. When the tools carry out high-intensity attacks on the attack target, problems such as the service collapse of the target host are prone to occur, and at this time the originally feasible path nodes become infeasible. The control of the network is time-consuming and labour-intensive. If the initial information of the network is re-entered for path planning, it means that the path hosts that have been compromised will be abandoned, which is a waste for both the planning and execution stages. Therefore, considering the attack path finds problems, reduces the problem space of re-planning as much as possible, and improves the success rate of re-planning.

The great majority of existing attack path finding tools are based on the attack graph model [5] and the intelligent planner [6, 7]. As long as the network size is manageable and environmental factors remain stable, this method can identify effective attack pathways. However, when applied to a developing network, these fixes frequently break down. The ant colony approach has been widely adopted in the field of path planning due to its remarkable search capabilities, high concurrency, and adaptability when combined with other methods [8, 9]. The classic ant colony optimization method can easily provide a local maximum. Scholars have looked into the ant colony method for specialist usage, proposing a wide range of improvements to increase the algorithm's path-finding performance. These range from field-specific heuristic functions to the integration of diverse types of heuristic information. By dynamically modifying the pheromone volatilization coefficient [10, 11], the explorer's ability can be preserved. When compared to the ant colony algorithm with elite strategy [12], which only updates the pheromone on the optimal path of each iteration and sets the pheromone concentration within a certain range to avoid search stagnation, the maximum and minimum ant systems [13] only update the pheromone on the optimal path of each iteration. Researchers have also considered integrating ant colony algorithm with other algorithms such as the genetic algorithm. Particle swarm optimization [14] and particle swarm optimization [15] work together to maintain a certain concentration of particles of fitness level to ensure the diversity of the population, and the ant colony algorithm [16] and genetic algorithm [17] take advantage of the excellent global convergence rate and the ant colony algorithm's fast local convergence. The ant colony algorithm has ability to operate in parallel; incorporating the ant colony algorithm with the artificial potential field method [16], where the ant colony algorithm uses the direction of the resultant force obtained from the artificial potential field method as an incentive factor to encourage more targeted early-stage movement. The heuristic pheromone of the ant colony algorithm is improved and the global path is made smoother by using the evaluation function of the A algorithm [17–20]. Swarm algorithms, such as the ant colony method, are frequently used for path discovery in complex dynamic environments [21–23]. In Ref. [24], a rolling window is added to the planning process to better observe and predict dynamic obstacles, making the ant colony algorithm more adaptable to such environments; in Ref. [25], the ant colony algorithm of fuzzy control is adopted, allowing for the avoidance of obstacles and the determination of the shortest path in complex terrain.

The deployment of an artificial neural network (ANN)-based tool for calculating short circuit currents in power networks with a high penetration of power electronics-based renewables was the main emphasis of Aljarrah et al. (2023) [26]. Their research proved how well the ANN technique predicted short-circuit currents. Using supervised machine learning techniques, Ahmad Fauzi et al. (2022) [27] explored mobile network coverage prediction. They suggested a method for forecasting mobile network coverage by analysing the effectiveness of several methods. Using out-of-band data and beamforming design, Xiu et al. (2019) [28] investigated effective techniques for millimetre-wave cell finding in wireless communication networks.

In the literature, security in 5G networks also received a lot of attention. The Distributed Slice Mobility Attack (DSMA), a focused attack against network slices in 5G networks, was first described by Sathi and Murthy in 2021 [29]. They evaluated the effects of DSMA and suggested mitigation strategies. Khan et al. (2022) [30] looked into how Denial of Service (DoS) and Distributed DoS (DDoS) attacks affected 5G network slices and how they could be detected. To defend network slices from these attacks, they suggested SliceSecure as a security solution. A deep learning–based method for detecting and thwarting DDoS attacks in 5G and beyond mobile networks was proposed by Bousalem et al. in 2022 [31], demonstrating the efficiency of deep learning algorithms in doing so. Dey and Patra (2023) [32] discussed handover process vulnerabilities and suggested solutions to strengthen security in 5G-V2X networks in order to solve security breaches during the handover in 5G Vehicle-to-Everything (V2X) communication.

Studies also concentrated on certain security issues in 5G networks [33]. In their study of session management for security systems in 5G standalone networks, Park et al. (2022) [34] made recommendations for ways to guarantee secure session creation, upkeep, and termination. Li et al. (2022) [35] proposed ways to assure accurate and secure positioning information in 5G networks, addressing secure 5G positioning with truth finding, attack detection, and tracing. In softwarized 5G networks, Sathi et al. (2021) [36] established protocols to reduce network slice topology learning attacks and safeguard user service access behaviour privacy by preventing adversaries from deducing network slice topology and user behaviour through traffic analysis. A security analysis of systems connected to 5G networks was carried out by Saha et al. (2022) [37], who also proposed a framework to better identify and address security risks in 5G networks.

Additionally, unique security threats were looked into. Hussain et al. (2021) [38] demonstrated the efficiency of deep learning algorithms in detecting and mitigating such attacks by presenting a deep learning–based strategy for detecting DDoS attacks in cyber-physical systems over 5G networks. The security against pollution attacks in network coding-enabled 5G networks was addressed by Vasudevan et al. (2020) [39], who proposed methods to identify and counteract these assaults, which interfere with data transmission and reception in network coding-based communication systems. MSR-DoS, a Modular Square Root (MSR)-based strategy to withstand DoS attacks in 5G-enabled vehicle networks, was proposed by Al-Shareeda and Manickam (2022) [40], who also provided evidence of its efficiency in preventing DoS attacks and guaranteeing dependable communication.

The existing literature on 5G networks lacks in-depth exploration of the impact of network slice orchestration on the quality of service (QoS) provisioning. While network slicing enables efficient resource allocation and customized service provisioning, there is a research gap in investigating the dynamic allocation and optimization of resources to meet diverse QoS requirements in a multi-tenant environment.

The objective of this work is to establish a framework for intelligent resource allocation for network slicing in 5G networks. The framework intends to dynamically allocate network resources to network segments based on their individual QoS requirements and real-time network conditions.

This work contributes by proposing a novel algorithm for network slice resource allocation that takes into consideration QoS requirements and real-time network conditions. The algorithm intelligently allocates bandwidth, computing capacity, and storage to various slices based on their demand and priority. In addition, it takes into account the elasticity and scalability requirements of network slices, allowing them to dynamically modify their resource allocation in response to fluctuating demands. The proposed framework improves the overall efficacy and efficiency of network slicing in 5G networks, providing users with a more robust and reliable service experience and optimizing network operators' resource utilization. The experimental evaluation demonstrates the efficacy and superiority of the proposed framework compared to existing resource allocation strategies, emphasizing its potential for deployment in 5G networks in the real world.

8.2 ANT COLONY ALGORITHM

The ant colony algorithm was first presented in Ref. [20], and it was later widely utilized to tackle issues like travelling salesman, robot navigation, and optimization. It was inspired by the foraging behaviour of ants in the natural world. The ideal path is ultimately discovered by the ant colony algorithm, which makes use of the information on the path that this substance uses to direct the ants to preferentially pick the path with a high pheromone concentration. The information initialization, ant Path finding, and pheromone updating are the three main phases of the ant colony algorithm. Ant colony state initialization and parameter initialization settings are the two primary components of information initialization. Ant path finding means that each ant transfers in turn according to a certain transfer probability until it reaches the target point. Among them, ant k is at t the probability $P_{ij}^k(t)$ of moving from waypoint i to waypoint j at any time, as shown in formula (8.1).

$$P_{ij}^k(t) = \begin{cases} \dfrac{\left[\tau_{ij}(t)\right]^\alpha \left[\eta_{ij}(t)\right]^\beta}{\displaystyle\sum_{s \in \text{allowed}_k} \left[\tau_{ij}(t)\right]^\alpha \left[\eta_{ij}(t)\right]^\beta}, & j \in \text{allowed}_k \\ 0, & \text{otherwise} \end{cases}$$

(8.1)

Among them, allowed k represents the path point that can be selected in the next step, α and β represent the parameters of the importance of pheromone and heuristic function factor respectively, $\tau_{ij}(t)$ is the pheromone concentration between paths (i, j) at time t, $\eta_{ij}(t)$ is the heuristic information of the path (i, j) at time t, usually taken as

$$\eta_{i,j}(t) = \frac{1}{d(i,j)} \tag{8.2}$$

Where $d(i, j)$ is the distance between path points i and j.

Under the guidance of $P_{ij}^k(t)$, the ants update the pheromone concentration after completing the path finding. The update method is shown in Formulae (8.3) and (8.4):

$$\tau_{i,j}(t+1) = \rho\tau_{i,j}(t) + \sum_{n=1}^{N} \Delta\tau_{i,j}^n(t) \tag{8.3}$$

$$\Delta\tau_{i,j}^n(t) = \begin{cases} \dfrac{Q}{L_n}, & \{i,j\} \subset \text{path}_n \\ 0, & \text{otherwise} \end{cases} \tag{8.4}$$

Among them, $\tau_{i,j}$ is the pheromone concentration between path point i and j; $\Delta\tau_{i,j}^n$ is the pheromone left by the nth ant between path point i and j; N is the number of ants in the ant colony; L_n is the path length of the nth ant; ρ and Q are constants, respectively representing the pheromone volatilization coefficient and pheromone constant. This pheromone update method is the ant cycle model volume model and ant-dense model.

8.3 BIDIRECTIONAL ANT COLONY ALGORITHM FOR ATTACK PATH DISCOVERY

8.3.1 Network scene description

The purpose of network attack path planning is to find an attack sequence that can reach the target host, and use the exploit relationship between hosts to transfer until reaching the target. As shown in Figure 8.1, the attack workspace includes the discovery of the network and host, and the corresponding operating system, ports, services, compromised hosts, etc. This article assumes that the information of the workspace can be known in advance by means of detection and scanning. After exploiting a vulnerability on a host, it is considered that the control of the host has been obtained, and the establishment of a C2 (Command & Control), escalation of local privileges, etc.

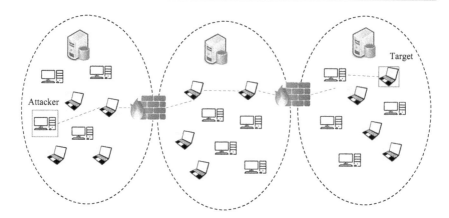

Figure 8.1 Schematic diagram of network attack path.

Network information can be represented by a directed acyclic graph $G = \langle V, E \rangle$, where $V = \{v_0, v_1, v_2, \cdots, v_n\}$. $E = \{e_{ij} \mid v_i, v_j \in V\}$ indicates the connection relationship between hosts, the connection mentioned here refers to the direct connection, that is, it only takes one hop to access the host v_j from the host v_i. In the robot path finding problem, the Euclidean distance is usually used as the edge cost, but in the penetration testing environment, the attack path is formed by exploiting relationships between hosts, and the path cost needs to be set in combination with the vulnerability information. Intrude into host j, use cost to represent the minimum attack cost in the exploit action, that is, the minimum attack cost for host i to intrude into host j, and the corresponding exploit action is *minact*. In this paper, the minimum attack cost is taken as the target of attack path discovery; the attack cost depends on the vulnerability information of the host. The Common Vulnerability Scoring System (CVSS) is an index used to evaluate the severity of the vulnerability small. In this paper, the path cost between path hosts i and j is defined as Formula (8.5).

$$\text{cost}_{ij} = \min\left\{100 - 10 * \text{CVSS}\left(a_{jk}\right)\right\} \tag{8.5}$$

Among them, a_{jk} means that host j has vulnerability k and can be exploited; if host j has multiple vulnerabilities $\langle k_1, k_2, \cdots, k_n \rangle$. The action is *minact*.

8.3.2 Network attack path discovery method based on bidirectional ant colony algorithm

In the classic ant colony algorithm, all ants in the population search from the starting point and end at the end point. Although the probability-based routing strategy is adopted, taking into account a certain balance between exploration and utilization, at the beginning of the algorithm, due to the lack of guidance, the ant's path quality is low, which affects the distribution of pheromone, and the ants are easy to fall into the local optimal solution.

Two-way ant search strategy

In order to enable ants to better explore unknown areas and avoid falling into local optimal solutions while speeding up the convergence speed, this paper uses a bidirectional ant colony algorithm for path discovery. Two populations of ants are set, and the forward ants start searching from the initial host, the search path is expressed as $L_1 = \langle f_0, f_1, \cdots, f_s \rangle$; the reverse ant conducts a reverse search from the target host and for the convenience of a unified description, the search path is expressed as $L_2 = \langle b_0, b_1, \cdots, b_t \rangle$. Among them, f_i, $i \in [0, s]$ is the host of the forward path, f_0 is the starting host, fs is the target host; b_i, $i \in [0, t]$ is the host of the reverse path, b_0 is the starting host, b_t is the target host. In this paper, different path transfer strategies are set for the forward ant colony and the reverse ant colony respectively. The path strategy uses roulette to select the path host to be transferred in the next step, ensuring that ants can explore unknown areas with a certain probability; the reverse ant colony selects the candidate path host with the highest transfer probability, and takes it as the next transfer path The host ensures that ants prefer to choose the local optimal path, which improves the path quality. The forward search will reduce the search efficiency due to too many branches, and the reverse search starts from the target host, which can reduce the number of nodes visited to a certain extent. And it is guaranteed to have a certain difference from the forward search path.

(1) Path crosses optimization operation

After both the forward ant Ant_{m1} and the reverse ant Ant_{m2} search for a path, this paper refers to the idea of cross mutation of genetic algorithm [21], and performs cross operation on the paths found by two different path finding strategies to obtain a better path after the cross. Assume that the two paths L_1 and L_2 have the same host, that is, when $f_p = b_q$,

$$L_2 = \langle b_0, b_1, \cdots, b_q, \cdots, b_t \rangle$$

$$L_1 = \langle f_0, f_1, \cdots, f_p, \cdots, f_s \rangle$$

Segment the original path according to the intersection point,

$$L_{1-1} = \langle f_0, f_1, \cdots, f_{p-1} \rangle, L_{1-2} = \langle f_{p+1}, f_{p+2}, \cdots, f_s \rangle$$

$$L_{2-1} = \langle b_0, b_1, \cdots, b_{q-1} \rangle, L_{2-2} = \langle b_{q+1}, b_{q+2}, \cdots, b_t \rangle$$

If

$$\sum_{i=0}^{p-2} \cos t\left(e_{i,i+1}\right) \leq \sum_{i=0}^{q-2} \cos t\left(e_{i,i+1}\right) \tag{8.6}$$

Then $L_{newl} = L_{1-1}$, otherwise $L_{newl} = L_{2-1}$; similarly, if

$$\sum_{i=p+1}^{s-1} \cos t\left(e_{i,i+1}\right) \leq \sum_{i=q+1}^{t-1} \cos t\left(e_{i,i+1}\right) \tag{8.7}$$

Then $L_{new\,2} = L_{1-2}$, otherwise $L_{new\,2} = L_{2-2}$. The updated path $L = L_{new\,1} \cup f_p \cup L_{new2}$.

If the two paths do not have the same host, directly select the path with the smallest total cost as the path after crossover. If there are multiple common path hosts in the two paths, in order to make the effect of crossover optimization more obvious, take the path host in the middle position as the crossover path Point. First, the public host list of the two paths is obtained as $[h_0, h_1, \cdots, h_g]$, where $h_i \in L_1 \cap L_2, i \in [0, g]$, i. The closer to the target host takes the intersection point $h_{\lceil g/2 \rceil}$, and the updated path L is used as the mth search path of the ant.

(2) Pheromone updates strategy

After the ants complete the search in an iterative process, the pheromone distribution needs to be updated. If the update is based on all ants, the reverse ant colony can quickly converge to a better solution, and the algorithm's exploration ability will decline, and it is easy to be premature; if only based on updating forward ants cannot make full use of the ant's path finding information, the accumulation of pheromone concentration in the optimal path is slow, and the final operation result is also poor. In order to solve this contradiction, this paper proposes a new pheromone update scheme. The path finding results of the ant colony are updated with pheromone, and then the optimal path generated by this iteration is enhanced with additional pheromone by referring to the elite ant colony strategy.

$$\tau_{i,j}\left(t+1\right) = \rho\tau_{i,j}\left(t\right) + \sum_{n=1}^{N} \Delta\tau_{i,j}^{n}\left(t\right) + E \times \Delta\tau_{i,j}^{best} \tag{8.8}$$

$$\Delta\tau_{i,j}^{n}\left(t\right) = \begin{cases} \dfrac{Q}{L_n}, & \{i,j\} \subset path_n \\ 0, & \text{otherwise} \end{cases} \tag{8.9}$$

$$\Delta\tau_{i,j}^{best} = \begin{cases} Q/L_{best}, & \{i,j\} \subset path_{best} \\ 0, & \text{otherwise} \end{cases} \tag{8.10}$$

Among them, t represents the number of iterations, $\tau_{i,j}$ is the phero-mone concentration between path point i and j, $\Delta\tau_{i,j}^n$ represents the pheromone left by all forward ants between path point i and j, $\Delta\tau_{i,j}^{\text{best}}$ is the most pheromone between path points i and j in the optimal path. N is the number of positive ant colonies, E is the adjustment param-eter of the elite path, L represents the total cost of the path, and path represents the set of path hosts. This update scheme avoids the reverse Part of the path pheromone brought by ants accumulates too quickly, and the optimization ability is improved by additionally updating the pheromone of the optimal path. The optimal path here is taken from the path set after cross optimization. Finally, the scheme in this paper is verified by experiments effectiveness.

(3) Re-planning mechanism

Regarding the selection of the starting point of re-planning, the tra-ditional re-planning algorithm directly takes the path point closest to the fault point as the starting point, and plans a path to the tar-get point. However, if the host on the current path has fewer con-nections, the host on its adjacent path fails afterwards; there may be nowhere to go when planning the new starting host, resulting in failure of re-planning. For example, suppose the current agent has captured host h_1, h_1 belongs to the same local area network as h_2 and h_3, but the mutual the hosts accessible by h_1 are h_4 and h_5, h_1 has a vulnerability dependency with h_4, and has no vulnerability depen-dency with h_5. Both h_2 and h_3 and h_4 and h_5 have vulnerability de-pendencies. In the original planning route, h_1's the next attack target is h_4. When h_4 fails, if h_1 is used as the starting host for re-planning, the planning will fail because there are too few attackable hosts for the next hop of h_1; as the starting point of re-planning, the host can finally attack h_5 through h_2 or h_3 to realize the re-planning of the attack path. In the field of robot navigation, the distance to the target point is often used as the heuristic value information to select the starting point of re-planning [22, 23], while in the automation penetration in the test; such "distance" information is difficult to estimate. In this paper, the out-degree of the path host is considered as the basis for the selection of the re-planning starting point. The greater the out-degree of the path host, the more next-hop hosts can be selected, and the easier it is to jump out of the "Partial dead end", to avoid re-planning failure.

Assuming that the agent has moved to the host $h_{\text{ob}-1}$ along the planned route, and the h_{ob} crashes when trying to attack the host h_{ob}, the list of captured hosts $L_{\text{control}} = [h_0, h_1, \cdots, h_{\text{ob}-1}]$, h, $h_{\text{ob}-1}]$, h rep-resents the initial planning path Host. Select the path host with the largest out-degree as the starting host for re-planning, and the host closest to the obstacle host as the target host for re-planning, and re-call the bidirectional ant colony algorithm to quickly find the best path around the obstacle, and then continue to move along the original planned route until reaching the target host.

(4) Algorithm design

Figure 8.2 shows the flow of the network attack path discovery method based on the bidirectional ant colony algorithm, and the specific path finding algorithm is shown in Algorithm 1.

The initial value of *localbest_ant* in each round of iteration is ∞. With the continuous update of the path finding of ants, it is kept as the minimum path cost, which is mainly used to find elite paths and update pheromones. *best_ant* is a global variable, and the initial value is ∞, it is updated every time

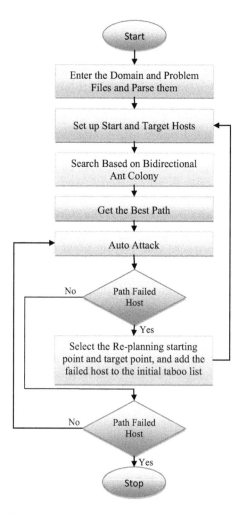

Figure 8.2 APD-BACO algorithm flow.

ALGORITHM 1   BIDIRECTIONAL ANT COLONY ALGORITHM

Input: *domain. pddl, problem. pddl* /∗ the specific content is introduced in the experimental chapter∗/

Output: *Attack path hosts* ‹ h_0, h_1,.., h_n›, corresponding exploit actions and attack costs

{(h_i, h_{i+1}): [νul, cost]}

1. *H, E, C* ← *pddlParser(domain. pddl, problem. pddl)*/∗Analyze network information to get host, edge and attack cost corresponding to edge∗/

2. *Initialize(pheromone_graph)* /∗ Initialize the pheromone concentration of the edge∗/

3. *Initialize(best_ant)* /∗ Save global optimal path information∗/

4. *for i* ← 1 *to iterNum do* /∗ *iterNum is the number of iterations*∗/

5. *for j* ← 1 *to antNum/2 do* /∗*antNum is the number of ant populations, which are equally divided into forward ant colony and reverse ant colony*∗/

6. *Initialize(forward_ant, backward_ant)* /∗ initialize forward ant and reverse ant∗/

7. *forward_ant. searchPath()* /∗ Forward path finding for ants∗/

8. *backward_ant. searchPath()* /∗ Reverse∗/

9. *Cross_Path()* /∗ Perform path cross optimization∗/

10. *localbest_ant* ← *mincost(ANT)* /∗ Save the optimal path information of this iteration for pheromone update∗/

11. *Update_Pheromone()* /∗ pheromone update∗/

12. *IFlocal best_ant < best_ant THEN*

13. *best_ant* ← *localbest_ant* /∗ Record global optimal path information∗/

14. *end*

FUNCTION searchPath()/∗ Ant pathfinding ∗/

1. *next_host* ← *start_host*

2. *While next_host not goal_host do*

3. *pre_host* ← *next_host*

4. *IF pre_host. hasConect() THEN*

5. *next_hosts ← getNeighbor(pre_host)*

6. *next_host ← getNext(pre_host, next_hosts, id)*

7. *IF next_hostis NULL THEN*

8. *break*

9. *host_parent[next_host] ← pre_host*

10. *ELSE*

11. *path. remove(next_host)*

12. *open_table_host[next_host] ← False*

13. *next_host ← host_parent[next_host]*

14. *continue*

15. *Move()*

FUNCTION getNext(pre_host, next_host, id)

1. *for each host ∈ next_hosts do*

2. *IF open_table_host[host] THEN*

3. *(pre_host, host). prob ← getProb()*

4. *IFidisforward_ant THEN*

5. *return next_host ← Roulette()*

6. *ELIFidis backward_ant THEN*

7. *return next_host ← Maxprob()*

an iteration ends, and it is kept as the minimum path cost. When the iteration stops, it is the optimal path cost found by the algorithm. In the function *searchPath()*, *pre_host. hasConect()* is used to determine whether the current host is connected to other hosts. If not, you need to go back and reselect the path; *open_table_host* is a taboo table, which saves the visited hosts; host _ parent is used to record the parent-child node relationship, when backtracking It will be used; *Move()* means move, add *next_host* to the path path and add a taboo list, when the target host is reached, the path and path cost found by the ant will be obtained. The function *getNext()* returns the host that the ant will move to next, *getProb()* is the probability calculated according to Formula (8.1). After obtaining the probabilities of all candidate hosts, if it is a forward ant, return the host selected by roulette; if it is a reverse ant, return the host with the highest probability.

8.4 EXPERIMENT

The vulnerability information used in this experiment comes from the public vulnerability database and *Metasploit*, and the network information and vulnerability information have been formally described using the planning domain definition language PDDL. The PDDL language is a bridge connecting planning problems and planning solvers [24], including domain files and problem files. *do − main. pddl* is a description of the model, such as actions, pre-conditions and post-conditions of actions, etc. *pddl* is a description of the problem domain, including initial state and target state. The initial state mainly describes the hosts contained in the network, the connection relationship between hosts, the attributes of the hosts, etc. The workspace of the penetration test environment is transformed into the initial state described by *pddl*, vulnerability exploitation and attack modules are converted into actions, and the corresponding *pddl* description examples are listed in Tables 8.1 and 8.2.

The usefulness of the enhanced ant colony method is first tested by utilizing it to locate the network assault path. Both the original ant colony algorithm (Ant Colony Algorithm, ACO) and its more advanced descendant, the Elite Ant Colony Algorithm (EACO), are contrasted with the APD-BACO. The ideal path cost is broken down into six sub-components: the success rate of optimal path discovery, the number of iterations required to find the optimal path for the first time, the average path cost, the average running time, and the running time range. In this paper the experiments were carried out on networks with different host scales, among which network 1 contained 50 hosts, and network 2 contained 100 hosts. The experiment used python as the

Table 8.1 Example of *domain. pddl*

(: *action Dell_SonicWALL_Plixer_Scrutinizer_9_SQL_Injection*)

:*parameters*(? *srcIP*? *dstIP*)

:*precondition*(*and* (*connectivity. srcIP*? *dstIP*) (*compromised*? *srcIP*) (*iswindows*? *dstIP*)
   (*isscrutinizer8_6_5*? *dstIP*)

:*effect* (*and* (*compromised*? *dstIP*)(*increase* (*total − cost*) 45.0)))

Table 8.2 Example of *problem. pddl*

(*isunix host_36*)

(*iszimbra_collaboration_suit6_0_4 host_36*)

|*slifesize_room_appliance_softwareIs_rml_3_5_9 host_36*

(*iscakephp1_3_0 host_36*)

(*isgec_2fged1_4_3 host_36*)

(*isxml_rpc1_0_10 host_36*)

Table 8.3 Parameter settings for algorithm

Parameter	Information factor α	Heuristic factor β	Pheromone evaporation coefficient ρ	Pheromone concentration enhancer factor Q	Elite Path adjustment parameter E
Value	1.0	2.0	0.5	100	0.5

programming language, and the experimental platform included Inteli9, 2.59 GHz processor and 128 GB memory. Combined with recent work based on literature research and experimental experience, the selected parameters are listed in Table 8.3.

Due to the inherent randomness of the algorithm, 100 iterations of each of the three algorithms are performed for statistical purposes. Each run is given 200 iterations, all three algorithms have the same total number of ants (30 for Network 1), and Network 2 has the same amount of ants (20 for Network 2). Network 2 has its total number of ants increased to 50, while all other settings are kept the same. Figures 8.3 and 8.4 depict the results of an experiment conducted on network 2 that compared the optimal path cost of APD-BACO, ACO, and EACO as a function of the number of iterations.

The network scale is large, the optimal path finding success rate of EACO and APD-BACO is much higher than that of ACO, effectively avoiding the algorithm from falling into local optimum. EACO adds the additional update of the optimal path pheromone increases the amount of calculation, and the time consumption increases significantly when the network scale expands; APD-BACO also has an additional update of the optimal path pheromone, but compared with the other two algorithms, it only updates the positive path pheromone. The path pheromone to the ant colony, the number of updates is half of the other two algorithms; although the cross-optimization operation

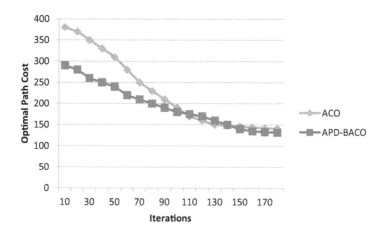

Figure 8.3 ACO and APD-BACO optimal path cost changes with the number of iterations.

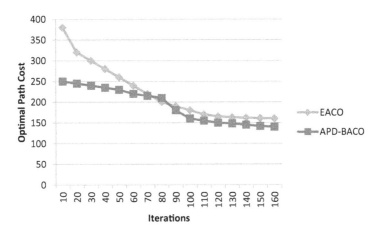

Figure 8.4 The optimal path cost of EACO And APD-BACO changes with the number of iterations.

increases the amount of calculation, the path quality is improved in the iterative process, and the reverse ant path finding strategy is simple, the final algorithm. The running time is shorter, and the success rate of finding the optimal path is guaranteed. From Figures 8.3 and 8.4, it can be seen that compared with ACO, EACO iterates to the optimal solution in a shorter time, and the optimal number of iterations of APD-BACO is higher than that of ACO. The other two algorithms are less. From the initial moment, the quality of the path finding of ants has been improved, and the high concurrency of the ant colony algorithm is retained, which is convenient for parallel computing.

Metric-FF planner [25] is the latest version of the famous FF planner, which integrates a variety of path planning algorithms and can handle numerical effects. The $D * (D\_star)$ algorithm is an efficient heuristic search algorithm, which was used in Mars Pathfinding algorithm at the core of the detector. Comparing APD-BACO with Metric-FF planner and D* algorithm, the attack path discovery is carried out in networks of different scales respectively. Figure 8.5 shows the running time and Comparison of memory usage.

Figure 8.5 depicts the algorithm's execution time (red solid line) and memory consumption (blue dotted line). It is clear that the Metric-FF algorithm requires ever-increasing amounts of time to run. Metric-FF takes 6 279 25 seconds to complete when the number of hosts is 400; the D method takes the least time and is the most consistent, going from 1.41 seconds to 6.21 seconds. When the number of hosts is low, the APD-BACO and D algorithms use about the same amount of memory as the Metric-FF algorithm; when the number of hosts is high, the D algorithm uses the most memory, and the Metric-FF algorithm uses the least. The algorithm is rapidly expanding, despite taking up less memory. APD-BACO falls in the middle of the other two algorithms in terms of both running time and memory usage. This is due to the fact that the D algorithm must keep track of the OPEN and CLOSE

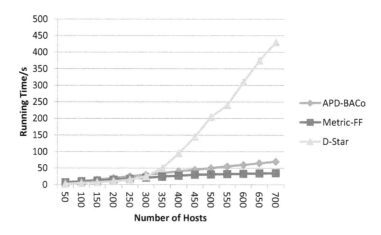

Figure 8.5 The running time of the three algorithms vary with the number of hosts.

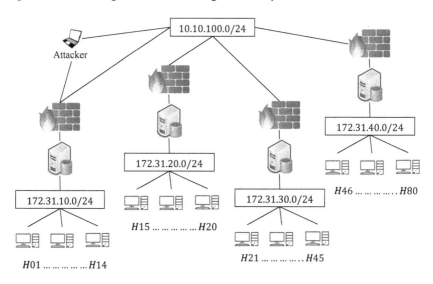

Figure 8.6 Experimental environment setting and attack path display.

tables, as well as reduce the time required for each operation by recording and updating the statistical information of all nodes. At runtime, Graph-plan completes the heuristic evaluation of the Metric-FF algorithm, and the state space expands at an unmanageable rate of the asymptotic convergence algorithm APD-BACO. The rise is happening somewhat slowly.

Set up the experimental network as shown in Figure 8.6, simulating the attack situation where layers of fortifications and the target host are located deep in the intranet. The left side of the firewall is the attacker's network, and the right side of the firewall is the penetration test scene host. The network connection rules are set as follows: hosts in each subnet can visit each other, and can only

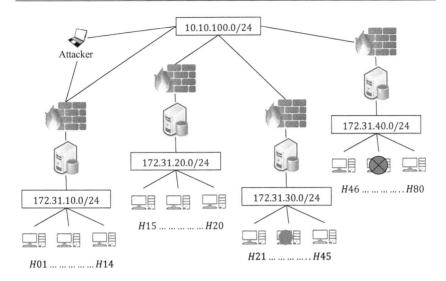

Figure 8.7 Attack path display after path host failure.

be accessed by hosts in the previous subnet. For example, Host-15 can only access subnet 172.31.20.0/24 and172.31.30.0/24 host, unable to access subnet 172.31.10.0/24 host; Attacker can only access subnet 172.31.10.0/24 hosts. The host configuration information is randomly generated by the preconditions required for exploiting the vulnerability. First, APD-BA-CO is used for path discovery, and the obtained attack path sequence is shown in Figure 8.6, and the red line represents the attack path sequence.

Assuming that when the agent uses Host-71 as a springboard to attack Host-74, the host-74 host crashes due to too frequent access, and the environmental information has changed; if the host-81 closest to the failed host is directly selected as a new starting point, it is necessary to add Host-74 to the initial Taboo list is used for re-planning. When the running status of Host-71 and Host-73 does not meet the preconditions of exploiting the vulnerability, re-planning will fail. In order to avoid multiple re-planning caused by re-planning failure and improve the success rate of re-planning, this paper chooses the path host Host-22 with the largest out-degree is used as the starting point of re-planning, and the host near the faulty host is used as the end point of re-planning. This method can quickly find local paths and avoid re-planning failure again. The final planned route is shown in Figure 8.7.

8.5 CONCLUSION

This study suggests a technique for finding attack vectors that works well in dynamic network settings. To begin, we model the network data and establish the attack price. The next step is to suggest a novel two-way ant colony method for finding global attack paths. The APD-BACO algorithm has been shown to have a shorter running time, lower average path cost during the search process, and faster convergence speed when compared to the ACO and EACO algorithms in experimental benchmarks. The results show that the APD-BACO method is highly flexible and has reasonably stable time and space costs as the number of hosts rises, in contrast to the Metric-FF planning algorithm and the D algorithm. The paper's re-planning technique improves APD-BACO's suitability for attack path discovery in dynamic network settings by increasing the success rate of local re-planning and instructing the agent to attack and move in a dynamic environment.

REFERENCES

[1] Nikolaos Polatidis, Michalis Pavlidis, "Haralambos Mouratidis, Cyber-Attack Path Discovery in a Dynamic Supply Chain Maritime Risk Management System," *Computer Standards & Interfaces*, vol. 56, pp 74–82, ISSN 0920-5489, 2018,.

[2] Antoine Boudermine, Rida Khatoun, Jean-Henri Choyer, "Dynamic Logic-Based Attack Graph for Risk Assessment in Complex Computer Systems," *Computer Networks*, vol. 228, p. 109730, ISSN 1389-1286, 2023.

[3] Ferhat Arat, Sedat Akleylek, "Attack Path Detection for IIoT Enabled Cyber Physical Systems: Revisited," *Computers & Security*, vol. 128, p. 103174, ISSN 0167-4048, 2023.

[4] Alisson R. Svaigen, Azzedine Boukerche, Linnyer B. Ruiz, Antonio A.F. Loureiro, "Trajectory Matters: Impact of Jamming Attacks Over the Drone Path Planning on the Internet of Drones," *Ad Hoc Networks*, vol. 146, p. 103179, ISSN 1570-8705, 2023.

[5] J. Bhayo, S. A. Shah, S. Hameed, A. Ahmed, J. Nasir, D. Draheim, "Towards a Machine Learning-Based Framework for DDOS Attack Detection in Software-Defined IoT (SD-IoT) Networks," *Engineering Applications of Artificial Intelligence*, vol. 123, 106432, 2023.

[6] R. C. Meena, S. Bhatia, R. H. Jhaveri, L. Cheng, A. Kumar, A. Mashat, "HyPASS: Design of Hybrid-SDN Prevention of Attacks of Source Spoofing with Host Discovery and Address Validation," *Physical Communication*, vol. 55, p. 101902, 2022.

[7] P. Cigoj, B. J. Blazic, "An Intelligent and Automated WCMS Vulnerability-Discovery Tool: The Current State of the Web," in *IEEE Access*, vol. 7, pp. 175466–175473, 2019, doi: 10.1109/ACCESS.2019.2957573

[8] T. Cody et al., "Discovering Exfiltration Paths Using Reinforcement Learning with Attack Graphs," *2022 IEEE Conference on Dependable and Secure Computing (DSC)*, Edinburgh, United Kingdom, pp. 1–8, 2022, doi: 10.1109/DSC54232.2022.9888919

[9] G. Vidhyalakshmi, P. Vaishnavi, "A Trusted Security Approach to Detect and Isolate Routing Attacks in Mobile Ad hoc Networks," *Journal of Engineering Research*, p. 100149, 2023, doi: 10.1016/j.jer.2023.100149

[10] N. Schweitzer, L. Cohen, A. Dvir, A. Stulman, "Persuasive: A Node Isolation Attack Variant for OLSR-Based MANETs and its Mitigation," *Ad Hoc Networks*, vol. 148, P. 103192, 2023.

[11] S. Suma, B. Harsoor, "An Approach to Detect Black Hole Attack for Congestion Control Utilizing Mobile Nodes in Wireless Sensor Network," *Materials Today: Proceedings*, vol. 56, pp. 2256–2260, 2022.

[12] B. Yiğit, G. Gür, F. Alagöz, B. Tellenbach, "Network Fingerprinting via Timing Attacks and Defense in Software Defined Networks," in *Computer Networks*, vol. 232, p. 109850, 2023.

[13] S. Q. Ali Shah, F. Zeeshan Khan, M. Ahmad, "The Impact and Mitigation of ICMP Based Economic Denial of Sustainability Attack in Cloud Computing Environment Using Software Defined Network," in *Computer Networks*, vol. 187, p. 107825, 2021.

[14] T. Yi, X. Chen, Y. Zhu, W. Ge, Z. Han, "Review on the Application of Deep Learning in Network Attack Detection," in *Journal of Network and Computer Applications*, vol. 212, p. 103580, 2023.

[15] H. Kalghatgi, M. Dhawle, U. Raut, "Defense Techniques Against Spoofing Attacks in Wireless Sensor Networks," *Materials Today: Proceedings*, 2023.

[16] Hritika Kalghatgi, Malhar Dhawle, "Umesh Raut, Defense Techniques Against Spoofing Attacks in Wireless Sensor Networks," *Materials Today: Proceedings*, ISSN 2214-7853, 2023.

[17] A. Galal, X. Hesselbach, "Probability-Based Path Discovery Protocol for Electromagnetic Nano-Networks," IN *Computer Networks*, vol. 174, p. 107246, 2020.

[18] Sharma, D. K., S. K. Dhurandher, S. Kumaram, K. Datta Gupta, P. K. Sharma, "Mitigation of Black Hole Attacks in 6LoWPAN RPL-Based Wireless Sensor Network for Cyber Physical Systems," IN *Computer Communications*, vol. 189, pp. 182–192, 2022.

[19] K. Kurniawan, A. Ekelhart, E. Kiesling, G. Quirchmayr, A. M. Tjoa, "KRYSTAL: Knowledge Graph-Based Framework for Tactical Attack Discovery in Audit Data," in *Computers & Security*, vol. 121, p. 102828, 2022.

[20] D. Kong et al., "Combination Attacks and Defenses on SDN Topology Discovery," in *IEEE/ACM Transactions on Networking*, vol. 31, no. 2, pp. 904–919, April 2023, doi: 10.1109/TNET.2022.3203561

[21] K. Wu, J. Li, Y. Zhu, S. Miao, S. Zhu, C. Zhou, "Interactive Visual Analysis on the Attack and Defense Drill of Grid Cyber-Physical Systems," in *CSEE Journal of Power and Energy Systems*, vol. 7, no. 1, pp. 45–56, Jan. 2021, doi: 10.17775/CSEEJPES.2020.05030

[22] P. De, U. Parampalli, C. Mandal, "Secure Path Balanced BDD-Based Pre-Charge Logic for Masking," in *IEEE Transactions on Circuits and Systems I: Regular Papers*, vol. 67, no. 12, pp. 4747–4760, Dec. 2020, doi: 10.1109/TCSI.2020.3019921

[23] P. De, U. Parampalli, C. Mandal, "Secure Path Balanced BDD-Based Pre-Charge Logic for Masking," in *IEEE Transactions on Circuits and Systems I: Regular Papers*, vol. 67, no. 12, pp. 4747–4760, Dec. 2020, doi: 10.1109/TCSI.2020.3019921

[24] H. Mouratidis, V. Diamantopoulou, "A Security Analysis Method for Industrial Internet of Things," in *IEEE Transactions on Industrial Informatics*, vol. 14, no. 9, pp. 4093–4100, Sept. 2018, doi: 10.1109/TII.2018.2832853

[25] B. Donnet, P. Raoult, T. Friedman, M. Crovella, "Deployment of an Algorithm for Large-Scale Topology Discovery," in *IEEE Journal on Selected Areas in Communications*, vol. 24, no. 12, pp. 2210–2220, Dec. 2006, doi: 10.1109/JSAC.2006.884019

[26] R. Aljarrah et al., "Application of Artificial Neural Network-Based Tool for Short Circuit Currents Estimation in Power Systems With High Penetration of Power Electronics-Based Renewables," in *IEEE Access*, vol. 11, pp. 20051–20062, 2023, doi: 10.1109/ACCESS.2023.3249296

[27] M. F. Ahmad Fauzi, R. Nordin, N. F. Abdullah, H. A. H. Alobaidy, "Mobile Network Coverage Prediction Based on Supervised Machine Learning Algorithms," in *IEEE Access*, vol. 10, pp. 55782–55793, 2022, doi: 10.1109/ACCESS. 2022.3176619

[28] Y. Xiu, J. Wu, C. Xiu, Z. Zhang, "Millimeter Wave Cell Discovery Based on Out-of-Band Information and Design of Beamforming," in *IEEE Access*, vol. 7, pp. 23076–23088, 2019, doi: 10.1109/ACCESS.2019.2898261

[29] V. N. Sathi, C. S. R. Murthy, "Distributed Slice Mobility Attack: A Novel Targeted Attack Against Network Slices of 5G Networks," in *IEEE Networking Letters*, vol. 3, no. 1, pp. 5–9, March 2021, doi: 10.1109/LNET.2020.3044642

[30] M. S. Khan, B. Farzaneh, N. Shahriar, N. Saha, R. Boutaba, "SliceSecure: Impact and Detection of DoS/DDoS Attacks on 5G Network Slices," *2022 IEEE Future Networks World Forum (FNWF)*, Montreal, QC, Canada, 2022, pp. 639–642, doi: 10.1109/FNWF55208.2022.00117

[31] B. Bousalem, V. F. Silva, R. Langar, S. Cherrier, "Deep Learning-based Approach for DDoS Attacks Detection and Mitigation in 5G and Beyond Mobile Networks," *2022 IEEE 8th International Conference on Network Softwarization (NetSoft)*, Milan, Italy, 2022, pp. 228–230, doi: 10.1109/NetSoft54395.2022. 9844053

[32] M. R. Dey, M. Patra, "Hand it Over Carefully: Security Breach during Handover in 5G-V2X," *2023 15th International Conference on COMmunication Systems & NETworkS (COMSNETS)*, Bangalore, India, 2023, pp. 360–363, doi: 10.1109/ COMSNETS56262.2023.10041381

[33] V. N. Sathi, C. S. R. Murthy, "Distributed Slice Mobility Attack: A Novel Targeted Attack Against Network Slices of 5G Networks," in *IEEE Networking Letters*, vol. 3, no. 1, pp. 5–9, March 2021, doi: 10.1109/LNET.2020.3044642

[34] S. Park, S. Kwon, Y. Park, D. Kim, I. You, "Session Management for Security Systems in 5G Standalone Network," in *IEEE Access*, vol. 10, pp. 73421–73436, 2022, doi: 10.1109/ACCESS.2022.3187053

[35] Y. Li, S. Liu, Z. Yan, R. H. Deng, "Secure 5G Positioning With Truth Discovery, Attack Detection, and Tracing," in *IEEE Internet of Things Journal*, vol. 9, no. 22, pp. 22220–22229, 15 Nov., 2022, doi: 10.1109/JIOT.2021.3088852

[36] V. N. Sathi, M. Srinivasan, P. K. Thiruvasagam, C. S. R. Murthy, "Novel Protocols to Mitigate Network Slice Topology Learning Attacks and Protect Privacy of Users' Service Access Behavior in Softwarized 5G Networks," in *IEEE Transactions on Dependable and Secure Computing*, vol. 18, no. 6, pp. 2888–2906, 1 Nov.–Dec. 2021, doi: 10.1109/TDSC.2020.2968885

[37] T. Saha, N. Aaraj, N. K. Jha, "Machine Learning Assisted Security Analysis of 5G-Network-Connected Systems," in *IEEE Transactions on Emerging Topics in Computing*, vol. 10, no. 4, pp. 2006–2024, 1 Oct.–Dec. 2022, doi: 10.1109/TETC. 2022.3147192

[38] B. Hussain, Q. Du, B. Sun, Z. Han, "Deep Learning-Based DDoS-Attack Detection for Cyber–Physical System Over 5G Network," in *IEEE Transactions on Industrial Informatics*, vol. 17, no. 2, pp. 860–870, Feb. 2021, doi: 10.1109/TII. 2020.2974520

[39] V. Adat Vasudevan, C. Tselios, I. Politis, "On Security Against Pollution Attacks in Network Coding Enabled 5G Networks," in *IEEE Access*, vol. 8, pp. 38416–38437, 2020, doi: 10.1109/ACCESS.2020.2975761

[40] M. A. Al-Shareeda, S. Manickam, "MSR-DoS: Modular Square Root-Based Scheme to Resist Denial of Service (DoS) Attacks in 5G-Enabled Vehicular Networks," in *IEEE Access*, vol. 10, pp. 120606–120615, 2022, doi: 10.1109/ACCESS.2022.3222488

Chapter 9

Enhancing electric vehicle charging efficiency in urban areas with 5G network integration and network attack mitigation

Chintureena Thingom
Alliance University, Bangaluru, India

Arijeet Chandra Sen
MSc (Independent Researcher), BITS Pilani, Pilani, India

Amit Jain
O P Jindal, University, Raigarh, India

Krishan Dutt
Lovely Professional University, Phagwara, India

9.1 INTRODUCTION

The evolution of human society has been accompanied by a substantial increase in energy consumption. Consumption of fossil fuels has steadily increased over the past century, leading to environmental problems such as the greenhouse effect and a deteriorating environment. In the past few years, electric vehicles (EVs) have become very common as a solution to these problems. EVs are better for the environment than standard locomotives with internal combustion engines because they use electricity as an extra source of power. This means that they emit less carbon dioxide and other harmful gases. Also, because fossil fuel supplies have dropped so quickly over the past few decades, EVs are now a must for future transportation [1].

Even though EVs have a lot of good things going for them, they can't fully replace traditional locomotives with internal combustion engines for a number of reasons. EVs need to be charged so they can go farther. However, due to current limitations in electric vehicle charging technology, the charging time for EVs is significantly lengthier than that for conventional vehicles. As a result, EV drivers are frequently subjected to lengthy charging wait periods, which negatively impact their travel experience. Moreover, the improper distribution of charging stations (CS) can have a negative impact on the charging efficacy of electric vehicles and the stability of charging services and security

DOI: 10.1201/9781003470281-9

against potential network attacks. Currently, the distribution of charging stations is largely dependent on urban policies and regional planning, resulting in situations in which EVs may need to spend more time searching for available charging stations in certain regions. These two issues, charging congestion and inefficient distribution of charging stations, are the primary impediments to the widespread adoption of electric vehicles. Consequently, resolving charging congestion becomes a crucial issue for the widespread adoption of EVs [1] for the successful implementation of the Internet of Things facilitated by 5G communication technologies.

The application of traditional computer queuing theory is essential to solving this research problem. Existing literature on EV charging concentrates primarily on the parking mode of EVs, in which they are parked at fixed locations such as charging stations or communities with charging facilities [2–4]. In this mode, optimizing charging scheduling, such as determining when and if to charge electric vehicles, is essential. Some investigations have used first-come, first-served (FCFS) to determine the charging order of electric vehicles [2]. However, the FCFS strategy lacks flexibility when dealing with EVs with uncertain charging energy and duration requirements. Thus, more adaptable charge scheduling strategies are required. For example, a charging scheduling strategy has been proposed that prioritizes the charging sequence of electric vehicles based on their power demand (the difference between the battery's maximum capacity and its current capacity) rather than their arrival time [5]. In addition, charging demand for a significant number of EVs in motion presents a different set of challenges than charging demand for EVs in parking mode. EVs in motion must locate charging stations in order to obtain charging services. As the charging demand of EVs varies dynamically in time and space, this can result in a large number of concurrent charging requests [6] and a decrease in the quality of experience (QoE) for EV users.

To alleviate charging congestion, it is essential to coordinate the charging needs of travelling EVs. A component of this coordination is the selection scheme for charging stations, which aims to redirect electric vehicles to stations with greater availability, thereby reducing wait periods. Consequently, precise knowledge of the charging station and EV status within the charging network becomes crucial. The extensive and delay-sensitive data processing capabilities of charging network communication, especially in the context of the Internet of Things, necessitate advancements in wireless communication and network technologies, such as the implementation of 5G technology [7–10]. Several studies have proposed charging station selection schemes based on criteria such as the shortest waiting time (i.e., the EV waits the least amount of time before a charging slot becomes available) and have demonstrated their superiority over selection schemes based on the shortest distance [9]. Due to the unpredictability of the charging service status at charging stations, however, these decision-making schemes still require refinement. Some studies have incorporated reservation information into the system, whereby EVs provide their own reservation information in order to increase the accuracy of predicting charging station availability and charging service times [11]. In addition, EVs typically have predetermined travel routes and cannot remain at charging stations for an extended period of time [12, 13]. Consequently, the limited parking time for EVs at charging stations adds another dimension to EV charging requirements [12, 13].

The goal of this paper is to solve the problems that are stopping electric vehicles from becoming more popular by suggesting ways to improve EV charging in cities. The goal of this paper is to look into how long charging times and charging congestion affect the way EV users move, with a focus on the importance of charging service, station choice, and scheduling strategies. It looks at the possible benefits of using a smart system to make EV charging even more efficient. The paper presents a preemptive charging scheduling strategy called charging priority (CP). CP puts EVs in order of priority based on how much charging they need and how much time they still have to park, which lets them charge faster. A reservation-based system for choosing charging stations is also suggested. This system takes reservation information into account to choose the charging station with the fastest trip time for EVs. The study shows how important it is for EVs to share information about their charging reservations so that charging station crowding can be predicted and charging resources can be used efficiently. Simulation-based validation using the urban traffic scene in Helsinki shows that the proposed methods work to reduce the average time it takes for EVs to charge and provide full charging services in a short amount of parking time. Overall, the goal is to improve EV charging, make it easier for people to move with EVs, and get more people to use EVs as a sustainable way to get around. The main contributions of this paper are as follows:

1. In order to maximize the quality of electric vehicle charging experiences within a constrained parking time, this study suggests a charging scheduling technique that takes charging priority into account. Furthermore, in order to address the issue of charging congestion in large-scale electric car applications, this research additionally suggests a charging station selection method based on CP charging scheduling strategy in the reservation mode. This research specifically proposes a CP charging scheduling approach that utilizes the charging priority as the preemption measurement for CP scheduling. The charging priority is determined by calculating the charging demand of electric vehicles and the remaining parking time.

2. The central global controller allows electric vehicles with higher charging priority to perform preemptive charging. The innovation of CP scheduling strategy lies in the fact that the previous literature research (such as literature [2, 3, 5]) did not consider the remaining parking time and does not provide preemptive charging service (such as literature [2, 12]). This paper introduces the CP charging scheduling strategy to ensure that as many electric vehicles as possible are fully charged before departure and security against potential network attacks.

3. By estimating the total charging journey time (combining the sum of the charging time spent at the charging station, the journey time to and

from the charging station to the destination), this paper proposes a charging station selection scheme based on reservation.

4. This scheme is used in estimating charging the CP charging scheduling strategy is applied to the charging time of the station, which can further improve the overall charging service performance of electric vehicles per unit time. Compared with the previous charging station selection scheme based on static historical data (such as literature [9, 11]), this paper proposes the charging station selection scheme of [10] considers the real-time charging service status of charging stations. In this scheme, electric vehicles need to send their own charging reservations. The reservation information is beneficial to the overall charging allocation for electric vehicles in the charging network, and significantly improves the electric vehicle the user's overall charging experience.

This paper presents innovative solutions to address EV charging challenges, ultimately promoting the widespread adoption of electric vehicles in urban settings while incorporating network attack mitigation measures for enhanced security and reliability.

9.2 RELATED WORK

Solving the problem of how to charge electric cars focuses on two main use cases. The first use case is to solve the charging scheduling problem for electric vehicles in parking mode. This is needed because a single charging station may not be able to meet the parallel charging needs of a large number of parked electric vehicles. In another application case, an electric car is going on the road, but it needs to find a charging station (charging station selection) because it doesn't have enough power.

9.2.1 Charging strategy

Even though a lot of studies (like literature [2, 3, 14]) have looked at the charging scheduling strategy of electric vehicles, these studies are based on the arrival time of electric vehicles, and the charging priority is set by the FIFS strategy, which limits the flexibility of charging services. So, some studies try to find ways to make the charging schedule better. Literature [11] suggested a rough model for optimizing the distributed charging scheduling strategy based on figuring out the waiting time. Literature [15] suggested a way to do things that is based on the idea of dynamic programming game this method uses a distributed system to plan the charging of electric vehicles. But none of the above research looked at how long it takes electric cars to fully charge. Literature [5] came up with two ways to schedule things: the earliest start time strategy (EST) and the earliest finish time strategy (EFT). In the EST strategy, the order in which electric vehicles are charged depends on the order in which they arrive. In the EFT strategy, the order in which electric vehicles are charged depends on the order in which they are charged the earliest. Note that the above research didn't look at how long electric cars can stay parked for the most part. Literature [16] introduced the length of time a car is parked as a charging optimization index and suggested a charging optimization strategy based on the length of time a car is parked so that more electric cars can be fully charged in a short amount of time. The waiting time is a simulation of how long it takes to charge an electric car in real life. At the same time, to take into account how the type of electric vehicle affects things, literature [17] optimized the scheduling problem of multi-model electric cars in public transportation. It took into account how long it takes to charge different models and how much energy they use when scheduling their charging. Based on this, literature [13] suggested a scheduling strategy for electric vehicles with different charging priorities, in which electric vehicles with higher charging priorities (based on the type of vehicle) can charge first.

9.2.2 Charging options

By comparing two different ways to choose a charging station based on the shortest distance and the shortest waiting time, literature [18] showed that choosing the charging station with the shortest waiting time worked better in urban settings. At the same time, the simulation of how charging stations are chosen in this situation shows that the scheme for choosing charging stations based on the expected wait time is the best way to get the best global results for charging electric vehicles. In order to predict the charging service status of charging stations after a certain amount of time more accurately, [19] combined the expected waiting time and charging intention. The charging intention took into account the past charging station preferences of electric vehicles and where they were at the time. So that charging stations don't get too crowded, this piece [20] modelled the choice of charging stations as a multi-objective optimization problem and took the charging time, travel time, and charging cost into account when choosing the best charging station. Part of the work [21, 22] was to include the cost of charging in the measurement index and set prices based on how busy the charging station was. When there are a lot of cars at a charging point, the price will go up. These pricing tactics can keep electric cars from filling up charging stations that are already busy and help charging stations make the most money possible. Literature [23] looked at energy demand response, which tries to keep the supply and demand of energy in balance. But balancing supply and demand can't ensure that the charging service will be good. By introducing electric car charging prediction [24], the overall charging performance can be made sure. Literature [25] suggested a navigation system that would allow electric vehicle users to tell other electric vehicle users about their charging plans (which charging station they want to use, which route they want to take, etc.). This would improve the accuracy of charging station state estimations. Also, adding information about charging reservations can help the central global controller better predict the state of electric cars (such as how much energy they need and where they are right now) and choose the best charging stations. This study [11] mimicked how electric cars are charged on the highway and introduced information on how to reserve charging. In addition, literature [26] simulated how charging and reservations work in urban settings. The charging station selection method above, which is based on charging reservation information, improves the overall charging performance of electric vehicles by a large amount (it shortens the average amount of time electric vehicles have to wait to charge, which makes charging less crowded).

9.3 SYSTEM MODEL

9.3.1 Participants in the EV charging network

Figure 9.1 shows the participants in the charging network.

Electric vehicle (EV): The electric vehicle contains wireless communication equipment for charging request communication with the central global controller. When the electric vehicle is driving, the ratio of the current battery power to the battery power is lower than the preset charging state (Status of Charge, SOC) threshold, the electric vehicle will send a charging request to the central global controller to select a charging station for charging.

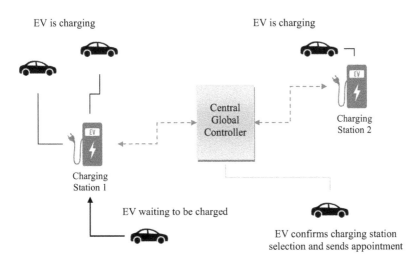

Figure 9.1 Participant in the charging network.

Charging station (CS): The charging station is fixedly deployed in various areas of the city, and communicates with the central global controller to provide its charging service status. Among them, the charging station is equipped with multiple charging slots to support parallel charging.

Central global controller (GC): The central global controller is able to communicate with EVs and charging stations simultaneously (via 5G communication network). The central global controller is based on aggregated information from charging stations and EVs (charging service status from charging stations information and charging request information from EVs), manage charging station selection decisions for EVs and charging scheduling decisions at charging stations.

9.3.2 Priority-based charging scheduling strategy

The schematic diagram of CP charging priority scheduling strategy is shown in Figure 9.2.

Due to the uncertainty of charging energy and duration requirements of electric vehicles, some electric vehicles with high charging priority have preemptive charging requirements. In order to optimize the above problems, this paper proposes the CP strategy as the underlying charging scheduling strategy (when to charge electric vehicles). The CP charging scheduling strategy takes into account the parking duration and charging energy demand of electric vehicles, and allows electric vehicles with higher "charging priority" to preemptively charge. Here, the charging priority is determined by the estimated charging time of electric vehicles minus the electric the difference calculated

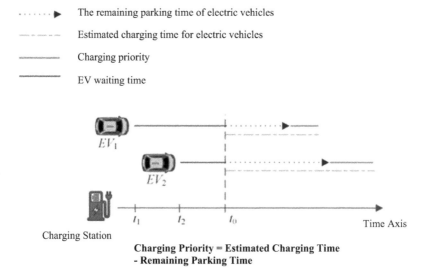

Figure 9.2 CP charging priority scheduling strategy.

from the remaining parking time of the car is given. As an index to determine the charging sequence between different electric vehicles, the charging priority V_{ev} can be expressed as:

$$V_{ev} = T_{ev}^{cha} - \left(T_{ev}^{arr} + D_{ev} - T_{ev}^{sta}\right) \tag{9.1}$$

Among them, T_{ev}^{arr} indicates the moment when the electric vehicle arrives at the charging station; T_{ev}^{cha} indicates the charging time; T_{ev}^{sta} is the waiting time for the electric vehicle to arrive at the charging station until the charging slot is available, and the calculation formula is $\left(T_{cur} - T_{ev}^{arr}\right)$; $\left(T_{ev}^{arr} + D_{ev} - T_{ev}^{sta}\right)$ refers to the remaining parking time of electric vehicles.

In Figure 9.2, when the charging slot at the charging station is available at t_0, both EV_1 and EV_2 have arrived and waiting at the charging station. Here, t_1 and t_2 refer to the arrival time of EV_1 and EV_2 respectively. Since EV_1 arrives earlier than EV_2 and the upper limit of the parking time is a fixed value, it can be concluded that the remaining parking time of EV1 is relatively short.

However, by comparing the charging demands of EV_1 and EV_2, it is found that the estimated charging time of EV_2 is much longer than that of EV_1. At this time, although the arrival time of EV_2 is later than that of EV_1, according to the calculation of the charging priority formula, the charging priority of EV_2 (Figure 9.2 the red line) is higher. Therefore, EV_2 can preemptively obtain the charging service, while EV_1 will charge when the latter charging slot is available. At this time, the electric vehicle can achieve the best overall charging effect by scheduling charging through the CP strategy.

If electric cars need to charge more often and have less time left to park, the CP charging scheduling approach will make it more likely that electric cars can get charging services. At the same time, the CP strategy can fix the problem of electric cars that aren't fully charged. It's important to note that advance charging only plans the charging order for electric vehicles that haven't started charging yet. It won't stop the service for electric vehicles that are already charging and security against potential network attacks.

9.3.3 Algorithm assumption

In this paper, the charging stations are spread out around the city, and a central global controller handles the charging service for electric vehicles around the world. The car-mounted system of electric vehicles can talk to the central global controller through wireless devices (like 5G/5G networks) that are built into the vehicle. Charging station decision is asked of and answered by the central global controller. This paper uses a centralized communication system. The central global controller handles charging requests centrally and makes sure that charging services in the cloud are spread out in the best way possible. When the electric car is in motion and its SOC is below the set level, it sends a request to charge to the central global controller. The electric vehicle's charging request is processed by the central global manager, which starts to sort the charging stations and predicts how long the charging trip will take (mainly based on how long it takes to charge).So that more electric cars can be fully charged (full charge), the central global controller looks at both the charging demand of electric cars and the charging service state of charging stations. The CP scheduling strategy is one of them. It lets electric cars with a high charging priority be charged first. Service based on CP scheduling, the central global controller estimates how long it will take the electric car to charge at each charging station and then chooses the station where the total charging journey will end the earliest.

9.3.4 Problem description

This section improves the charge optimization formula by defining the symbols and objective functions in order to make more efficient use of charging station resources and reduce charging congestion. Following is a list of symbols that can be used to help frame the issue.

(1) $\delta_{l_{CS}}$: the number (times) of fully charged electric vehicles at a single charging station.
(2) vl_{CS}: The average total charging trip time of fully charged electric vehicles at a single charging station.
(3) N_{CS}: The number of charging stations in the charging station queue.
(4) CS: Total travel time of electric vehicles fully charged at all charging stations.
(5) X: The number (times) of electric vehicles fully charged at all charging stations.

The objective function is as follows:

$$Maximize\ X = \sum_{l_{CS} \in N_{CS}} \delta_{l_{CS}} \tag{9.2}$$

$$Minimize\ M = \sum_{l_{CS} \in N_{CS}} \delta_{CS} \times vl_{CS} \tag{9.3}$$

When the maximum allowed parking time has been reached, for example, the electric car must leave the charging station. To maximize the number of times all electric vehicles are fully charged, as specified by the objective function (2), it is important to optimize the charging scheduling within the constrained parking period. As more and more EVs are charged, the charging network will benefit from an increase in the $\delta_{l_{CS}}$ of each charging station. The objective function (3) aims to minimize the total charging trip time of all fully charged EVs in the network, so as $\delta_{l_{CS}}$ in the objective function (2), vl_{CS} needs to decrease. νl_{CS} and $\delta_{/CS}$ are related to N_{CS}, and a larger NN_{CS} will lead to a smaller νl_{CS}, because electric vehicles can be distributed in more charging stations for charging services. However, since N_{CS} (referring to the total number of charging stations) is immutable, so νl_{CS} can only be reduced by evenly distributing EV charging services among charging stations;

9.4 TECHNICAL DESCRIPTION

The central global controller determines which charging station is optimal based on the total charging time of the electric vehicle's travel through all charging stations. The following procedures will help you determine when the reserved electric car EV_r will be fully charged with reference to Figure 9.3. Cost of one full charge of time.

* The first step is for the central global controller to estimate the available moment of the charging slot by monitoring the charging state at each individual charging location.
* The subsequent procedure involves forecasting the charging timetable for the EV_r upon its arrival at the charging station, utilizing the CP charging scheduling strategy. This is accomplished by consolidating the results obtained in the first step, which include the electric vehicle queue currently stationed at the charging station, as well as the queue of electric vehicles in transit that have been reserved for charging.
* Third, the central global controller uses the scheduling output data to determine the charging station's available charging time.
* Compute the anticipated end time of the complete charging trip by adding the available charging time acquired in step 3 and the journey time of EV_r arriving at and leaving the charging station.

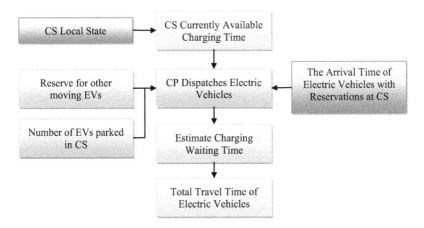

Figure 9.3 Charging station selection logic flow chart.

9.4.1 Charging station charging service current status

The calculation of the current charging service queuing status of the charging station is shown in Algorithm 1.

ALGORITHM 1   CALCULATION OF THE CURRENT CHARGING SERVICE QUEUE STATUS OF THE CHARGING STATION

Input: NC
Output: LIST

1. if no EV is charging then

2. add T_{cur} into LIST with δ times (number of charge slots)

3. return LIST

4. end if

5. for $(n=1; n \leq N_c; n++)$ do

6. if $\left(\left(T_{cur} - T_{ev(n)}^{arr} + \dfrac{E_{ev(n)}^{max} - E_{ev(n)}^{cur}}{\beta} \right) \leq \left(T_{ev(n)}^{arr} + D_{ev(n)} \right) \right)$ then

7. LIST.ADD $\left(\left(\dfrac{E_{ev(n)}^{max} - E_{ev(n)}^{cur}}{\beta} \right) + T_{cur} \right)$

8. else

9. LIST.ADD $\left(T_{ev(n)}^{arr} + D_{ev(n)} \right)$

10. end if

11. end for

12. if $(N_c < \delta)$ then

13. for$(m = 1; m \leq (\delta - N_c); m + +)$ do

14. LIST.ADD (T_{cur})

15. end for

16. end if

17. Sort LIST in ascending order

18. return LIST

There are multiple charging slots at the charging station to charge multiple electric vehicles at the same time, so the electric vehicles currently being charged are represented as N_C queues. The current moment in the network is represented by T_{cur}. If no electric vehicles are currently parked at the charging station Charging, T_{cur} will be added to LIST(the list of available charging times for charging slots), and will be added to LISTδ (representing the number of charging slots) times in total. This indicates that the charging station is available at the current moment, and all charging slots are available the charging time is T_{cur}, as shown in the second line of Algorithm 1. Lines 5–11 of Algorithm 1 show the charging process of EV$_n$ (electric vehicles in queue N_C), and line 6 compares whether EV$_n$ can meet the upper limit of parking time. Fully charged within, that is, comparing $D_{ev(n)}$ and the full charging time $\left(\dfrac{E_{ev(n)}^{max} - E_{ev(n)}^{cur}}{\beta} \right)$. If EV$_n$ can be fully charged before leaving, it is expressed as

$$\left(\left(T_{cur} - T_{ev(n)}^{arr} + \frac{E_{ev(n)}^{max} - E_{ev(n)}^{cur}}{\beta} \right) \leq \left(T_{ev(n)}^{arr} + D_{ev(n)} \right) \right),$$ at this time it can leave at the

end of full charging, and the charging completion time $\left(\dfrac{E_{ev(n)}^{max} - E_{ev(n)}^{cur}}{\beta} \right)$ will be

added to the LIST; if EV$_n$ is not fully charged, the charging completion time (departure time) will be replaced by $\left(T_{ev(n)}^{arr} + D_{ev(n)} \right)$, indicating that EV$_n$ must be within the upper limit of the allowable parking time Arrive and leave.

9.5 EXPERIMENTAL VERIFICATION

This paper uses the Opportunistic Network Environment (Opportunistic Network Environment, ONE) [27–29] to build the simulation scene of the urban charging network. A 4500 × 3400 m² regional scene is built through ONE simulation. The charging network in the urban area the electric vehicle in the simulation is configured with Coda Automotive [30], and its maximum battery capacity is 33.8 kWh, the maximum driving distance is 193 km, and the average energy consumption is 0.1751/(kWh/km). At the beginning of the simulation, the batteries of all electric vehicles are at full capacity.

In order to distinguish different electric vehicles and enrich the simulation environment, the simulation divides electric vehicles into three categories, corresponding to three SOC thresholds of 30%, 40%, and 50%. The electric vehicles start with a random initial position in the scene, and the moving speed is at the speed fluctuates between 30km/h and 50 km/h. Among them, the speed of the electric vehicle will change on each route to reflect the influence of different traffic conditions. In addition, each electric vehicle will randomly choose the end point of its journey. Whenever it reaches the end point, the electric vehicle will randomly select a new journey end point again until its SOC is lower than the preset threshold.

The results of the change of parking duration are shown in Figure 9.4. In the first set of simulations, the number of electric vehicles is set as a constant value. Adjust the parking duration to observe its impact on different

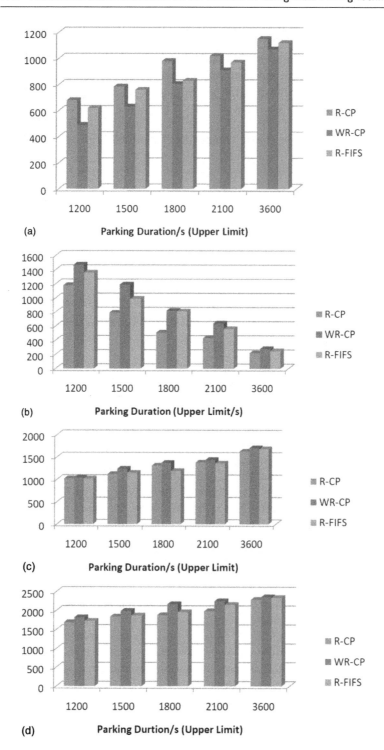

Figure 9.4 (a) Full charge times, (b) not fully charged, (c) average charging waiting time, (d) average charging trip time.

charging management schemes. The parking duration is set to 1200s, 1500s, 1800s, 2100s, and 3600s respectively. In order to reflect the impact of parking time, in the simulation setting, the charging slot will disconnect its charging service and force the electric vehicle to leave when the electric vehicle reaches the parking limit.

In the case of extended parking time, all three charging management schemes promote more EVs to be fully charged, as shown in Figure 9.4. The EACT estimation is more accurate, and it also enables the central global controller to allocate electric vehicles with charging requests to charging stations with lower congestion when the central global controller selects charging stations, which improves the utilization rate of global charging stations. In addition, R-CP The scheme considers the priority of electric vehicle charging and allows preemptive charging, which effectively prevents some electric vehicles from leaving the charging station without being fully charged, especially avoids the long waiting time of some electric vehicles without receiving any charging service This also means that thanks to the CP charging scheduling strategy, compared with the R-FIFS scheme, R-CP can fully charge more EVs.

In Figure 9.4(b), the R-CP scheme clearly outperforms the R-FIFS and WR-CP schemes in terms of results. When parking time is the primary constraint condition (a short parking period), the charging station will experience charging congestion. Preemptive charging is provided by electric vehicles with charging priority, which can significantly improve total charging performance. Figure 9.4(b) also demonstrates the significance of charging scheduling schemes. Figure 9.4(c) shows that the WR-CP scheme has the longest average waiting time of the three schemes, regardless of whether the parking time is shortened or extended. Simultaneously, the average charging waiting time of the R-CP scheme and the R-FIFS scheme is similar, because both introduce charging reservation information, allowing the central global controller to more accurately predict the potential charging state of the charging station and distribute charging demand evenly congestion. The comparison of the R-CP and R-FIFS schemes demonstrates that the R-CP CP strategy, as shown in Figure 9.4(a), can fully charge more electric vehicles while keeping the charging waiting time to a minimum. When the average charging time is examined in Figure 9.4(d), it is clear that R-CP and R-FIFS continue to emphasize the necessity of introducing reservation information. When the charging station and driving time from the charging station to the destination are both 3600 seconds, the impact on the overall charging travel time is reduced, but the influence on charging scheduling is enhanced. As a result, the advantages of the CP charging scheduling method are represented in how to plan the charging scheduling within the parking period at this moment. At 3600s, both R-CP and WR-CP achieved a shorter average charging trip duration than R-FIFS.

9.5.1 Consequences under change in the number of electric vehicles

Figure 9.5 depicts the outcomes of varying the quantity of EVs. In the second set of simulations, we restrict electric vehicles to charge for no more than

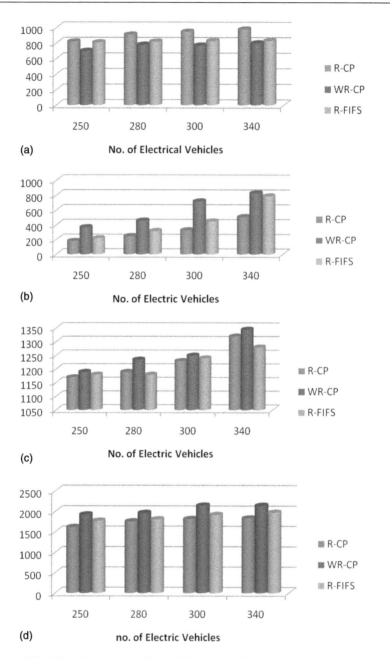

Figure 9.5 (a) Full charged time, (b) not fully charged, (c) average charging waiting time, and (d) average charging trip time.

1800 seconds at a time. By varying the amount of EVs, we can see the results of three distinct charging management strategies. Figure 9.5(a) demonstrates that compared to the other two methods, the R-CP system is superior in terms of obtaining fully charged EVs in the shortest amount of time. To make sure enough EVs can get fully charged even in congested charging scenarios, the R-CP scheme takes into consideration priorities charging and allows preemptive charging.

Figure 9.5(b)'s results also show the benefits of the R-CP method. It's important to note that when there are 330 electric cars, the effects of the R-CP and R-FIFS schemes are very different. This is because there are more electric cars on the road. It will lead to more charging service congestion, which means that a lot of electric cars will be parked at charging stations but won't be able to start charging. At this point, electric cars can be charged while parked, which makes the charging scheduling approach more important. CP's plan for charging takes the electric vehicle into account. When there are a lot of people charging, the importance of charging can be used to better plan the order of charging so that people can charge ahead of time. As shown in Figures 9.5(c) and (d), as the number of electric vehicles goes up, so does the number of cars waiting to charge. As a result, both the average time to charge and the average time to wait to charge go up. The average wait time for the R-CP and R-FIFS methods is one of them. The duration is shorter than that of the WR-CP scheme (see Figure 9.5(c)), because the WR-CP scheme doesn't take the charging reservation information of the electric vehicle into account when calculating EACT. This means that it can't accurately predict the charging state of the charging station, which could lead to the central global controller. Give the electric cars that start the request to charge to the stations that are already full. Figure 9.5(d) shows that because Algorithm 1 takes driving time and charging time into account, the R-CP scheme promises that the average journey of electric cars will be the shortest of the three schemes.

9.6 CONCLUSION

The goal of this study is to improve the charging experience for consumers of electric cars by presenting a charging scheduling technique based on CP. This approach takes into account the obstacle that the congestion of charging services poses to the widespread adoption of electric vehicles. The suggested approach is predicated on ranking the order of importance for electric vehicle charging, accounting for the duration of the vehicle's parking as well as its charging requirements. It efficiently arranges electric cars' charging priorities when they are in park mode, enabling proactive charging and offering defence against possible network intrusions. In order to facilitate the widespread integration of electric vehicles in urban settings, this study presents innovative approaches to address the challenges related to EV charging. Furthermore, it integrates methods to lessen network intrusions, improving the security and stability of EV charging networks. This paper presents a charging station selection technique based on the CP scheduling strategy framework. This strategy, which primarily aims to maximize travel time, makes use of reservation data to decrease the amount of time that electric vehicles need to be charged. In conclusion, this study offers an integrated method that combines an algorithm for choosing charging stations and a charge scheduling strategy into a charging management scheme that is dependent on reservation data and charging priority. Improving the entire charging service experience is the goal. The goal is to build and simulate an environment for a charging network using the road network structure. The results indicate that the charge management strategy put forward in this study successfully raises the average waiting time for charging while decreasing the average length of charging trips. It also keeps charging services at a high completion rate, which essentially stops electric vehicles from leaving the charging station before they are fully charged.

REFERENCES

[1] N. Odkhuu, M. A. Ahmed and Y. -C. Kim, "Priority Determination Based on Fuzzy Logic for Charging Electric Vehicles," *2019 Eleventh International Conference on Ubiquitous and Future Networks (ICUFN)*, Zagreb, Croatia, 2019, pp. 295–299, doi: 10.1109/ICUFN.2019.8806184

[2] S. B. Fahmy, S. E. Guirguis, O. M. Shehata and E. I. Morgan, "Investigation of an Optimal Charging/Discharging Policy for Electric Vehicles Parking Station in a Smart Grid Environment," *2020 8th International Conference on Control, Mechatronics and Automation (ICCMA)*, Moscow, Russia, 2020, pp. 138–143, doi: 10.1109/ICCMA51325.2020.9301484

[3] Y. Zheng and L. Jian, "Smart Charging Algorithm of Electric Vehicles Considering Dynamic Charging Priority," *2016 IEEE International Conference on Information and Automation (ICIA)*, Ningbo, China, 2016, pp. 555–560, doi: 10.1109/ICInfA.2016.7831884

[4] M. N. B. Anwar, R. Ruby, Y. Cheng and J. Pan, "Time-of-Use-Aware Priority-Based Multi-Mode Online Charging Scheme for EV Charging Stations," *2022 IEEE International Conference on Communications, Control, and Computing Technologies for Smart Grids (SmartGridComm)*, Singapore, Singapore, 2022, pp. 166–171, doi: 10.1109/SmartGridComm52983.2022.9961019

[5] Y. Ota, H. Taniguchi, T. Nakajima, K. M. Liyanage, J. Baba and A. Yokoyama, "Autonomous Distributed V2G (Vehicle-to-Grid) Satisfying Scheduled Charging," in *IEEE Transactions on Smart Grid*, vol. 3, no. 1, pp. 559–564, March 2012, doi: 10.1109/TSG.2011.2167993

[6] E. Veldman and R. A. Verzijlbergh, "Distribution Grid Impacts of Smart Electric Vehicle Charging From Different Perspectives," in *IEEE Transactions on Smart Grid*, vol. 6, no. 1, pp. 333–342, Jan. 2015, doi: 10.1109/TSG.2014.2355494

[7] E. Veldman and R. A. Verzijlbergh, "Distribution Grid Impacts of Smart Electric Vehicle Charging From Different Perspectives," in *IEEE Transactions on Smart Grid*, vol. 6, no. 1, pp. 333–342, Jan. 2015, doi: 10.1109/TSG.2014.2355494

[8] G. Binetti, A. Davoudi, D. Naso, B. Turchiano and F. L. Lewis, "Scalable Real-Time Electric Vehicles Charging With Discrete Charging Rates," in *IEEE Transactions on Smart Grid*, vol. 6, no. 5, pp. 2211–2220, Sept. 2015, doi: 10.1109/TSG.2015.2396772

[9] S. -A. Amamra and J. Marco, "Vehicle-to-Grid Aggregator to Support Power Grid and Reduce Electric Vehicle Charging Cost," in *IEEE Access*, vol. 7, pp. 178528–178538, 2019, doi: 10.1109/ACCESS.2019.2958664

[10] C. B. Saner, A. Trivedi and D. Srinivasan, "A Cooperative Hierarchical Multi-Agent System for EV Charging Scheduling in Presence of Multiple Charging Stations," in *IEEE Transactions on Smart Grid*, vol. 13, no. 3, pp. 2218–2233, May 2022, doi: 10.1109/TSG.2022.3140927

[11] A. S. Al-Ogaili et al., "Review on Scheduling, Clustering, and Forecasting Strategies for Controlling Electric Vehicle Charging: Challenges and Recommendations," in *IEEE Access*, vol. 7, pp. 128353–128371, 2019, doi: 10.1109/ACCESS.2019.2939595

[12] Z. Zhang, Z. Chen, Q. Xing, Z. Ji and X. Huang, "Comprehensive Optimal Scheduling Strategy of Multi-Element Charging Station for Bounded Rational Users," in *IEEE Access*, vol. 9, pp. 9442–9452, 2021, doi: 10.1109/ACCESS.2021.3049565

[13] Y. Cao, H. Wang, D. Li and G. Zhang, "Smart Online Charging Algorithm for Electric Vehicles via Customized Actor–Critic Learning," in *IEEE Internet of Things Journal*, vol. 9, no. 1, pp. 684–694, 1 Jan., 2022, doi: 10.1109/JIOT.2021.3084923

[14] E. ElGhanam, H. Sharf, Y. Odeh, M. S. Hassan and A. H. Osman, "On the Coordination of Charging Demand of Electric Vehicles in a Network of Dynamic Wireless Charging Systems," in *IEEE Access*, vol. 10, pp. 62879–62892, 2022, doi: 10.1109/ACCESS.2022.3182700

[15] L. Yao, W. H. Lim and T. S. Tsai, "A Real-Time Charging Scheme for Demand Response in Electric Vehicle Parking Station," in *IEEE Transactions on Smart Grid*, vol. 8, no. 1, pp. 52–62, Jan. 2017, doi: 10.1109/TSG.2016.2582749

[16] A. Mehrabi, H. S. V. S. K. Nunna, A. Dadlani, S. Moon and K. Kim, "Decentralized Greedy-Based Algorithm for Smart Energy Management in Plug-in Electric Vehicle Energy Distribution Systems," in *IEEE Access*, vol. 8, pp. 75666–75681, 2020, doi: 10.1109/ACCESS.2020.2987970

[17] N. I. Nimalsiri, C. P. Mediwaththe, E. L. Ratnam, M. Shaw, D. B. Smith and S. K. Halgamuge, "A Survey of Algorithms for Distributed Charging Control of Electric Vehicles in Smart Grid," in *IEEE Transactions on Intelligent Transportation Systems*, vol. 21, no. 11, pp. 4497–4515, Nov. 2020, doi: 10.1109/TITS.2019.2943620

[18] Z. Liu, Q. Wu, S. Huang, L. Wang, M. Shahidehpour and Y. Xue, "Optimal Day-Ahead Charging Scheduling of Electric Vehicles Through an Aggregative Game Model," in *IEEE Transactions on Smart Grid*, vol. 9, no. 5, pp. 5173–5184, Sept. 2018, doi: 10.1109/TSG.2017.2682340

[19] J. Liu, H. Guo, J. Xiong, N. Kato, J. Zhang and Y. Zhang, "Smart and Resilient EV Charging in SDN-Enhanced Vehicular Edge Computing Networks," in *IEEE Journal on Selected Areas in Communications*, vol. 38, no. 1, pp. 217–228, Jan. 2020, doi: 10.1109/JSAC.2019.2951966

[20] G. Wenzel, M. Negrete-Pincetic, D. E. Olivares, J. MacDonald and D. S. Callaway, "Real-Time Charging Strategies for an Electric Vehicle Aggregator to Provide

Ancillary Services," in *IEEE Transactions on Smart Grid*, vol. 9, no. 5, pp. 5141–5151, Sept. 2018, doi: 10.1109/TSG.2017.2681961

[21] S. Yoon and E. Hwang, "Load Guided Signal-Based Two-Stage Charging Coordination of Plug-In Electric Vehicles for Smart Buildings," in *IEEE Access*, vol. 7, pp. 144548–144560, 2019, doi: 10.1109/ACCESS.2019.2945483

[22] F. Berthold, A. Ravey, B. Blunier, D. Bouquain, S. Williamson and A. Miraoui, "Design and Development of a Smart Control Strategy for Plug-In Hybrid Vehicles Including Vehicle-to-Home Functionality," in *IEEE Transactions on Transportation Electrification*, vol. 1, no. 2, pp. 168–177, Aug. 2015, doi: 10.1109/TTE.2015.2426508

[23] L. Yan, X. Chen, J. Zhou, Y. Chen and J. Wen, "Deep Reinforcement Learning for Continuous Electric Vehicles Charging Control With Dynamic User Behaviors," in *IEEE Transactions on Smart Grid*, vol. 12, no. 6, pp. 5124–5134, Nov. 2021, doi: 10.1109/TSG.2021.3098298

[24] H. Li, Z. Wan and H. He, "Constrained EV Charging Scheduling Based on Safe Deep Reinforcement Learning," in *IEEE Transactions on Smart Grid*, vol. 11, no. 3, pp. 2427–2439, May 2020, doi: 10.1109/TSG.2019.2955437

[25] S.J. Sultanuddin, R. Vibin, A. Rajesh Kumar, Nihar Ranjan Behera, M. Jahir Pasha, K.K. Baseer, "Development of Improved Reinforcement Learning Smart Charging Strategy for Electric Vehicle Fleet," in *Journal of Energy Storage*, vol. 64, p. 106987, 2023, ISSN 2352-152X.

[26] Keonwoo Park and Ilkyeong Moon, "Multi-Agent Deep Reinforcement Learning Approach for EV Charging Scheduling in a Smart Grid," in *Applied Energy*, vol. 328, p. 120111, 2022, ISSN 0306-2619.

[27] Sarthak Mohanty, Subhasis Panda, Shubhranshu Mohan Parida, Pravat Kumar Rout, Binod Kumar Sahu, Mohit Bajaj, Hossam M. Zawbaa, Nallapaneni Manoj Kumar, and Salah Kamel, "Demand Side Management of Electric Vehicles in Smart Grids: A Survey on Strategies, Challenges, Modeling, and Optimization," in *Energy Reports*, vol. 8, pp. 12466–12490, 2022, ISSN 2352-4847.

[28] Omid Sadeghian, Arman Oshnoei, Behnam Mohammadi-Ivatloo, Vahid Vahidinasab, and Amjad Anvari-Moghaddam, "A Comprehensive Review on Electric Vehicles Smart Charging: Solutions, Strategies, Technologies, and Challenges," in *Journal of Energy Storage*, vol. 54, p. 105241, 2022, ISSN 2352-152X.

[29] Muhammad Shahid Mastoi, Shengxian Zhuang, Hafiz Mudassir Munir, Malik Haris, Mannan Hassan, Mohammed Alqarni, and Basem Alamri, "A Study of Charging-Dispatch Strategies and Vehicle-to-Grid Technologies for Electric Vehicles in Distribution Networks," in *Energy Reports*, vol. 9, pp. 1777–1806, 2023, ISSN 2352-4847.

[30] A. Kapoor, V. S. Patel, A. Sharma and A. Mohapatra, "Centralized and Decentralized Pricing Strategies for Optimal Scheduling of Electric Vehicles," in *IEEE Transactions on Smart Grid*, vol. 13, no. 3, pp. 2234–2244, May 2022, doi: 10.1109/TSG.2022.3141261

Chapter 10

Next-generation intrusion detection system for 5G networks with enhanced security using updated datasets

Komal Shyamsundar Jakotiya, Vishal Shirsath, and Raj Gaurav Mishra

School of Engineering, ADYPU, Pune India

10.1 INTRODUCTION

The proliferation of connected devices and the advent of fifth generation (5G) wireless networks have ushered in a new era of technological innovation, enabling seamless communication, ultra-low latency, and unparalleled data speeds. The fusion of these two domains has given rise to the Internet of Things (IoT) in the 5G landscape, where a multitude of devices are interconnected, sharing data and insights to streamline processes and enhance user experiences. However, this integration of IoT and 5G networks also introduces a host of complex security challenges that demand careful analysis and mitigation.

The security concerns surrounding 5G-connected IoT systems are multifaceted. The sheer volume and diversity of connected devices, coupled with the unique characteristics of 5G networks such as network slicing and massive machine-type communication, create a dynamic and heterogeneous environment that requires a new level of security awareness. The potential consequences of security breaches in such an ecosystem can be dire, ranging from compromised user privacy to disruptions in critical infrastructure as shown in in Figure 10.1.

To address these challenges, researchers and practitioners turn to datasets specifically crafted to emulate real-world scenarios, providing a platform for analyzing security vulnerabilities and devising effective defensive strategies. The CIC-IOT 2023 dataset stands as a prime example of such a resource, designed to capture the intricacies of IoT device interactions within a 5G network. This dataset encompasses a wide array of IoT device types, communication protocols, and network behaviors, offering a comprehensive foundation for exploring security concerns unique to 5G-connected IoT systems.

DOI: 10.1201/9781003470281-10

183

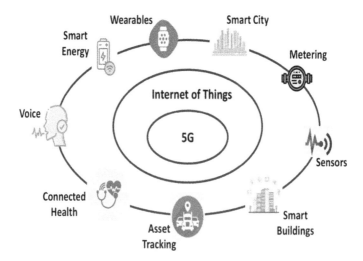

Figure 10.1 Applications of IOT using 5G.

In this context, the present study undertakes a detailed analysis of the CIC-IOT 2023 dataset, aiming to uncover patterns of abnormal behavior, identify potential attack vectors, and shed light on vulnerabilities that might be exploited by malicious actors within a 5G IoT network. By employing machine learning algorithms, statistical techniques, and anomaly detection methods, this research seeks to contribute to the body of knowledge surrounding 5G network security.

The subsequent sections of this analysis will delve into the dataset's structure, characteristics, and composition, followed by a detailed exploration of the methodologies employed to extract meaningful insights. Additionally, the study will elucidate the relevance of the findings in the broader context of 5G network security and propose recommendations for enhancing the resilience of IoT systems within this evolving landscape. Through this analysis, we endeavor to advance the understanding of security challenges in 5G-connected IoT environments and facilitate the development of strategies that safeguard the integrity and confidentiality of these systems.

10.2 5G NETWORK SECURITY ARCHITECTURE

With its significantly enhanced speed, capacity, and low latency, 5G networks will play a pivotal role in enabling innovations like autonomous vehicles, the Internet of Things, augmented reality (AR), and much more. However, as the capabilities of 5G networks expand, so do the potential threats to security. To counteract these threats, a robust 5G network security architecture is crucial. This article explores the key components and strategies that constitute a secure 5G network.

10.3 NETWORK SLICING

One of the fundamental features of 5G security architecture is network slicing. Network slicing enables the creation of isolated virtual networks on a single physical infrastructure, allowing different services and applications to run securely and independently. Each network slice can have its unique security policies and configurations, ensuring that resources are allocated optimally while maintaining the highest level of security.

10.4 AUTHENTICATION AND IDENTITY MANAGEMENT

In a 5G network, robust authentication and identity management mechanisms are essential. Techniques like multifactor authentication, digital certificates, and biometrics are employed to strengthen identity verification, protecting against unauthorized access and identity theft.

10.5 ENCRYPTION

Encryption is a cornerstone of 5G network security. End-to-end encryption secures data transmission between devices and applications, preventing eavesdropping and data interception. Advanced encryption algorithms and protocols are employed to protect sensitive information, both in transit and at rest.

10.6 SECURITY AT THE EDGE

5G's low latency capabilities enable edge computing, where data processing occurs closer to the source of data. While this offers significant performance benefits, it also presents new security challenges. A robust security framework at the edge is essential to protect against potential threats and vulnerabilities, ensuring the integrity and confidentiality of data processed at the edge.

10.7 SECURITY ORCHESTRATION

Security orchestration involves the coordination of various security measures and responses to potential threats in real time. Machine learning and artificial intelligence (AI) are leveraged to detect and respond to security incidents promptly. Automated security orchestration streamlines threat mitigation, reducing the impact of cyberattacks and enhancing network resilience.

10.8 IOT SECURITY

5G networks will facilitate the proliferation of IoT devices, each of which presents a potential security risk if not adequately protected. To secure the IoT ecosystem within 5G networks, robust device authentication, secure boot processes, and over-the-air (OTA) updates are implemented to ensure the integrity and security of IoT devices and their data.

10.9 CONTINUOUS MONITORING AND THREAT INTELLIGENCE

5G networks require continuous monitoring and threat intelligence gathering to stay ahead of emerging threats. Security operations centers (SOCs) employ advanced analytics and machine learning to detect anomalies and potential security breaches. Access to real-time threat intelligence feeds helps network operators respond proactively to new threats.

The deployment of 5G networks represents a remarkable leap in connectivity and technological advancement. However, it also brings forth an array of security challenges. A robust 5G network security architecture is essential to mitigate these challenges and ensure the confidentiality, integrity, and availability of data and services. By implementing network slicing, robust authentication, encryption, edge security, security orchestration, IoT security, NFV/ SDN, and continuous monitoring, 5G network operators can build a secure foundation for the future of communication and innovation.

10.10 RELATED WORK

IoT security datasets have been the subject of several published contributions during the last few years. In actuality, data has been generated with various objectives and utilizing various techniques and resources. We evaluate a number of approaches found in the literature and contrast them with the latest CICIoT2023, in order to give clear insight of the features of existing datasets.

In Ref. [1], the authors introduce N-BaioT (2018), an innovative network-based dataset tailored for the detection of botnet attacks within the IoT ecosystem. They conducted attacks on nine industrial IoT devices, employing the BASHLITE and Mirai botnets for this purpose. To identify these attacks, the authors employed a deep-learning autoencoder that extracted a multitude of network traffic features.

In Ref. [2], the same authors present another dataset called IoTHIDS (2018), which is host-based and comprises real data from IoT devices. was created using tests that took into account the topology of three devices that were infected with the malware botnets Doflo, BASHLITE, Adira, Hajime, Wroba, Tsunami, and Mirai.

In Ref. [3], the IoT-SH dataset from 2019 is described, consisting of captures of twelve attacks targeting eight unique smart home scenarios categorized into four classes. To categorize these assaults, a three-stage Intrusion Discovery System is employed, integrating diverse combinations of rule-based and machine learning methods.

In Ref. [4], BoT-IoT (2019) is presented as a practical, industry-focused dataset, carefully designed to encompass diverse network scenarios. This dataset focuses on five scenarios that are subjected to a variety of attacks, including DDoS, DoS, data theft, and reconnaissance. The authors employ correlation measures and common entropy methods to select a novel set of features for the evaluation process. Various deep learning and machine learning models are trained to evaluate the precision of attack detection.

Kitsune dataset (2019), which consists of four different sorts of assaults carried out against nine IoT devices, is introduced by the authors in Ref. [5]. A real sample is the Mirai botnet for infecting a security camera. The main goal of this dataset is to aid in the creation of resilient Network Intrusion Detection Systems (NIDS) that can differentiate between legitimate and malicious activities within the corporate landscape.

Similarly, IoTNIDS (2019) [6] is a project that aims to collect real-time IoT network data by facilitating interactions between two IoT devices, specifically a speaker and a camera. This project comprehensively analyzes various types of attacks, including Mirai, Man-in-the-Middle (MITM), Denial of Service (DoS), and scanning attacks. Another valuable resource is the IoT network design architecture dataset based on MedBIoT (2020) [7]. In this dataset, the authors extracted 100 statistical features from IoT network data and conducted extensive testing with various machine learning algorithms. Furthermore, the authors of Ref. [8] recommend using the IoT-23 dataset, which consists of botnet traffic data acquired in a real network environment, encompassing both legitimate and malicious network traffic.

In Ref. [9], you'll find the IoTIDs dataset from 2020, featuring flow-based attributes related to IoT. These attributes were carefully selected and ranked using the Shapiro-Wilk algorithm and the correlation coefficient technique. The study involved subjecting speakers and cameras of two IoT devices to four distinct attacks, from which data was collected. In the assessment process, a variety of machine learning techniques, including LDA, SVM, LR, and G-NB, were employed, with a particular focus on detection and categorization of attacks.

In Ref. [10], the authors introduced the MQTT dataset from 2020, designed with main aim of furnishing accurate data tailored to IoT network scenarios, leveraging the MQTT protocol. Additionally, this dataset includes 33 distinct features extracted from 8 IoT devices linked to the MQTT broker, which were then subjected to diverse machine learning algorithms. Likewise, MQTT-IoT-IDS (2020) [11] is another valuable resource aiming to create a dataset utilizing MQTT, a lightweight protocol frequently employed in IOT networks, following a similar approach as the aforementioned MQTT dataset.

In Ref. [12], the authors introduced TON-IoT (2020), an acronym representing a novel telemetry-driven dataset for IoT/IIoT applications. This comprehensive dataset includes both typical and samples of attacks collected
in diverse scenarios. It includes sub-categories of attacks, data extracted
from network traffic data, and operating system logs, all designed to create
a realistic dataset. During the evaluation phase, a range of deep learning
and machine learning algorithms are employed, and the findings are thoroughly documented. Additionally, to facilitate the advancement of Intrusion
Diagnosis Systems (IDS), the author introduced the Edge-IIoTSet (2022)
dataset, serving as a real-time security assets specifically tailored for IIoT and
IoT solutions.

To facilitate the advancement of Intrusion Diagnosis Systems (IDS) in both
decentralized and consolidated systems, the Edge-IIoTSet dataset, introduced
in 2022, serves as a practical cybersecurity asset for IIoT and IoT applications
[13]. The publication offers a detailed insight into the testbed utilized, along
with an in-depth explanation of the dataset creation framework as provided
by the authors [14]. Furthermore, the publication delves into the discussion
of centralized and federated learning concepts in the context of the machine
learning evaluation process.

10.11 DATASETS

The DARPA dataset, initially made publicly available in February 1998
[15] and published by the Massachusetts Institute of Technology's Lincoln
Laboratory, was meticulously crafted over a seven-week period, employing
various techniques such as DoS and R2L attacks. However, it's worth noting
that DARPA has been regarded as antiquated or obsolete for evaluating contemporary networks since 2008 [16]. Although it continues to be utilized for
evaluating the performance of new anomaly detection systems [17, 18], it's no
longer deemed suitable for contemporary network evaluations [19].

The KDD99 dataset, which emerged in 1999 [20], was constructed using the
DARPA dataset as its foundation. It encompasses various types of attacks,
including User to Root (U2R), Denial of Service (DoS), and ports weep incidents. However, the KDD99 dataset presents inherent challenges, notably the
presence of duplicate records. It has been identified that approximately 78% of
records are repeated in the training set and about 75% in the testing set [19].
This redundancy in data can introduce bias concerns in AI learning techniques.

NSL-KDD, an improved iteration of KDD99, was introduced in 2009
[21]. It was developed by utilizing a subset of the original KDD99 dataset to
rectify certain shortcomings. However, the authors of NSL-KDD cautioned
that this updated version may not offer a flawless representation of presently
operational real-world networks [19].

The UNSW-NB15 dataset, crafted by the University of New South Wales
in 2015 [22], encompasses nine distinct attack categories, such as Backdoors,

DOS, and Worms. While it contains a substantial 2,218,761 instances of normal traffic, it comprises a relatively small subset of 321,283 records related to attacks. Despite the limited number of entries for each attack type, this dataset presents a diverse spectrum of anomalous traffic patterns. Consequently, an Intrusion Detection System (IDS) trained on this data may exhibit a bias toward normal traffic.

In 2017, the Canadian Institute for Cybersecurity introduced the CIC-IDS2017 dataset [19]. This dataset was compiled during a five-day period and comprises a wide range of network traffic, encompassing both legitimate and malicious activities. Among the malicious activities are DDoS and DoS attacks, which utilize tools like GoldenEye [23], as well as SQL Injection attacks. Additionally this involves using the Low Orbit Ion Cannon (LOIC) program [24] to initiate UDP, TCP along with HTTP requests aimed at the target server.

The dataset creators assert that CIC-IDS (2017) offers a comprehensive representation of contemporary attack scenarios, drawing from a study published by McAfee in 2016 to ensure the inclusion of the most prevalent and up-to-date attack techniques at that time. However, it's worth noting that the CIC-IDS (2017) dataset does not incorporate IoT devices within its testbed.

In 2018, the Dispatches Security Establishment of Canada and the Canadian Institute for Cybersecurity collaborated to develop the CSE-CIC-IDS2018 dataset as an update to its predecessor, CIC-IDS2017. This enhanced dataset encompasses contemporary attack scenarios, such as Denial of Service (DoS) assaults employing GoldenEye and Decentralized Denial of Service (DDoS) assaults utilizing LOIC. Notably, a significant departure from the real CIC-IDS2017 is the inclusion of a most expansive testbed. This testbed comprises hundreds of Windows machines hosted on Amazon Web Services (AWS), organized into five distinct subnets, mirroring the structure of organization departments. However, it is essential to acknowledge that the CSE-CIC-IDS2018 dataset does not account for IoT devices, as it still lacks representation of these elements in the network topology.

In 2019, the University of New South Wales introduced the Bot-IoT dataset [25]. This dataset replicates a smart home environment featuring five simulated IoT equipment: garage door, refrigerator, thermostat, motion-activated lighting, and a weather monitoring system [26]. The dataset encompasses various attacks, including DDoS and DoS, which employ GoldenEye to target HTTP traffic and Hping3 to target TCP and UDP traffic [27]. To generate regular traffic between the virtual machines, tools like Ostinato [28] and data collection tools were employed, particularly when transferring files between these virtual devices. It's worth noting that despite its IoT focus, this dataset's testbed does not incorporate any actual IoT devices.

One noteworthy aspect of this dataset is the considerable class imbalance, with only around 9,000 instances of regular flows compared to millions of attack flows, posing significant challenges in terms of class balancing.

TON_IOT, released in 2020 [29] by the University of New South Wales, features a blend of genuine and simulated IoT devices. Among the physical gadgets, there are two smart fridges, smartphones, and a smart TV, while the simulated devices utilize Node-RED [30]. This dataset encompasses a range of attacks, including DDoS and ransomware, directed at IoT devices. The normal traffic patterns emerge from the subscribing and publishing methods employed by these devices to communicate with both private and public MQTT gateways [31].

However, it's important to note that despite its inclusion of genuine and simulated IoT devices, along with various threat scenarios, TON_IOT primarily stems from local testbed operations and is not intended for practical use by real users in actual service environments.

The CIC IoT program, unveiled in 2022 year [32] by the Canadian Institute for Cybersecurity, offers insights into the activities of real-world IoT devices in diverse context, including simulations of smart homes with devices like cameras, lamps, and coffee makers. These devices were subjected to various attacks, such as LOIC-based assaults utilizing UDP, HTTP, and TCP protocols, as well as brute force attacks exploiting the Real-Time Streaming Protocol (RTSP) used by the cameras. Notably, this dataset features actual IoT devices, although it focuses solely on DoS attacks and is primarily designed to facilitate the behavioral analysis of different IoT devices, particularly in their idle and powered-on states.

CIC IoT 2022, created by the Canadian Institute for Cybersecurity in 2022 [33], scrutinizes the behaviors of genuine IoT devices across various scenarios, including simulations of smart homes equipped with cameras, lighting, and coffee makers. These devices were subjected to attacks like LOIC, utilizing TCP, UDP, and HTTP protocols, as well as brute force attacks exploiting the Real-Time Streaming Protocol RTSP used by the cameras [34]. While this dataset features real IoT devices, it exclusively considers DoS attacks and is primarily designed for in-depth behavioral analysis of diverse IoT devices, particularly when they are in their powered-on and idle states.

The concept of the Internet of Things holds immense significance for society, offering diverse sectors newfound capabilities. IoT solutions are increasingly prevalent, especially in industries like transportation and healthcare, with promising new services on the horizon. Over the past decade, the number of IoT connections in our society has experienced a remarkable surge, and this trend is expected to continue in the coming years.

However, despite these remarkable advantages, there remain several pressing issues that need to be addressed to ensure effective and secure IoT operations. These challenges encompass concerns such as security, standards, interoperability, and server technologies. Moreover, despite ongoing efforts to create datasets that document attacks on IoT devices, there are still numerous potential threats that have not been adequately accounted for. Most current initiatives also fall short when it comes to comprehensively considering the intricacies of network topology involving genuine IoT devices.

Based on our research findings, we assert that Denial of service and distributed denial of service DDoS attacks remain prevalent concerns in network security. These attacks predominantly exploit the UDP, HTTP, and TCP protocols, often employing tools such as Hping3, LOIC, and GoldenEye. However, as our study underscores, there is a clear need for openly accessible IoT datasets that incorporate real user interactions, similar to the one detailed in this research.

To evaluate the effectiveness of our latest dataset in constructing robust security measures, we conducted a comparative analysis with the most widely recognized IoT datasets found in existing literature. To our knowledge, the CIC-IoT-2023 dataset stands alone in its inclusion of genuine physical IoT devices within a real production network, encompassing DDoS attacks and genuine external user-generated regular traffic interacting with real services. The incorporation of DDoS attacks is crucial as it mimics authentic distributed behaviors observed in attacks against physical IoT devices. Furthermore, the inclusion of the "typical" category facilitates the modeling of genuine user traffic patterns.

10.12 IMBALANCE RATIO ABOUT DATASET

These datasets exhibit significant imbalances, which necessitate addressing in order to accurately assess the system's efficiency. The metric used to quantify this imbalance is the Imbalance Ratio, denoted as ρ and calculated as shown in Equation (10.1):

$$\text{Imbalance Ratio}(\rho) = \text{maxi}\{C_i\} / \text{mini}\{C_i\} \tag{10.1}$$

Here, C_i represents the size of data in class i. In essence, the imbalance rate is characterized by the disparity between the count of occurrences in the majority (maximum) class and the minority (minimum) class.

For the CIC-IOT-2023 dataset, the data imbalance rate is notably high, at 7,000,000: 10,000. Such substantial differences between data classes significantly impact the system's effectiveness. Additionally, it's important to highlight that skilled hackers frequently concentrate on exploiting the less common data types to accomplish their goals.

10.13 MACHINE LEARNING ALGORITHM

10.13.1 Algorithm Adaboost

To address classification challenges, the community employs a machine learning technique called adaptive boosting, commonly known as AdaBoost [32]. "Boosting" involves the process of aggregating weak predictions from the data to yield a robust and accurate outcome. In its initial phase, AdaBoost uniformly distributes the data before performing classification.

During this process, it identifies the weakest classifier and adjusts the weights accordingly. Throughout the iterative updating procedure, it prioritizes addressing the worst-performing predictions. Ultimately, it combines multiple underperforming classifiers to form a strong and effective classifier. The primary aim of AdaBoost is to enhance its overall categorization success rate. Equation (10.2) is utilized to create the ultimate equation for classifying the dataset.

$$F(x) = sign\left(\sum_{i=1}^{N} \theta_i f_i(x)\right) \tag{10.2}$$

10.13.2 Decision tree (DT)

The supervised learning approach employed to classify of both numerical and categorical data is the Decision Tree (DT). This method utilizes predefined variables with leaf nodes to aid in its top-down decision-making process [33]. Decision Trees are favored for their ability to rapidly process data and their straightforward structure. However, in some cases, when dealing with more complex datasets, decision trees can become intricate, making it challenging to achieve desired outcomes. Another concern with decision tree algorithms is the risk of overfitting, which can be mitigated by pruning certain leaf nodes. To guide decision trees effectively, it is essential to evaluate concepts like entropy and information gain.

Equation (10.3) illustrates the calculation of entropy.

$$E(S) = \sum_{x \in X} -p(a) E(a) \tag{10.3}$$

The calculation of information gain is based on the formula

$$E(S) = X^* p(a) * E(a) \tag{10.4}$$

Where X represents a set of classes within the dataset S. In this equation, S denotes the dataset, p is a ratio denoting the number of entries in class X, and $E(a)$ refers to the entropy associated with class X. Equation (10.4) is utilized to compute the information gain.

The calculation of Gain (A, S) is expressed as follows:

$$\text{Gain}(A,S) = E(S) * \Sigma(a \in M) p(a) * E(a), \tag{10.5}$$

Where M represents the subsets generated from the dataset S.

10.13.3 Algorithm random forest

A supervised machine learning architecture known as Random Forest (RF) can effectively address both regression problems and classification [35]. This approach is straightforward to implement, utilizing Decision Trees to form a decision forest and addressing problems in this manner. It achieves this by generating a diverse set of trees, each making multiple decisions during the process. These trees are trained to provide the most accurate classifications, often yielding satisfactory results even without the need for hyperparameters. Random Forest is widely favored for its ability to produce outcomes rapidly and accurately, even when dealing with mixed, imperfect, or noisy datasets.

ALGORITHM K NEAREST NEIGHBOR

A supervised learning method known as K Nearest Neighbor (KNN) is distinct from other supervised learning algorithms as it does not involve a dedicated training phase [36]. Instead, KNN leverages information from the original sample class to make classifications. It determines the appropriate class assignment for new data by considering the K nearest data points, which are the new data's closest neighbors. The properties of these K nearest neighbors are used to compute the distance between the new data point and the existing sample class groups. Various distance metrics, such as Minkowski functions, Euclidean and Manhattan, are employed for distance calculations. The formulas for calculating these distances are given in Equations (10.6) to (10.8).

$$\text{Minkowski} = \left(\sum_{i=1}^{N} \left(|x_i - y_i| \right)^k \right)^{\frac{1}{k}} \tag{10.6}$$

$$\text{Euclidean} = \sqrt{\sum_{i=1}^{N} \left(x_i - y_i \right)^2} \tag{10.7}$$

$$\text{Manhattan} = \sum_{i=1}^{N} |x_i - y_i| \tag{10.8}$$

In these equations, N represents the size of dataset, k denoted as a positive integer, and x_i and y_i denote the coordinates of the ith data point. It's worth noting that K Nearest Neighbor (KNN) can encounter challenges when dealing with straightforward, but noisy, training data. Additionally, a drawback of this approach is its high memory usage since it stores all instances for distance computations.

10.13.4 Algorithm for gradient boosting

The Gradient Boosting Algorithm (GB) is employed for regression, and challenges related to categorization are discussed [37]. A set of weak classification models, like the Adaboost-ing algorithm, usually builds a decision tree model. To achieve the lowest possible error values, the gradient is increased by updating the estimates in accordance with the learning rate.

10.13.5 Proposed architecture

The study employed the CIC-IOT-2023 benchmark dataset as its primary data source. In the initial phase of data preprocessing, columns containing null values were removed to create a refined dataset. This cleaned dataset was subsequently used for feature selection and feature scaling. During this stage, the Pearson correlation technique played a crucial role in identifying significant attributes, as depicted in Figure 10.2 and 10.3 which illustrates the attack categories analyzed as in Table 10.1.

To facilitate the modeling process, categorical features were transformed into numeric ones through the one-hot encoding technique, following the identification of key features. Subsequently, feature normalization and standardization procedures were applied to ensure appropriate scaling. Finally, a diverse array of deep learning and machine learning algorithms were employed to train the model. Specifically, 80% of the dataset was allocated for model training, with the remaining 20% reserved for testing and evaluating the model's performance (Figure 10.4).

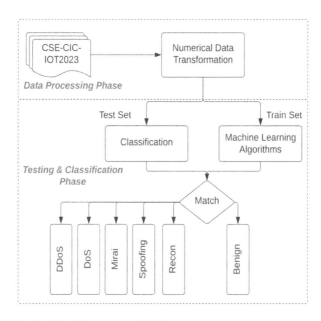

Figure 10.2 Flowchart for the proposed IDS.

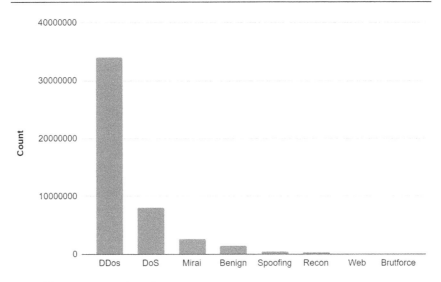

Figure 10.3 Variations of attacks.

Table 10.1 Data description of CIE CIC-IOT2023

	Attack	Size
DDoS	ACK Fragmentation	285,104
	UDP Flood	5412287
	SlowLoris	23426
	ICMP Flood	7,200,504
	RSTFIN Flood	4,045,285
	PSHACK Flood	4,094,755
	HTTP Flood	28,790
	UDP Fragmentation	286,925
	IDMP Fragmentation	452,489
	TCP Flood	4,497,667
	SYN Flood	4,059,190
	SynonimousIP Flood	3,598,138
DoS	TCP Flood	2,671,445
	HTTP Flood	71,864
	SYN Flood	2,028,834
	UDP Flood	3,318,595
Recon	Ping Sweep	2262
	OS Scan	98,259
	Vulnerability Scan	37,382
	Port Scan	82,284
	Host Discovery	1,34,378

(Continued)

Table 10.1 (Continued)

	Attack	Size
Web Based	SQL Injection	5245
	Command Injection	5409
	Backdoor Malware	3218
	Uploading Attack	1252
	XSS	3846
	Browser Hijacking	5859
BrutForce	Dictionary BrutForce	13,064
Spoofing	Arp Spoofing	307,593
	DNS Spoofing	178,911
Mirai	GREIP Flood	751,682
	Greeth Flood	991,866
	UDPPlain	890,576

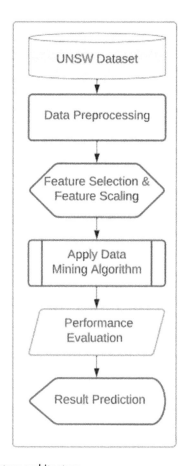

Figure 10.4 Proposed system architecture.

10.13.6 Python SCIKIT-LEARN

Python, currently one of the most widely embraced application development platforms across various domains, is a versatile and user-friendly general-purpose programming language. Its efficient design simplifies application development and seamless integration with diverse systems. Python finds utility in an array of domains, including the creation of desktop and web applications, the development of tools for analyzing and visualizing data, programming networks, developing database applications, and building machine learning systems.

One notable advantage of Python is its compiler-free nature, allowing it to run seamlessly across different platforms. It offers compatibility with a broad spectrum of operating systems, encompassing Windows, Linux, Mac, and Symbian. Furthermore, Python enhances system performance through additional parallel execution libraries and robust code support, facilitating efficient processing across single or multiple CPUs/GPUs.

10.14 RESULT AND CONCLUSION

The implementation utilizes the CIE CIC-IOT-2023 dataset, which contains a total of 46,686,579 rows and comprises 48 features. To begin with, the dataset underwent a preprocessing phase where null values were systematically removed. This step led to a reduction in the dataset size, roughly halving it from its original state. Furthermore, encoding techniques were applied to manage categorical features effectively. Subsequently, a normalization technique was employed to scale the features appropriately.

Figure 10.2 provides insights into the assault categories included within the dataset. Notably, the implementation of the suggested model was conducted on a high computation architecture featuring a Windows 10 with 64-bit, RAM of 16 GB, a 6 GB GTX 1660 TI GPU, and AMD RYZEN 9 CPU with 9 cores This robust configuration was instrumental in achieving effective results during the implementation process.

REFERENCES

[1] Meidan, Y., Bohadana, M., Mathov, Y., Mirsky, Y., Shabtai, A., Breitenbacher, D., & Elovici, Y. (2018). N-baiot—Network-based detection of IoT botnet attacks using deep autoencoders. *IEEE Pervasive Computing*, *17*(3), 12–22.

[2] Bezerra, V. H., da Costa, V. G. T., Martins, R. A., Junior, S. B., Miani, R. S., & Zarpelao, B. B. (2018, October). Providing IoT host-based datasets for intrusion detection research. In *Anais do XVIII Simpósio Brasileiro de Segurança da Informaçao e de Sistemas Computacionais* (pp. 15–28). SBC.

[3] Anthi, E., Williams, L., Słowińska, M., Theodorakopoulos, G., & Burnap, P. (2019). A supervised intrusion detection system for smart home IoT devices. *IEEE Internet of Things Journal*, *6*(5), 9042–9053.

[4] Koroniotis, N., Moustafa, N., Sitnikova, E., & Turnbull, B. (2019). Towards the development of realistic botnet dataset in the internet of things for network forensic analytics: Bot-IoT dataset. *Future Generation Computer Systems, 100*, 779–796.

[5] Mirsky, Y., Doitshman, T., Elovici, Y., & Shabtai, A. (2018). Kitsune: an ensemble of autoencoders for online network intrusion detection. *arXiv preprint arXiv:1802.09089*.

[6] Kang, H., Ahn, D. H., Lee, G. M., Do Yoo, J., Park, K. H., & Kim, H. K. (2019). IoT network intrusion dataset. IEEE Dataport.

[7] Guerra-Manzanares, A., Medina-Galindo, J., Bahsi, H., & Nõmm, S. (2020, February). MedBIoT: Generation of an IoT botnet dataset in a medium-sized IoT network. In *ICISSP* (pp. 207–218).

[8] Parmisano, A., Garcia, S., & Erquiaga, M. J. (2020). *A labeled dataset with malicious and benign IoT network traffic*. Stratosphere Laboratory.

[9] Ullah, I., & Mahmoud, Q. H. (2020, May). A scheme for generating a dataset for anomalous activity detection in IoT networks. In *Canadian Conference on Artificial Intelligence* (pp. 508–520). Springer International Publishing.

[10] Vaccari, I., Chiola, G., Aiello, M., Mongelli, M., & Cambiaso, E. (2020). MQTTset, a new dataset for machine learning techniques on MQTT. *Sensors, 20*(22), 6578.

[11] Hindy, H., Bayne, E., Bures, M., Atkinson, R., Tachtatzis, C., & Bellekens, X. (2020, September). Machine learning based IoT intrusion detection system: An MQTT case study (MQTT-IoT-IDS2020 dataset). In *International Networking Conference* (pp. 73–84). Springer International Publishing.

[12] Alsaedi, A., Moustafa, N., Tari, Z., Mahmood, A., & Anwar, A. (2020). TON_IoT telemetry dataset: A new generation dataset of IoT and IIoT for data-driven intrusion detection systems. *IEEE Access, 8*, 165130–165150.

[13] Ferrag, M. A., Friha, O., Hamouda, D., Maglaras, L., & Janicke, H. (2022). Edge-IIoTset: A new comprehensive realistic cyber security dataset of IoT and IIoT applications for centralized and federated learning. *IEEE Access, 10*, 40281–40306.

[14] Sharafaldin, I., Lashkari, A. H., & Ghorbani, A. A. (2018). Toward generating a new intrusion detection dataset and intrusion traffic characterization. In *ICISSP, 1*, 108–116.

[15] 1998 Darpa Intrusion Detection Evaluation. Accessed: May 9, 2022. [Online]. https://www.ll.mit.edu/rd/datasets/1998-darpaintrusion-detection-evaluation-dataset

[16] Thomas, C., Sharma, V., & Balakrishnan, N. (2008, March). Usefulness of DARPA dataset for intrusion detection system evaluation. In *Data Mining, Intrusion detection, information assurance, and data networks security 2008* (Vol. 6973, pp. 164–171). SPIE.

[17] Garg, S., Kaur, K., Kumar, N., Kaddoum, G., Zomaya, A. Y., & Ranjan, R. (2019). A hybrid deep learning-based model for anomaly detection in cloud datacenter networks. *IEEE Transactions on Network and Service Management, 16*(3), 924–935.

[18] Indre, I., & Lemnaru, C. (2016, September). Detection and prevention system against cyber attacks and botnet malware for information systems and Internet of Things. In *2016 IEEE 12th International Conference on Intelligent Computer Communication and Processing (ICCP)* (pp. 175–182). IEEE.

[19] Tavallaee, M., Bagheri, E., Lu, W., & Ghorbani, A. A. (2009, July). A detailed analysis of the KDD CUP 99 data set. In *2009 IEEE Symposium on Computational Intelligence for Security and Defense Applications* (pp. 1–6). IEEE.

[20] Cup, K. D. D. (1999). http://kdd.ics.uci.edu/databases/kddcup99/kddcup99. html *The UCI KDD Archive*.

[21] NSL-KDD Dataset. Accessed: May 9, 2022. [Online]. https://www.unb.ca/cic/datasets/nsl.html

[22] Moustafa, N., & Slay, J. (2015, Nov.). UNSW-NB15: A comprehensive data set for network intrusion detection systems (UNSW-NB15 network data set). In *Proceedings of the Military Communications and Information Systems Conference (MilCIS)* (pp. 1–6).

[23] Goldeneye Layer 7 (Keepalive+Nocache) Dos Test Tool. Accessed: May 9, 2022. [Online]. https://github.com/jseidl/GoldenEye

[24] Low Orbit Ion Cannon (LOIC). Accessed: May 9, 2022. [Online]. https://www.cloudflare.com/learning/ddos/ddos-attacktools/low-orbit-ion-cannon-loic

[25] Koroniotis, N., Moustafa, N., Sitnikova, E., & Turnbull, B. (2019). Towards the development of realistic botnet dataset in the internet of things for network forensic analytics: Bot-IoT dataset. *Future Generation Computer Systems, 100,* 779–796.

[26] A Realistic Cyber Defense Dataset (CSE-CIC-IDS2018). Accessed: May 9, 2022. [Online]. https://registry.opendata.aws/cse-cicids2018

[27] hPing. Accessed: May 11, 2022. [Online]. http://www.hping.org

[28] Ostinato. Accessed: May 11, 2022. [Online]. https://ostinato.org

[29] Alsaedi, A., Moustafa, N., Tari, Z., Mahmood, A., & Anwar, A. (2020). TON_IoT telemetry dataset: A new generation dataset of IoT and IIoT for data-driven intrusion detection systems. *IEEE Access, 8,* 165130–165150.

[30] Node-RED. Accessed: May 11, 2022. [Online]. https://nodered.org

[31] Al-Fuqaha, A., Guizani, M., Mohammadi, M., Aledhari, M., & Ayyash, M. (2015). Internet of Things: A survey on enabling technologies, protocols, and applications. *IEEE Communications Surveys and Tutorials, 17*(4), 2347–2376, 4th Quart.

[32] Dadkhah, S., Mahdikhani, H., Danso, P. K., Zohourian, A., Truong, K. A., & Ghorbani, A. A. (Aug. 2022). Towards the development of a realistic multidimensional IoT profiling dataset. In *The 19th Annual International Conference on Privacy, Security & Trust (PST2022)* (pp. 1–11). Los Alamitos, CA, USA.

[33] Wyner, A. J., Olson, M., Bleich, J., & Mease, D. (2017). Explaining the success of adaboost and random forests as interpolating classifiers. *The Journal of Machine Learning Research, 18*(1), 1558–1590.

[34] Ke, G., Meng, Q., Finley, T., Wang, T., Chen, W., Ma, W., ... & Liu, T. Y. (2017). Lightgbm: A highly efficient gradient boosting decision tree. *Advances in Neural Information Processing Systems, 30.*3154.

[35] Frosst, N., & Hinton, G. (2017). Distilling a neural network into a soft decision tree. *arXiv preprint arXiv:1711.09784.*

[36] Belgiu, M., & Drăguţ, L. (2016). Random forest in remote sensing: A review of applications and future directions. *ISPRS Journal of Photogrammetry and Remote Sensing, 114,* 24–31.

[37] Zhang, S., Li, X., Zong, M., Zhu, X., & Wang, R. (2017). Efficient kNN classification with different numbers of nearest neighbors. *IEEE Transactions on Neural Networks And Learning Systems, 29*(5), 1774–1785.

Index

Pages in *italics* refer to figures and pages in **bold** refer to tables.